KLONDIKE TRAIL:
The complete hiking and paddling guide

Also by Jennifer Voss

Stikine River: A guide to paddling *The Great River*

KLONDIKE TRAIL:
The complete hiking and paddling guide

by Jennifer Voss

THE
MOUNTAINEERS
BOOKS

Published by
The Mountaineers Books
1001 SW Klickitat Way, Suite 201
Seattle, WA 98134

First published in Canada by Lost Moose, the Yukon Publishers, Whitehorse, Yukon

Library of Congress Cataloguing-in-Publication Data
A catalog record for this book is available at the Library of Congress

ISBN 0-89996-797-5

All photos by Jennifer Voss unless otherwise noted.

Production: K-L Services, Whitehorse, Yukon

Cover design: Catalyst Communications, Whitehorse, Yukon

Printed in Canada

PREFACE

A re you ready for the adventure of a lifetime? For most, a trip along the historic gold rush trail to the Klondike is a dream come true. This guidebook was written to help you get as much out of your northern quest as I did when I hiked the Chilkoot and paddled the Yukon in recent years. The book contains information on access, history and the environment so you are able to learn about the magnificent land you are passing through.

Travel along the 934 kilometres from Dyea, Alaska to Dawson City, Yukon is a lot safer today than it was 100 years ago when gold rush "stampeders" first arrived by the tens of thousands to meet little-known challenges head-on. Road access and plentiful supplies at key points make your journey a breeze compared to what people faced in the early days. As with travel through any wilderness, there are some risks, so this guidebook puts first priority on your safety and comfort. Good preparation is the key to success and you are urged to think and act carefully at all times.

This guide is just that — a guide. No author can be responsible for the safety of individuals or groups travelling along this or any other wilderness route. The best advice I can give is to first prepare yourself through good research, then hone your skills through practice for the hiking and paddling challenges that lie ahead. Your group must include people with sufficient wilderness travel experience; you may want to seek quality instruction beforehand, or qualified guides for the trip itself. A further caution is that rivers and trails may change in certain places from year to year. Experienced people are able to make good on-the-spot decisions based on a visual inspection of a given situation and an assessment of the skill level of the entire group.

Overall, the Klondike Trail is among the best outdoor adventures in the world. People of relatively modest skill levels can travel safely and have an amazing experience that will last the rest of their lives. For others, one trip along the Klondike Trail will be but the first of many return visits to explore the vast northern wilderness over and over again.

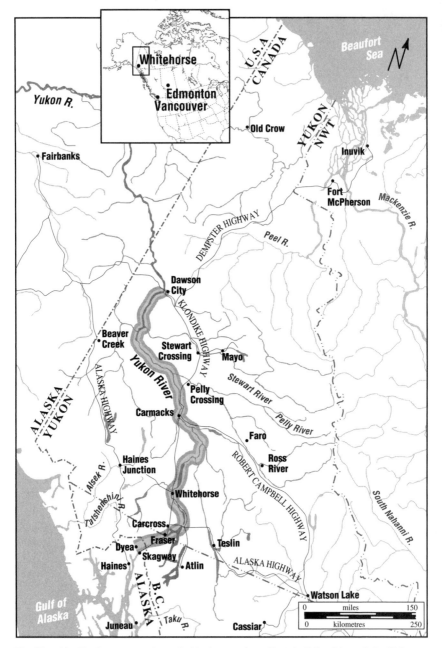

The Klondike Trail as it runs through Alaska, northern British Columbia and the Yukon.

To my lovely daughters
Kelsey and Katrina,
for whom I wish many years
of wandering the wilds of Canada

ACKNOWLEDGMENTS

It is not possible to produce a book such as this in isolation. Support, guidance, assistance, advice and information came to me from many different people. Above all shines my husband, Jan, who has encouraged, supported and assisted me throughout. My Mom and my family have always been behind me with love, encouragement and excitement. And there's Martha Meimetis, without whose caregiving for my two beautiful daughters, this book could not have been done. Of course there's Carl Anderson, Christine Hoffman, Ernie Kunz and Mariette Leppert, who experienced with me, first hand, the joys of the Klondike Trail. And the many others whose support and assistance are invaluable: all my friends for their encouragement and support; Wynne Krangle, Peter Long, Max Fraser and Alison Reid of Lost Moose Publishing for guidance and support; Tracey Jacobs, Peter Jacobs and Ray Falle of Waterfront Jet Boat Tours in Whitehorse for their skill and knowledge; Paul Shakotko and John van Hove for their awesome help in field testing the manuscript; Hilary Brown for incredible support, encouragement and assistance with the maps; Charlie Roots for his input on geology and his patience with my constant questions; Brian Slough for input on amphibians; Hugh Danks for information on bugs; Bruce Bennett and Peter Long for their photographs; David Neufeld for his editorial comments; Natural Resources Canada and the U.S. Geological Survey for the use of topographic maps as a basis for creating the strip maps in this book; and MSCUA University of Washington Library, Yukon Archives, University of Alaska Fairbanks, Department of Canadian Heritage, Yukon Energy Corporation, PR Services, Alaska State Library, Anchorage Museum of History and Art, Museum of History and Industry, and National Archives of Canada for permission to use various photographs and maps.

CONTENTS

INTRODUCTION 1

Chapter 1...WHERE, WHEN & HOW 7

Chapter 2...TRIP TIPS...27

Chapter 3...ROUTES & RAPIDS 45

  Chilkoot Trail, Dyea to Bennett 53

  Headwater Lakes, Bennett to Whitehorse..81

  Yukon River, Whitehorse to Carmacks 101

  Yukon River, Carmacks to Dawson 127

Chapter 4...MAPS 153

  Chilkoot Trail, Dyea to Bennett 155

  Headwater Lakes, Bennett to Whitehorse.. 163

  Yukon River, Whitehorse to Carmacks 172

  Yukon River, Carmacks to Dawson... 186

Chapter 5...THEN & NOW 207

  First Nations 208

  The newcomers 216

  Modern times 225

  Protection 227

Chapter 6...ROCKS, RABBITS & RAINFOREST... 229

  Coastal rainforest 231

  Alpine 235

  Subalpine boreal forest... 239

  Northern boreal forest 247

Chapter 7...REFERENCE... 257

Chilkoot packers take a break on the Long Hill.

INTRODUCTION

*M*y legs ached, my lungs burned, and I was sure my heart would escape the confines of my chest. Yet some inexplicable feeling kept my spirits high and my energies focused on the summit. This was the high point, literally, of our four-week journey into the past, a pilgrimage through times gone by. The final ascent of the Chilkoot Pass, nicknamed the Golden Stairs, was marked by the footsteps of many before me. My pack of a mere 45 pounds paled in comparison to the 80- to 150-pound loads carried by Klondike goldseekers over 100 years before.

Once atop the pass, we looked back over the Taiya River valley towards the ocean and the winding trail up through the coastal forest. We also looked forward to times and places to come, a journey following the historic route down to Dawson City.

Ho for the Klondike!

An intimidating look up the Golden Stairs.

1

In the quiet years before the Klondike gold rush, First Nations people lived off the land, following a seasonal round of fishing, hunting, trapping and trading. A complex system of trails facilitated these activities, some of them jealously guarded. One of these was the Chilkoot Trail, the overland portion of the route from Dyea on the Pacific coast to the Klondike region.

The route to Dawson City via Dyea and the Chilkoot Trail was opened up to the world in the late 1800s with the cry of gold. The big gold strike was made by George Carmack, Skookum Jim and Tagish Charlie in August 1896. But it wasn't until the arrival of the *S.S. Excelsior* in San Francisco and the *S.S. Portland* in Seattle in the summer of 1897 that the word "Klondike" was on the lips of people throughout North America and beyond. As many as 100,000 people from all parts of the globe packed their belongings and headed out to the promised land, the Klondike. These adventurers established many arduous and long routes into the Klondike region. Over the next two years, most stampeders turned back and a few perished due to the hardships of wilderness travel. In the end, almost 30,000 made it to the goldfields, but most of them were far too late to even think of staking a claim given that Bonanza and Eldorado creeks were fully staked within a matter of weeks of discovery. Of those lucky enough to stake or purchase a claim, most would go home penniless, either due to a lack of gold or because they squandered their hard earned "colours" in the inflated economy of Dawson City. This book describes, for modern day adventurers, the most famous and infamous route taken into the Klondike goldfields — over the Chilkoot Pass and down the Yukon River to Dawson City.

Yukon Archives, MacBride Museum, 3626

Women and men in an endless line, carrying their immense loads up the Golden Stairs in the winter of 1898.

The clay cliffs near Whitehorse tower over the Yukon River.

The Klondike Trail passes through a vast land. The route is 934 kilometres long, almost 27 kilometres uphill from Dyea to the Chilkoot Pass at an elevation of 1,122 metres, and 907 kilometres from the pass through the watershed of the Yukon River to Dawson City, the city of gold. The Yukon River at Dawson City has an amazing typical July flow of about 5,000 cubic metres per second, draining an area of 264,000 square kilometres. On the Yukon River, you will pass by several major tributaries, many of them navigable, including the Teslin, Big Salmon, Little Salmon, Pelly and Stewart rivers. This watershed has a fascinating geological history, evidence of which you will see as you travel down the river.

This region has seen incredible things in its day. Most awe-inspiring are the geological events that have shaped the land over millions of years. In contrast, it was only very recently, approximately 10,000 years ago, that the first humans entered the picture, when the floor of Bering Strait was believed to be dry, joining Asia and North America. These few people in this vast land lived in relative peace and solitude until the 1700s, when the Russians began to move along the coast, setting up posts at Sitka and Ketchikan, both in modern-day Alaska. After some initial struggles, a new equilibrium developed where the coastal Tlingit Indians became traders between the Russians and the interior First Nations.

Voyageurs, explorers, prospectors and clerics began to arrive on the scene in the early to mid 1800s, the beginning of a slow invasion of the quiet north. These were hardy and unique souls, driven by a passion for both gold and various aspects of a northern life. They were quite a different breed than the cheechakos,

A canoeist takes a break at a beautiful spot on the Yukon River.

or greenhorns, who would arrive in the great stampede near the end of the century. Their presence had an impact on the lives of First Nations people. At first it was minimal, but, more importantly, it heralded a change to come.

The Klondike gold rush of 1896-1898 inaugurated profound changes in the Yukon. The population, although largely transient, exploded. Towns such as Dawson City and Whitehorse sprung up, and the territory was opened up to mining activities of all sorts. Communities were centred on waterways, which were the highways of that era. Riverboats plied the rushing waters of the Yukon rivers. It wasn't until the 1940s and 1950s, when highways were built, that the riverboats and many of the river communities disappeared, making way for a more road-based society.

Today, we float down the rivers in our modern boats, wearing advanced synthetic clothing and carrying global positioning systems (GPS). Although most of what you see may look superficially the same as it was more than a century ago, much of what you don't see is profoundly changed. Although some prospectors still seek out the "motherlode" by traditional means, pan in hand, most explorers and miners use more sophisticated technology. Most First Nation communities that lived off the land long before the "white" people came along, live different lives now. Many of the towns support a more varied economy, usually with an emphasis on tourism. Skagway, for instance, near the trailhead at Dyea, relies heavily on passengers from the cruise ships that dock each summer day at the foot of Broadway Street.

This book is intended to give you an appreciation for the land, the rivers and the people of the north.

■ HOW TO USE THIS BOOK

This book is sized so it can be packed into an easily accessible (and waterproofed!) space. It is a modern guide to enhance your enjoyment as you travel any part of the historic Klondike Trail from Dyea to Dawson. The guide contains specific information about the route and local services, and general information about trip planning and preparation. Certain sections are designed to help you in advance of your trip, while others are to be referenced while on the trail, lakes or river. You can use the guide each day to learn about specific features or the history of an area as you journey along. A glossary is located in the back to help you with new terms. An index is provided so you can find any specific information in which you may be interested.

The book is divided into seven chapters:

1...**Where, When & How** provides specific logistical information on planning a trip to the region. This includes information on shorter or longer trips, where to get maps, how to get to the area, arrangements to be made, and what the typical weather and river flow patterns are.

2...**Trip Tips** provides general information about trip planning and preparation, including safety and comfort. There are tips on reducing environmental impact, communicating in an emergency and appropriate clothing, gear and food.

3...**Routes & Rapids** is a detailed, stretch-by-stretch description of the route, including information on the special features shown on the strip maps in the following chapter. Place names are presented in bold type, so you can easily find the section you need.

4...**Maps** provides 52 pages of modified topographic maps of the route. These strip maps use a scale of approximately 1:50,000 for the trail section (eight maps), and 1:100,000 for the water sections (44 maps). These two scales give sufficient detail for general navigation, while featuring areas beyond the main route. Special features such as rapids, hikes, good camping spots and other significant natural, historical and cultural features are clearly marked. Each map has contour lines, route indicators and an arrow indicating magnetic north.

5...**Then & Now** provides an account of the rich human history of the area, including First Nation history, the gold rush period, the riverboat era and more recent times.

6...**Rocks, Rabbits & Rainforest** provides a description of the natural setting of the gold rush trail, including the geological, physical and biological world.

7...**Reference** provides additional information, including a glossary, list of contacts, references, specific area services, an index and a gear checklist.

So, be prepared and have fun! But keep in mind: weather, natural phenomena and even trail maintenance can change route conditions at any time. Rivers may change significantly from year to year, or even during a year, depending on water levels. The information in this guidebook is accurate to the summer of 2000.

One year after a forest fire.

Peter Long

CHAPTER 1...WHERE, WHEN & HOW

*G*etting to the Yukon is easier than most people realize, and certainly a lot simpler than during the Klondike gold rush. The most direct route is a two-hour plane ride from Vancouver, British Columbia to Whitehorse, Yukon. Hikers can reach Skagway, Alaska by road from Whitehorse or through air or ferry connections from Juneau, Alaska. It's suggested you check the web, Tourism Yukon or your travel agent to get the most up-to-date information on air carriers, schedules and prices.

Whitehorse, the Yukon's capital city, has everything a wilderness traveller needs — from camping equipment to canoe rentals. From here, it's a two-hour drive to the beginning of the trail at Dyea, Alaska, near Skagway.

Some people prefer to take the more historic and leisurely route to Skagway by ferry up the Inland Passage of coastal British Columbia and Alaska. It's a beautiful, breathtaking voyage and highly recommended.

The third access to the Yukon is via the Alaska Highway, another fantastic journey through great northern wilderness. In general, allow 30 hours driving time from either Vancouver or Edmonton, Alberta to reach Whitehorse.

This section of the book provides specific information about the logistics of planning and fulfilling a trip on the Chilkoot Trail and/or the Yukon River, including:

- trip options, for all or parts of the route from Dyea to Dawson;
- sources for additional maps;
- getting there and trip logistics;
- information details on the best weather and water levels; and
- other reading to enhance your northern experience.

The White Pass & Yukon Route railway has stunning views for its passengers.

■ OPTIONS – THE CHOICE IS YOURS

Not many people in this working world have enough vacation in a single summer to complete the full journey from Dyea to Dawson City. If you can swing it though, it is a most worthwhile adventure. There is something profoundly fulfilling in following those century-old footsteps and paddle strokes all the way to such a distant destination. The full trip combines many different experiences: backpacking over a coastal mountain pass, canoe-sailing along mountain-ringed lakes, and paddling and floating down a gentle river.

If you don't have enough time for the entire route in one trip, you should decide what experiences you would like to taste. Do you want to paddle, or would you like to throw in a little backpacking for fun? Would you prefer to paddle on lakes, on a river or both? As access to the route is possible at many points, there are many different options for shorter trips.

The table on the next page shows the main access points to the Klondike Trail. Five involve river travel on Yukon River tributaries: the Teslin, Big Salmon, Little Salmon, Pelly and Stewart rivers. These are briefly described on page 13 and in more detail in Chapter 3. Where the access point is a tributary or side trail, the distance indicates the kilometre mark where the tributary meets the main route.

The most common trips, by length of time available, are as follows.

One-week trips

- hike the Chilkoot Trail, from Dyea to Bennett or Log Cabin
- paddle the headwater lakes, Bennett to Whitehorse
- paddle the Yukon River, Whitehorse to Carmacks
- paddle the Yukon River, Carmacks to Dawson

Sunset on Lake Laberge

Road, trail and water access along the Klondike Trail			
Access to the Chilkoot Trail	**km**		
Dyea	0		
Log Cabin	50		
Bennett	53		

Access to the lakes and the river	**km**		**km**
Bennett	0	via Teslin River	305
Carcross	43	via Big Salmon River	358
Tagish	85	via Little Salmon River	421
Marsh Lake Campground	120	Little Salmon Village	422
M'Clintock River	125	Carmacks	477
Alaska Highway (Lewes River Bridge)	130	Minto	569
Schwatka Lake	159	via Pelly River	604
Whitehorse	163	Pelly Farm	604
Takhini River at Klondike Highway	183	via Stewart River	775
Policeman's Point	200	Dawson	881
Lake Laberge Campground	216		

Two-week trips

- hike and lake paddle Dyea to Whitehorse
- paddle Whitehorse to Dawson City
- paddle Lake Laberge to Dawson City (somewhat leisurely)
- paddle Carmacks to Dawson City (very leisurely)

Three-week trips

- hike and paddle Dyea to Carmacks
- paddle Bennett to Dawson City
- hike the Chilkoot Trail, then paddle Whitehorse to Dawson City
- paddle Whitehorse to Dawson City (quite leisurely)

Four-week trips

- hike and paddle Dyea to Dawson
- paddle Bennett to Dawson (quite leisurely)

The times given above assume ideal conditions; winds on the lakes can extend your journey by several days.

On the following pages are descriptions and approximate travel times for segments of the entire Klondike Trail. This will help you decide which sections you wish to travel. You can reference the corresponding maps in Chapter 4.

Alternate river trips on the Yukon River's tributaries, especially the Teslin River, are also very common. These trips involve travel first on the tributary, then on the Yukon River until the chosen take-out point at a road or community is reached. (See page 13 for information on these trips.)

■ THE KLONDIKE TRAIL, BY SEGMENT

1

WHEN, WHERE & HOW

Chilkoot Trail: Dyea to Bennett

53 kilometres, 3 to 6 days
Maps: 1 to 8
Difficulty: moderate backpacking with one very demanding day
Hazards: potential snow on the pass; intense rain and cold; some rough terrain
Scenery: spectacular, rugged coast mountain scenery
Wildness: sees lots of use; many artifacts; protected as historical parkland
Access: Dyea, Log Cabin, Bennett
History: an abundance of gold rush relics

Headwater Lakes: Bennett to Marsh Lake Outlet

118 kilometres, 6 to 8 days
Maps: 9 to 15
Difficulty: moderate to severe
Hazards: cold lakes; potential strong winds; large waves — travellers must stay close to shore
Scenery: spectacular — Coast Mountains and Teslin Plateau
Wildness: fairly settled — WP&YR tracks; Carcross; Klondike Highway; some cottages on lakesides
Access: Bennett, Carcross, Tagish, Marsh Lake Campground, M'Clintock River
History: little historical evidence, except at Carcross
Comments: stay close to shore; try canoe sailing; not an abundance of camping spots

Yukon River: Marsh Lake to Whitehorse

46 kilometres, 1 to 2 days
Maps: 15 to 17
Difficulty: easy, except a few tricky currents around Marsh Lake control structure, Miles Canyon and Whitehorse dam
Hazards: Whitehorse dam and rapids (easily avoided)
Scenery: rounded hills; pretty yellow cutbanks; clear, green water
Wildness: quite civilized — Alaska Highway; Marsh Lake control structure; some private property; Whitehorse dam; considerable float plane traffic; some tour boat activity; Whitehorse
Access: M'Clintock River, Lewes River Bridge, Schwatka Lake, Whitehorse dam, Whitehorse
History: sections of telegraph line; Canyon City
Comments: no wilderness camping within City of Whitehorse limits, from Wolf Creek to Takhini River (city bylaw); camping is available in Whitehorse at Robert Service Campground

Yukon River: Whitehorse to Upper Laberge

36 kilometres, 1 day
Maps: 17 to 19
Difficulty: easy
Hazards: minimal
Scenery: rounded hills
Wildness: fairly settled
Access: Whitehorse, Takhini River at Klondike Highway, Policeman's Point
History: Upper Laberge police post (Policeman's Point)
Comments: not an abundance of camping spots

Lake Laberge: Upper Laberge to Lower Laberge

58 kilometres, 2 to 3 days
Maps: 19 to 22
Difficulty: moderate
Hazards: possible sudden, strong winds and waves; cold water — travellers must stay close to shore
Scenery: beautiful — Miner's Range on west shore; Mount Laurier, Lime Peak and Teslin Mountain on east shore; limestone bluffs
Wildness: settled with cabins in south half, less so in north half
Access: Policeman's Point, Lake Laberge Campground at Deep Creek (no land access at Lower Laberge)
History: Upper Laberge village; some more recent history, such as boat wrecks
Comments: stay close to shore

The Thirty Mile: Lower Laberge to Hootalinqua

48 kilometres, 1 to 2 days
Maps: 22 to 24
Difficulty: moderate
Hazards: tricky currents around bends
Scenery: very scenic — moderate topographical relief; clear, green water
Wildness: quite wild, but popular; Canadian Heritage River
Access: no land access
History: abundant — Lower Laberge; Seventeen Mile Woodyard; steamer wreck locations; Hootalinqua
Comments: good camping opportunities

Yukon River: Hootalinqua to Carmacks

171 kilometres, 2½ to 4 days
Maps: 24 to 31
Difficulty: easy
Hazards: minimal
Scenery: moderate topographical relief
Wildness: quite remote, but popular; highway nearby between Little Salmon and Carmacks
Access: Big Salmon River, Little Salmon River, Little Salmon village, Carmacks (water access only to Hootalinqua)
History: abundant — Steamboat Island; wreck of the *S.S. Klondike*; two old gold dredges; Big Salmon and Little Salmon First Nations villages, Hootalinqua

Yukon River: Carmacks to Pelly River/Fort Selkirk

127 kilometres, 2 to 3 days
Maps: 31 to 37
Difficulty: easy to moderate
Hazards: Five Finger Rapids; Rink Rapids
Scenery: moderate topographical relief
Wildness: fairly remote except by Five Finger Rapids and the northern half
Access: Carmacks, Minto, Pelly Farm, Pelly River
History: Five Fingers Coal Company; some wood lots, abandoned settlements and steamer wrecks at Pelly Crossing (no land access to Fort Selkirk)
Comments: good camping opportunities

Yukon River: Pelly River/Fort Selkirk to White River

154 kilometres, 2 to 4 days
Maps: 37 to 45
Difficulty: easy
Hazards: minimal
Scenery: nice — Dawson Range to south, Klondike Plateau to north; lava cliffs for 20 kilometres downstream of the Pelly confluence
Wildness: quite remote, away from highway
Access: Pelly Farm, Pelly River, Pelly Crossing (no land access at White River)
History: Fort Selkirk; a few other old settlements
Comments: most remote section of the upper Yukon River

Yukon River: White River to Dawson City

123 kilometres, 1 to 2 days
Difficulty: easy
Hazards: gravel bars obscured by very silty water
Scenery: moderate topographical relief, good views up the White River valley
Wildness: frequent mining camps on side creeks; some river traffic
Access: Stewart River, Dawson City
History: mostly more modern development

ALTERNATE RIVER TRIPS VIA YUKON RIVER TRIBUTARIES

TESLIN RIVER
Johnson's Crossing to Hootalinqua
(see sidebar on page 116)
184 kilometres, 4 to 6 days
Difficulty: moderate
Hazards: class 1 riffles; some sweepers
Scenery: pretty Semenof Hills
Wildness: quite remote
Access: Johnson's Crossing
Earliest take-out point: Little Salmon
History: some small settlements, such as
  Mason's Landing along the Livingstone
  Trail
Comments: campsites are patchy

BIG SALMON RIVER
Quiet Lake to Big Salmon
(see sidebar on page 121)
235 kilometres, 6 to 8 days
Difficulty: difficult
Hazards: rapids up to class 2; sweepers;
  log jams; rocks
Scenery: beautiful — Big Salmon Range,
  Semenof Hills
Wildness: remote
Access: Quiet Lake via South Canol Road
Earliest take-out point: Little Salmon
History: little evident, although
  prospecting on the river and its
  tributaries has been carried out since
  1881

LITTLE SALMON RIVER
Robert Campbell Highway to
Little Salmon
(see sidebar on page 123)
50 kilometres, 1 to 2 days
Difficulty: easy
Hazards: rapids up to easy class 2,
  sweepers
Scenery: pretty — Pelly Mountains,
  Tatchun Hills

Wildness: highway parallels the river
Access: Little Salmon Lake via Robert
  Campbell Highway; take-out at Little
  Salmon; Little Salmon Village
History: little evident
Comments: limited camping

PELLY RIVER
Faro to Yukon River/Fort Selkirk
(see sidebar on page 137)
356 kilometres, 8 to 10 days
Difficulty: moderate
Hazards: some class 2-3 rapids
Scenery: pretty — Anvil Range, St. Cyr
  Range of Pelly Mountains, plateaus
Wildness: remote, despite some minor
  roads and cut lines
Access: Faro, rough road near Macmillan
  River, Pelly Crossing, Pelly Farm (no
  land access to Fort Selkirk)
Earliest take-out point: Pelly Crossing or
  Pelly Farm
History: little evidence on the Pelly River;
  major site at Fort Selkirk, on the Yukon
  River

STEWART RIVER
Stewart Crossing to Yukon River
(see sidebar on page 144)
190 kilometres, 4 to 6 days
Difficulty: easy
Hazards: minimal
Scenery: moderate topographical relief
Wildness: near highway from Stewart
  Crossing to the McQuesten River, then
  remote down to the Yukon River
Access: Stewart Crossing
Earliest take-out point: Dawson City
History: little evident

■ MAPS

The maps in Chapter 4 of this book provide what most travellers need to safely travel the route to the Klondike. They are based on topographical maps provided by national governments and are annotated with additional information supplied by the author. If you want to know more about the country alongside the route, you can purchase topographical maps from Canadian and United States governments or their authorized sales outlets in Whitehorse, Skagway and other major centres. Purchasing a complete set can be expensive, in which case you may want to be selective. It is a good idea to obtain these maps in advance, so they can be studied and waterproofed before your trip. I have found it useful to cut the maps into a readily accessible format, such as 8.5 inches x 11 inches (11 by 14 squares on the NTS grid), and then laminate them for protection.

The following list of 1:50,000 scale maps covers the Canadian portion of the route. If you desire 1:250,000 scale maps, which give you more information away from the river, take the first number and letter from the 1:50,000 codes to determine the required 1:250,000 map identification codes. For example, the corresponding 1:250,000 map that covers 94 E/4 is 94 E. Each 1:250,000 map covers 16 1:50,000 maps.

Chilkoot Trail, Dyea to Bennett
104 M/11 E   104 M/14 E   104 M/15 W

Headwater Lakes, Bennett to Whitehorse
104 M/15 W	105 D/2	105 D/1	105 D/8
105 D/9	105 D/10		

Yukon River, Whitehorse to Carmacks
105 D/10	105 D/11	105 D/14	105 E/3
105 E/6	105 E/11	105 E/10	105 E/15
105 E/14	105 E/13	105 L/3	105 L/4
115 I/1			

Yukon River, Carmacks to Dawson
115 I/1	115 I/8	115 I/7	115 I/10
115 I/11	115 I/14	115 I/13	115 J/16
115 J/15	115 J/14	115 O/3	115 O/4
115 O/6	115 O/5	115 O/12	
115 O/13	115 B/4	115 B/3	

The following maps cover the American portion of the Chilkoot Trail, from Dyea to the international border. They are offered in the scale of 1:25,000, as "1991 Provisional Editions," and are available through map distributors in Alaska or through the U.S. Geological Survey.

Skagway to Chilkoot Pass
Skagway (C-1) NW
Skagway (C-1) SW

A good map of the trail is also provided by Parks Canada as part of their park brochure. It can be obtained from the Trail Centre in Skagway or at bookstores in Whitehorse. Another good map of the Chilkoot Trail is put out by National Geographic Trails Illustrated, and is often carried by outdoor stores.

The NTS topographic maps can be ordered directly from the Canada Maps Office in Ottawa, or the Geological Survey of Canada in Vancouver. The American topographic series can be ordered through the U.S. Geological Survey in Fairbanks. The addresses can be found in Chapter 7 (Government Services, page 262).

■ GETTING TO THE NORTH

There are several locations that you can use to access the north and from which to base your trip. It all depends on which trip you plan to take. Whitehorse and Skagway are the most frequently used bases to start from, while Dawson is typically the end of the journey. Road, ferry and scheduled air flight are the main ways of accessing these locations.

Road

Regardless of where you are coming from, if you are coming to the region by road, you must travel the Alaska Highway. Built in 1942 for military purposes, it was originally called the "Alcan," or Alaska-Canada Military Highway. Visible and brave wildlife, hot springs and mountain vistas will mark this journey in your memory. From points east, you will access the Alaska Highway via Edmonton and Dawson Creek (595 kilometres from Edmonton to Dawson Creek, then another 1,475 kilometres to Whitehorse). From points south, the options are to go from Prince George up

Stone sheep on the Alaska Highway seem unconcerned about traffic.

Highway 97 to Dawson Creek (405 kilometres from Prince George to Dawson Creek, then another 1,475 kilometres to Whitehorse), or from Prince George up highways 16 and 37 to Watson Lake (1,200 kilometres from Prince George to the Alaska Highway west of Watson Lake, then another 454 kilometres to Whitehorse). All routes take you through gorgeous scenery.

Generally, the northern highways that access the region from the south are in good condition, having benefited from significant improvement over the past two decades. All main highways to the region are paved, with the exception of parts of the Stewart-Cassiar Highway (Highway 37) north of Meziadin Junction. Don't discount this route, though, since it is generally in good shape, and incredibly scenic.

In the Yukon, you must drive with your headlights on. In Alaska, the Yukon and British Columbia, seat belts are required for all occupants of your vehicle. *The Milepost*, which is published annually and available at many bookstores, is a good resource for local services and attractions for your road trip.

Ferry

The Alaska Marine Highway, the state's ferry system, is a great and different way to reach Skagway. The ferry may be boarded in Bellingham, Washington or Prince Rupert, British Columbia. You can travel to Bellingham by air, Amtrak, bus or car. Access to Prince Rupert is by air, car, bus, Via Rail or by B.C. Ferries from Port Hardy on Vancouver Island. Current ferry schedules and rates can be obtained by contacting the Alaska Marine Highway or B.C. Ferries at the addresses in Chapter 7 (Transportation, page 259). If you are taking a vehicle, reservations are required for both ferries.

The White Pass & Yukon Route train pulls up at Fraser, B.C.

A "speeder" train now takes hikers between Bennett and Fraser or Skagway.

Air

Whitehorse has a modern international airport with daily scheduled jet aircraft service — usually three flights per day from Vancouver in the summer. It's a trip of about two hours. You can reach Skagway by small plane from Juneau, connecting on to major airports in the U.S., including Seattle or to the Alaskan cities of Fairbanks and Anchorage. Dawson City can be reached by regional air carrier from Whitehorse, with connections to other points in the Yukon, Northwest Territories and Alaska.

◼ TRIP LOGISTICS

This section is designed to help you successfully plan the logistics of your trip to the north. Every traveller's plan must look at the distances involved, the need to deal with Customs to cross the international border between the U.S. and Canada, and the details of a journey involving different equipment for hiking and paddling. Below is information on:

- shuttles and movement of gear;
- booking and registration for the Chilkoot Trail;
- international customs; and
- accommodation, and other bookings such as rentals.

Shuttles and movement of gear

The first matter to plan is the movement of your group's members and their gear. Choose your start and stop points — either Whitehorse or Skagway. You need to get only the group and your backpacking gear to Dyea for the hiking portion of the trip. Your canoes and canoeing gear must arrive at Bennett for the day, or the

Water taxi is one way of exiting Bennett.

day before, you arrive there off the trail. (If you are renting canoes, see Chapter 7, page 260, to find out about rentals.) Then you need to have a way to get yourself and your gear back from Dawson City to your staging point at the end of the river portion of your trip.

Here's how we dealt with logistics for a trip for four. We chose Whitehorse as our start and stop point. Two of us flew from Vancouver to Whitehorse, while the other two drove a van up the Alaska Highway, stopping at Carcross to drop off the canoes and gear with a water taxi company. We then met up in Whitehorse where we spent a night. The next morning, two of us got up extremely early to drive to Dawson, dropping off the van with friends, before catching a plane back to Whitehorse. Meanwhile, the other two did last-minute chores in Whitehorse. The following morning, with only our backpacking gear, we all took the four-hour White Pass & Yukon Route (WP&YR) bus/train excursion to Skagway — a bit pricey but well worth it! After a night in a wonderful bed and breakfast in Skagway, we went to the trailhead at Dyea via a shuttle service. We then began our hike over the Chilkoot Pass. Our canoeing gear was delivered, on schedule, to meet us at Bennett, after which we had an enjoyable three-week paddle down to Dawson City, where our vehicle was waiting for us.

Logistics for your trip will be different, especially if you are doing only a portion of the route. You may wish to stage your trip through Skagway, instead of Whitehorse. You could get quite creative with cruise ships, trains, aircraft, rental vehicles and buses. If you are not continuing on past Bennett by canoe, you may want to take the WP&YR train from Bennett back to either Fraser or Skagway. You should book this well in advance.

There are three ways to get your canoeing gear to Bennett: by water taxi from Carcross; through a guide service in Whitehorse or Skagway; or by train from either Fraser or Skagway. If you are going to use the train, you should contact WP&YR to make arrangements for the service. (See Chapter 7, page 259, to contact water taxi operators or the WP&YR.) Whichever method you choose, ensure that all your arrangements are made at the time you drop off your gear, and that the arrival date for the gear being dropped off is clear to all parties. Giving the service-provider a written note of the arrangements is a good idea. The last thing you want to have happen is to arrive in Bennett with no canoes in sight and no food left!

There are two main ways to get a vehicle to Dawson City, one strictly by road and the other by both road and air (for the person returning to Whitehorse). The example cited above was by road and air, and took one full day. To do the shuttle strictly by road would require two vehicles and one very long day or two shorter days. Both vehicles would have to head north to Dawson City, each with a solo driver. One vehicle would be left in Dawson City while the other is driven back to Skagway. The Whitehorse-Dawson drive takes six to eight hours in each direction, plus it's another two hours to Skagway. Another alternative is to book a ride with a guiding company for the end of your trip, to return to Whitehorse with your canoe and gear. If you are renting canoes from a company in Whitehorse, bringing the canoes back to Whitehorse may be their responsibility.

To get yourself from Whitehorse to Skagway, you have a few options. Like we did, many take the WP&YR bus/train excursion. Others take a shuttle service provided by one of the local bus or tour companies. If you have your own vehicle, you will want to consider where the best place is for you to find long-term parking. Local service operators should be able to help you with this. Regardless of the arrangements for your canoeing gear, if it is crossing the border at any point, you should make Customs aware of the movement of your goods. They are used to travellers crossing the border several times to make arrangements between Skagway and Log Cabin or Bennett; be clear and straightforward at all times, and respect customs laws about when duty must be paid on goods purchased in either country.

Last, but not least, to get yourself (and your backpacking gear) to Dyea from Skagway, there is at least one shuttle company in Skagway that will do the honours. Please contact the Parks Canada Trail Centre or the Skagway Convention and Visitors Bureau for the names of companies that provide those services. (See Chapter 7, pages 261-262.)

Booking and registration

Before you climb the Chilkoot Trail, you must book and register for your trip well ahead of time. Parks Canada limits the number of hikers who cross the Chilkoot Pass each day to 50, and it requires that each party be booked into a specific campground on each of their nights. You should reserve well in advance to avoid the disappointment of full campgrounds.

When you finally arrive in Skagway, you must visit the Parks Canada Trail Centre on Broadway at 2nd Avenue to confirm your registration. It's also a great place to pick up information about the trail. (See Chapter 7, page 261, for contact information.) No booking or reservations are required for your travels along the waterways.

International customs

Hiking the Chilkoot Trail and moving yourselves and your gear between Alaska, British Columbia and the Yukon involve crossing the U.S.-Canada border. You must ensure, when you cross the border at any time, that you clear customs and immigration. When crossing by road, rail or air, this procedure is straightforward. By road you stop at the appropriate customs booth; by rail, a customs agent will board the train and clear everyone. By air, customs is handled at the airport. However, on crossing the border on the Chilkoot Trail, where no customs facilities exist, things are not as obvious. The official procedure is that you clear customs in Canada at your earliest convenience. If your trip is only the hike of the Chilkoot Trail, then, after you get out to Log Cabin, your earliest convenience will be to drive to Fraser and clear customs there, before going back to Skagway or Whitehorse. If you are paddling the lakes after the end of your hike at Bennett, then your earliest convenience will be in Whitehorse. Note that the customs office in Whitehorse is not open 24 hours, so special arrangements may have to be made if you are travelling through Whitehorse during an evening or weekend. As Canada Customs services may vary from year to year in certain places, it is recommended that you contact them well in advance of your arrival. (See Chapter 7, page 262.)

You must ensure that you have proper travel documents for crossing the border. For Canadian and U.S. citizens, a passport is your best bet, although often a birth certificate or citizenship card is adequate. For overseas visitors, contact your local consulate or embassy before travelling to determine appropriate visa requirements for both Canada and the U.S.

Travellers are reminded that Canada Customs officers vigorously enforce firearms importation laws, and may, at their discretion, do a search for firearms. Customs officials on both sides of the border do not have an issue with carrying bear spray for personal use, as long as it is clearly marked on the canister that it is for protection against animals. This does not allow for the small, personal pepper spray containers. It is possible that certain natural objects that may be legal in one country, may not be so in the other country, and may be confiscated at the border. Be sure to contact the appropriate customs office to check on restricted or controlled items. Indicate your citizenship in your inquiries, since procedures will differ depending on whether you are a resident or non-resident of the country you are entering.

Accommodations

There is a good range of accommodations in Skagway, Whitehorse and Dawson City — everything from bed and breakfasts to low-cost motels and higher-priced hotels. Some are turn-of-the century buildings that offer a special historic atmosphere. Lists of accommodations and room rates are available through Tourism Yukon and other sources. (See Chapter 7, pages 261-262.) You can check with the CAA (Canadian Automobile Association), the AAA (American Automobile Association) or a tourism agency for advice on accommodations. There are also campgrounds and RV parks in Skagway, Dyea, Tagish, Whitehorse, Carmacks and Dawson City.

■ WHEN TO GO

As the Yukon River is a northern river, and the Chilkoot Trail is a mountain pass of high elevations and abundant precipitation, the season for travelling the route is short. But one wonderful advantage of the northern locale is the long hours of daylight in summer. Certainly climate has the most bearing on when to travel this route, but river flows are also a consideration. Generally, the season for travel along the route is from June through September.

There are several factors people look at to help them decide when to make the trip. Each individual will have their own priorities. Bugs, weather, river flows, wildflowers, aurora borealis, fall colours — they all play a part in the enjoyment of the experience.

May is the earliest month for paddling after the river ice finally breaks up in the late northern spring. The last snow and nights of frost leave the interior in April and the days are warming up. Weather past the middle of May can be quite warm, and hours of sunlight are increasing noticeably each day, making outdoor travel very pleasant. Lakes are still locked in ice, however, limiting the kind of trips you can make. The Chilkoot is not yet ready for hikers.

Generally, **June** is a marginal month for travel over the Chilkoot. Significant quantities of snow will likely still lie in the alpine near the Chilkoot Pass, with the avalanche hazard running quite high. In the Yukon, the land is warm and green, wildflowers are in bloom and there is a fresh smell of new life in the air. The bugs are just making their appearance and can be quite plentiful, depending on water levels and conditions. The ice on Lake Laberge often doesn't go out until late May or early June. The water on the Yukon River is generally quite high, which, although it will carry you along quickly, also causes some tricky currents in some places, such as near the Marsh Lake control structure, around bends (of which there are plenty!), and at Five Finger Rapids and Rink Rapids. It also means the water is siltier, making it harder to see shallow areas. On the plus side, the days are *very* long, particularly around the summer solstice of June 21st. If you arrive in Dawson at that time, check out local celebrations by people who go to nearby high spots to watch the midnight sun. If you are still on the river, try floating through the shortest night of the year. Note that Yukon weather is influenced by systems in the Gulf of Alaska; this often leads to cloudy conditions in the southern Yukon while the central and northern Yukon regularly get much more sunshine and warmth.

July is better than June, especially towards the end of the month. It's the warmest month in the Yukon, and has the benefit of long hours of sunlight. Although still on the high side, the levels in the Yukon River have usually come down significantly from June, except higher upstream in the system where they stay high later in the season. By the end of the month, most of the snow should be gone on the Chilkoot Pass, and there should be the occasional sunny day in the pass. The wildflowers along the Yukon River will likely be spectacular in July, especially the brilliant fireweed, floral emblem of the Yukon. The Yukon is renowned for its short, intense growing season and July is a month of plentiful new vegetables. Restaurants in Dawson feature these on their menus.

August can be a nice month to travel. The levels are down quite a bit on the river. Although days are starting to get shorter, they are still fairly long, with the sun setting around 10:30 p.m. near the beginning of the month, and around 8:30 p.m. by the end of the month, depending on how far north you are located. When it's dark enough to see stars, it's dark enough for the aurora borealis – watch for it! The fireweed is in decline in August, but other wildflowers should be plentiful, and the Chilkoot Pass beautiful. By mid-August, most of the bugs are gone, thank goodness! By mid- to late August, the fall colours, which can be stunning, are starting to show. As the nights start getting cooler, there can be thick fog on the river in the morning, which usually burns off by mid-morning.

September is another marginal month. It's colder. No flowers. Shorter days. Lots of morning fog on the river. Fall rains have started on the coast, snow on the pass. Ice will be forming on the Yukon not long after the end of the month. But in the first half of the month, the fall colours in the south tend to be at their peak. There will be less river traffic. And as the month wears on, your chances of spotting aurora borealis increase.

Climate

Climate ranges greatly over the 934-kilometre length of this route, as it moves from coastal to interior, from south to north, from low to high elevation, and through variable topography.

Generally, the coast environment is wet, with long, cool summers and short, mild winters. This causes great amounts of snow to fall at the summit, which often remains late in the season and sometimes into the next winter. Winds over the pass are generally strong, from the north in the winter and from the

Average temperature (Celcius)

	Skagway	Whitehorse	Dawson
May	9.4	6.6	7.6
June	13.0	11.6	13.7
July	14.5	14.0	15.6
August	13.3	12.3	13.0
September	10.1	7.3	6.5

Average number of hours of daylight

	Skagway	Whitehorse	Dawson
May	16	16	18.5
June	18	18	21
July	19	19	20
August	17	17	16.5
September	14	14	13

south in the summer. It can snow on the pass at any time, and it is often cloudy, if not raining.

The interior, which encompasses most of the route, is a temperate and semi-arid environment. Winters are long and cold, with extreme temperatures dipping among the lowest on the planet. Summers are short, but with long hours of daylight they are very productive and often feature very warm days. The mountainous terrain causes great unpredictability in the weather, both from day to day and from year to year. So as with most wilderness adventures, be prepared for anything.

River flows

Given that the Yukon River, although swift, has a relatively mild and gentle nature, changes in flow do not greatly change your paddling experience. In higher water levels, the current will carry you along quicker, which can be pleasant. But around bends and at the rapids, tricky currents can catch unsuspecting paddlers off guard. The more technical tributaries, such as the Big Salmon and Pelly rivers, are not recommended in high water. Higher water levels generally also mean a higher sediment load in the river. High in the system, upstream of the Teslin River, the Yukon River is quite clear year-round due to the lakes' filtering capabilities. But as you travel down past the larger tributaries, the river will become dirtier. Below the White River, the Yukon River is incredibly murky no matter what time of year.

Generally, the river flows increase as you go downstream, due to the addition of flows from tributary rivers, streams and groundwater. The flows are low in winter, since much of the surface water is locked up as ice. Flows rise in spring due to snowmelt, and can sometimes maintain high levels if glacial melt is a factor. In Whitehorse, the river starts to rise in May, and may not peak until late September due to the high input of glacial melt from the mountains to the south. In

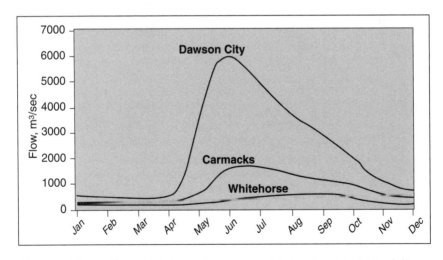

The Yukon River at Dawson City has a strong snowmelt-induced peak in June, while at Whitehorse, the peak is delayed until later when warm weather causes maximum glacial melt.

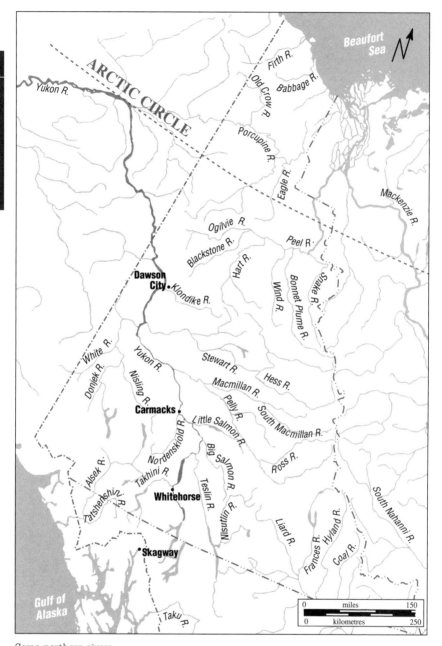

Some northern rivers.

Dawson City, the river begins to rise in April, and peaks in June. Most of the flow contributing to the peak flow at Dawson City is from the melting of the snowpack in the Yukon's interior.

■ EN ROUTE

Camping

Camping during your travels along the Klondike Trail will be a mixture of organized and primitive camping. Along the Chilkoot Trail, camping is allowed in designated areas only, into which you must be preregistered. Sites include outhouses, bear poles or caches, grey water pits for cleaning up, and group shelters at which you must cook, eat and wash up.

Along the waterway, primitive camping is free on public land. Respect standard minimal trace camping etiquette as outlined in Chapter 2. Some organized sites can be found. Territorial campgrounds are located in Tagish, Marsh Lake, Lake Laberge, Minto and Dawson. Camping permits are required; signs at each site will direct you to permit and pay procedures. Private sites can be found in Whitehorse, Carmacks and some other spots along the river. Along The Thirty Mile between Lake Laberge and the Teslin River, there are several free sites with facilities such as outhouses and picnic tables. Organized sites are marked on the maps and mentioned in Chapter 3.

Respect

While on your trip, please respect private property. Due to the history of the river, there are buildings along the way, some historic, others modern. Many of these are still owned by people who wish to maintain privacy. Assume that trespassers are unwanted unless it is clear otherwise. The same is true for old graveyards, which are sacred to the First Nations people. Occasionally, you will see signs for "fresh bread" or other items; this can be not only a welcome treat, but a good opportunity to meet people who live a special lifestyle in the wilderness.

Please also respect the environment. This northern climate is harsh, and the environment is slow to recover from harm. Please wash yourself far from the river so as not to contaminate it, and use the grey water pits provided in the parks. Respect the flora and the fauna. Do not remove any natural objects, such as feathers or bones, from the river or trail. Be scrupulous about making sure your campfire is out. More about minimizing environmental impacts is in Chapter 2.

Fishing and hunting

Northern fish taste great and can be a boon to any wilderness trip. You must first obtain a separate fishing license for any angling you plan to do while in the Yukon, British Columbia or Alaska. Fishing licenses can be purchased through most sporting goods stores and many other commercial facilities in the jurisdiction where you wish to fish. For fishing in transboundary lakes, including Bennett and Tagish, either a B.C. or Yukon fishing license will allow angling on either side of the border. This reciprocal agreement was to take effect on April 1, 2001.

Common species of fish that are found in the north include rainbow trout, steelhead, Dolly Varden, cutthroat, brook trout, northern pike, lake trout and Arctic grayling. Several species of salmon are also found in the Yukon watershed but, because of the need for conservation, usually are not available for sport fishing. Please respect fishing regulations and catch limits.

■ OTHER READING

There is an astounding amount of information written about the Yukon River and the history of the Klondike. You could spend years at a library and not read everything that has been written. When in Whitehorse, a visit to the public library is recommended for those who want to learn more. Likewise, the Yukon Archives has an extensive collection of books, maps and other historical resources available for interested people. And local bookstores carry a good collection of northern titles. There are a few writings that stand out among the others and can be helpful to enhance your appreciation of the area through which you will be travelling. Among these are:

- *Klondike*, by Pierre Berton;
- *Chilkoot Trail*, by David Neufeld and Frank Norris;
- *Law of the Yukon*, by Helene Dobrowolsky; and
- *The Best of Robert Service*, by Robert Service.

Klondike is a fascinating, easy reading non-fiction "novel" that chronicles much of the events of the Klondike gold rush. It's the authoritative work that many others have drawn from. Many groups travel down the river with this book in hand to learn about the places and people that made Yukon history.

Chilkoot Trail is a wonderful compilation of historical, cultural and natural information and photographs about the Chilkoot Trail. Working for Parks Canada and the U.S. National Park Service respectively, Neufeld and Norris together bring a quarter century of experience to this book, combining both research and field history.

Law of the Yukon is an extensive look at police and community history in the Yukon. Because much of that history was related to the opening of the territory, the gold rush, and life along the rivers, this highly illustrated volume presents a different take on the Yukon's past including relations between the NWMP and Yukon First Nations people.

Almost anyone who has heard of the Klondike gold rush has also encountered the name Robert Service. His poems of the era, including *The Cremation of Sam McGee* and *The Shooting of Dan McGrew* fill the mind with rich visions of a time gone by. It is fun to recite his poetry as you float down the mighty Yukon River following the path of the goldseekers.

Freshly caught fish make a nice treat.

CHAPTER 2...TRIP TIPS

*T*his section will help you plan your trip, and help you deal with changing circumstances as they occur. Safety and comfort in the backcountry are emphasized, as is minimizing negative impacts on the environment. You should remember that when it comes to survival in the wilderness, experience is the best teacher, and each group should include at least one person with sufficient experience. Dealing with emergencies in adverse conditions depends on your ability to make decisions, improvise and, most of all, remain calm.

Food and gear are aspects of every trip that can make or break your experience. When determining what to bring, you need to answer a number of questions. Will you travel every day or will there be rest days? What weather might you encounter? Will your group stay together or split up at some point along the way? Answers to questions like these may not only affect the list of gear and supplies you bring, but its distribution among group members. For your assistance, a typical checklist is provided on page 258.

Save your back! A canoe flipped over on two barrel packs makes a great table.

■ SAFETY & COMFORT

Have the necessary skills and know your limits

Few things are potentially more dangerous than an ill-equipped, unprepared wilderness traveller. For your safety and that of others, ensure you have the experience and appropriate skills for a backcountry wilderness trip. If everyone in your group does not have these skills, there should be enough people in the group with the experience or skill to ensure the safety of all. Although, for the most part, the river portion of this trip is not challenging, the trail is quite arduous. Previous backpacking experience — at least several weekend trips — is essential before attempting the Chilkoot Trail. While the Yukon River is considered fairly easy and suitable for beginners, good flatwater and basic moving water skills, as well as outdoor living skills, are required for any section of this magnificent waterway. It is important for both safety and comfort that these skills are up to date, and that you are in shape.

First aid training is essential on a wilderness trip. Your group must be able to deal with any emergency, since immediate outside help will not be available on most parts of the route. Good wilderness first aid courses are available at agencies such as St. John's Ambulance and the Red Cross, as well as some community colleges.

It is not recommended that you travel alone in the wilderness without a full understanding of all the risks involved. The ideal group size for safety is about six people. The chances of a bear attack are severely minimized, and evacuation of one injured person is more readily undertaken with a sufficient group size. However, too many in a group can make it difficult to find suitable camping spots.

Make sure that each traveller's basic gear is in good condition and suitable for the circumstances. Sleeping bags and tents, for example, should be good quality. Once on the river, you won't have an opportunity to shop to replace most things. (See more about gear, beginning on page 37.)

Treat water before drinking

Although many people think the northern environment is largely pure, the Taiya River along the Chilkoot Trail and the Yukon River are not always drinkable. The risk of picking up giardiasis (beaver fever) or another condition from the water is significant within the parks due to the amount of foot traffic. On the Yukon River, the risk increases below Whitehorse (due to effluent discharge), below the Teslin River, and especially below the White River due to the sediment load, which can carry contaminants. Your choices for maintaining a safe drinking water supply include:

- stocking up on fresh drinking water in communities;
- boiling the water (five minutes should do);
- chemical treatment (such as chlorine or iodine tablets, which should not be taken over long periods);
- mechanical filtering (with a hand pump); or
- purification (a combination of chemical treatment and mechanical filtering).

Beyond the White River, getting water in a bucket and letting it sit a while so sediment can settle will help your water filter last longer. A good outdoor equipment store can help you make the right water treatment decision for your needs.

Bring appropriate safety gear

Important safety gear when backpacking includes a whistle for alerting others if you need help, matches to start an emergency fire, and (optional) bear spray. Canoeing requires a bit more gear than backpacking. In addition to the items listed under backpacking, mandatory safety gear includes a lifejacket or personal floatation device (PFD) with a whistle and knife attached, bailer, and well-secured painters (floating ropes) at both ends of the canoe.

The importance of a PFD cannot be overstated. Any water, no matter how gentle it seems, carries the potential to harm. Northern waters are very cold, and even a short time in the water can lead to mild cases of hypothermia. A PFD will not only keep you more buoyant, but gives your body core some protection from the cold and from hard objects such as rocks and logs. Even on a lake, a PFD can help you fight against wind, waves or a long, cold swim to shore (which, of course, nobody ever plans). However, the PFD is only useful if it is on, zipped and tied!

Leave an itinerary with someone

This "someone" could be a family member or friend at home, or the operator of a local lodge or float plane company. The RCMP used to take itineraries of travellers, but no longer provides that service. Give your contact a detailed description of your route, approximate timetable, and an agreed-upon date and time after which the outside party would initiate a search. Information on who to contact in the event you do not return by the chosen date is given in Chapter 7, page 263.

A sample trip plan is shown on the next page. Leave a completed form with your contact so they can show it to officials if need be.

Sunset on Steamboat Slough.

TRIP PLAN: KLONDIKE TRAIL, DYEA TO DAWSON

Start point _____ Start date _____
dd   mm   yy

Destination point _____ Target date _____
dd   mm   yy

Trip description _____

_____

_____

Vehicle   Plate _____ Make/model _____ Year _____

          Colour_____ Location _____

First contact at destination   Name _____

             Company _____ Phone _____

Equipment   Tent make_____ Fly colour_____

             Watercraft_____ Colour _____

Name, age and emergency phone number of each member in the party

_____   _____

_____   _____

_____   _____

Medical conditions_____

_____

_____

Allergies_____

_____

_____

Please notify police if we do not return by: Date _____ Time _____
dd   mm   yy

Respect local wildlife

It is a good idea to know the types of wildlife that may be encountered where you are travelling. This knowledge has many advantages, including increasing your chances of viewing wild creatures (from a safe distance), and decreasing your risk of an unpleasant wildlife encounter. Please respect all the wildlife you see — do not chase or harass animals to get that perfect picture, or for any other reason. Give animals a wide berth and give them a chance to slip away quietly. A telephoto lens will help you get a good photo without getting too close. Chapter 6 has more information about the wildlife you may see on your trip.

Bears

The animal you should be the most aware of is the bear. There are two types of bears you may encounter: the black and the grizzly. Black bears are by far the most common, especially in valley bottoms where you are most likely to be.

In the wild, bears are likely to run in the opposite direction if they see or smell you. They want to avoid contact with humans and for this reason, the majority of human-bear encounters are non-injurious, with both parties getting no more than a rapidly beating heart and, I hope, more respect for the other. This said, bears are also very unpredictable. A bear that has become accustomed to humans, especially those humans with poor wilderness ethics, can be dangerous. Out of respect for

Grizzly tracks are most recognizable by the length of the claws.

yourself and others passing after you, you should take every possible precaution to minimize the risk of a negative bear encounter. These include the following:

- Travel in large groups and stay close (bears are unlikely to attack a group of six or more);
- Remain aware of your surroundings, and cautious at all times;
- Make lots of noise while travelling on land (use a bear bell, sing, chant or yell "yo bear!");
- Carry a bear retardant (pepper spray), bear bangers or an air horn while hiking. (This is optional and a personal preference; pepper spray may not be allowed on a flight. See Chapter 1, page 20.);
- If you sight a bear, give it lots of room, and calmly let it know you are there;
- Don't jump around and shout; a bear may see this as threatening behaviour. Standing may also be seen as a sign of aggression;
- Do not get between a mother bear and her cubs;
- Avoid using smelly foods such as fish and bacon;
- Cache all food in a bear cache when provided in parks, or strung from a tree, at least four metres in the air and at least two metres from the trunk, when away from your site or sleeping;
- Do not keep anything smelly in the tent; this includes food, deodorant, toothpaste, medications, and clothes you have cooked in;
- Cook, eat and clean up at shelters in parks, and use grey water pits for dish water;
- Make sure your kitchen or cooking area is far away and downwind from your tent;
- Do not bring dogs along; bear country is no place for your pet; and
- Remember — you are a visitor here; respect their privacy, do not harass the wildlife.

Grizzly bear and cub. Note the hump along the back as a means of distinguishing a grizzly bear from a black bear.

The manner in which you react to a bear depends on whether it is a black or a grizzly. The **grizzly** tends to be larger than the black. Generally a "grizzled" brown in appearance, colour can range from near black to silver-blonde. Northern grizzlies typically weigh between 225 and 275 kilograms. The grizzly has a concave nose and a wide head with two small, furry ears. It has a pronounced shoulder hump and has longer claws than the black bear. The **black bear** tends to be smaller than the grizzly bear, averaging about 135 kilograms in the Yukon. The colour of its coat is most commonly black, but ranges from almost white to very black, with many colour phases in between, including the common cinnamon. The black bear is missing the large shoulder hump of the grizzly bear, instead having a back and shoulders that form almost a straight line. Its straight or roman nose also distinguishes it from the grizzly.

Black bear (above) and grizzly bear (below).

There are no rules that are guaranteed to work when faced with a threatening bear. The book *Bear Attacks: Their Causes and Avoidance* by Stephen Herrero gives much insight into bear avoidance and defence techniques. The general guide to dealing with any threatening bear includes the following:

- Do not run! Bears can run 14 metres in a second (yes, that's considerably faster than you can!);
- Stand your ground if it charges; bears will often give false charges;
- Back away, talking in soft tones and dropping something as a distraction as you back up;
- If you have a pack on, leave it on for protection; and
- As a last resort, discharge your bear spray directly at the bear's face, if within four metres and given the correct wind conditions.

In addition to the above guidelines, if the threatening bear is a grizzly, heed the following:

- If there is a climbable tree, climb it, but climb it high; grizzlies have some tree climbing capabilities where there are large, weight-supporting branches;
- If the bear attacks, play dead, dropping into a spread-eagle position with your hands protecting the back of your neck (it will be harder for the bear to roll you over and access your vulnerable areas); and
- If the attack is a result of stalking, is unprovoked or lasts more than a couple minutes, fight back, concentrating your blows to the bear's face.

If the threatening animal is a black bear, these tactics are different:

- Do not bother climbing a tree, black bears are great climbers;
- Do not swim away, bears are great swimmers; and
- If the bear attacks, fight back with vigour.

The best tactic is to avoid the situation in the first place. Just remember, bears are unpredictable and there are no hard and fast rules. No encounter is better than a bad encounter.

Yes, there are bugs!

Biting bugs you may (or are likely to) encounter include mosquitoes, black flies, horse flies, deer flies and biting midges. So hang on to your bug hat — you're in for a ride!

Generally, mosquitoes make their first appearance in the southern and low-lying areas of the region in the first half of June, especially in wet areas. Higher areas in the south see these critters around the middle of the month. The northern, arctic regions experience the first wave in the last week or two of June. Usually by the middle of August, mosquitoes are in decline, with September generally free of the little nippers.

There are several methods that can be used to defend yourself from bugs. High on the list is a good bug repellent. A repellent containing citronella, a natural insect repellent, or DEET will work well. Which one works best on you may depend on body chemistry, since everyone seems to report different results. If you can, test them out before your trip. Keep your skin covered with clothing, avoiding dark colours, which most bugs are attracted to. Bug jackets and bug hats are an incredibly good invention — they are lightweight, vented, and keep the bugs out. Standing or sitting near a smoky fire or in a windy place can keep bugs at bay. Hence, islands are good camping locations to avoid bugs. Unfortunately, rain does not drive them away. It seems they can dodge the raindrops! Keep your tent zipped up at all times except briefly when entering or exiting.

■ ENVIRONMENTAL CONSIDERATIONS

Since we are travelling in the backcountry to enjoy a pristine environment, it is likely other people are too. Leaving campsites in good condition is not only considerate to fellow travellers, but is also an important safety concern due to bears. Along the Chilkoot Trail, your care of the site is regulated: no fires, use established tent sites, use the grey water pits for washing, and cook and clean at the group shelters. Along the lakes and river, it is up to you to take appropriate care.

In general, along on the Yukon River, campsites are found on sand and gravel bars, or in clearings on raised benches over the river. The remains of a firepit built on a gravel bar will be swept out during higher water levels, leaving the site in a more natural state. In higher areas, you will often find sites with several established firepits. Where they exist, you should use existing firepits to minimize further impact. Where no previous firepit exists, build a new pit below the high water mark.

The Canadian Recreational Canoe Association developed *A Canoeist Manual for the Promotion of Environmental and Ethical Concerns*, which has good ideas about backcountry camping. The highlights of this manual are listed below, and form a basis for minimizing the impact of canoe camping. These can also be applied to backpacking.

General and planning

- Become a responsible guardian of the land and waterway;
- Keep numbers small to minimize soil compaction and vegetation damage;
- Do not take a pet when in known animal habitat;
- Avoid unnecessary disturbance of wildlife;
- Stay on existing trails and portages, do not shortcut switchbacks; and
- Leave plants and rocks in their place.

Camping

- Choose campsites that will minimize your impact; and
- Use camping practices and gear that minimize your impact.

Cooking and fires

- Use a stove when travelling in sensitive areas such as alpine regions;
- Do not light a campfire when forest conditions are dry; the Yukon is a semi-arid climate and often a no-burn policy may be in effect to protect against wildfire;
- Keep campfires small;
- Use existing firepits when possible, otherwise remove evidence of fire after use;
- When building a fire pit, dig to mineral soil, away from burnable soils, roots and overhanging trees;
- Use only deadfall for firewood; cutting dead branches off standing trees is unacceptable;
- Burn to a white ash and remove any non-burnable items such as tin foil, cans and glass; and
- Douse your fire thoroughly before going bed and before departure.

Waste

- Clean up all litter you create, plus that left behind by others;
- Carry out what you carry in; you can dispose of waste at various access points along the route;
- When nature calls, move at least 35 metres from any surface water, bury human waste between 14 and 18 centimetres, and burn or carry out toilet paper;
- Use biodegradable soap; and
- Wash dishes and yourself at least 15 metres from water, not in the river or lake, even when using biodegradable soap.

In addition to the above, please resist the temptation to remove natural or cultural artifacts that you may find along the way. Archaeological sites, which are quite common along this route, are of historical significance and should not be disturbed. Plants and animal remains all play a part in the survival of a healthy ecosystem and should remain where they are found. Within the parks, it is illegal to remove any natural or historical objects. In the Yukon, it is illegal to remove any historical artifact.

If we leave our special places in better shape than when we found them, then we have truly done our part for all who visit after us, both two- and four-legged.

■ COMMUNICATING IN AN EMERGENCY

2

TRIP TIPS

Although some feel that carrying a radio takes away from that wilderness experience, it could also mean the difference between life and death in an emergency. Though park rangers are present on the Chilkoot Trail, the river has long sections that are far from services and, often, other people. Groups must weigh the pros and cons for their own circumstances and make their own decisions. Emergency communications can come in handy in case you encounter a person or group that needs more help than you can provide.

One risk of having a radio is that you may unconsciously take greater chances, believing that help could be on the way at the press of a button. You should remember that communication devices in remote locations are not always reliable, and should not be the only key to a rescue plan. A radio should also be used only in an absolute emergency; generally rescues consume huge amounts of resources at the expense of either you or the taxpayer. And after contact is made with emergency services, they may be some time away from reaching an injured person.

The choices you have in the Yukon for emergency communication consist of the single sideband radio, the land VHF radio, an emergency beacon such as an EPIRB (emergency position indicating radio beacon) or PLB (personal locator beacon), or a portable satellite telephone. A cell phone will not work along most of the route. The VHF radio is probably the most common device used today although satellite phones are coming into greater use. Both satellite phones and VHF radios can be rented in Whitehorse as well as larger centres at a reasonable cost; look under *Radio Communication Equipment and Systems* in the yellow pages. The dealer can preprogram emergency frequencies into the VHF radio before you head out. You can get these frequencies for the Yukon area from Northwestel by phoning your operator and asking for the Whitehorse operator. Explain your situation and state that you want the frequencies of the repeaters local to the Yukon River. Frequencies of each repeater come in the form of a transmit frequency, receive frequency and channel. Another source of repeater information is from the Yukon Amateur Radio Association. Details are in Chapter 7, under Emergency Services, page 263.

To avoid a situation where you need to use a radio or beacon, always be aware of hazards on your journey. Keep an eye on the weather at all times. Know the places that you can get off the river and to a highway (see chart on page 9 for route access points), and always know your location on the maps. Remember to have a contact who knows your route and itinerary, and who you feel confident will make rational decisions in the event that you fail to return on the specified date. Make sure that you and your contacts know the emergency numbers to call in the region. (See Chapter 7, Emergency services, page 263.)

If you are looking for further information on wilderness tripping, some recommended reading includes:

- *The Backpacker's Handbook*, by Chris Townsend
- *Bear Attacks: Their Causes and Avoidance*, by Stephen Herrero
- *Bush Basics*, by Glen Stedham
- *Path of the Paddle*, by Bill Mason
- *Planning a Wilderness Trip in Canada and Alaska*, by Keith Morton
- *Song of the Paddle,* by Bill Mason

■ WHAT TO BRING

It is imperative that you have enough suitable clothing and gear to meet your basic needs for food, warmth and shelter. It also makes your trip more comfortable and enjoyable. There is a huge assortment of materials and manufacturers to choose from when buying outdoor clothing and gear; the choices can be bewildering. Technologies are changing constantly. Your best bet when purchasing new outdoor equipment is to contact a well respected outdoor store to find out about the latest advances in gear.

Despite rapid changes in outdoor clothing and equipment, there are some basic guidelines that apply. The following is a discussion of these.

Blisters can be a hardship while on the trail.

Clothing

First, your clothing should be worn in layers to create insulating air pockets and allow for easy adjustment as conditions change. Each layer has a different function. The layer next to your skin should be quick drying, odour resistant and have moisture-wicking capabilities (forcing moisture away from your skin). Usually a synthetic material such as spun polyester does the best job. Avoid cotton for this layer as it holds the moisture against your skin and robs your body of heat. The outer layer should have wind and rain resistance, preferably with some breathability. One example of suitable material is Gore-Tex. Cuffs should be tight against the wrists or rain will work down to your elbows (and further) while paddling. The middle layers should provide warmth and moisture-wicking capabilities. Wool and synthetic piles are the best for this insulating layer, but remember that wool becomes very heavy when wet, and takes forever to dry. Protection for your extremities, such as a hat, mitts and good footwear, are essential. When you make camp each day, it's important to change into dry clothing and dry out the stuff that got wet during the day.

Footwear

Footwear is also very important for both canoeing and backpacking. For the trail, a good pair of sturdy hiking boots is essential, with its most important characteristics being a half shank, ankle support and a good tread. On such a rough

A sample of canoeing footwear: (left) rubber boots, inappropriate for moving water; (top, l-r) sneakers, wet suit booties; (bottom, l-r) river sandals, aqua socks.

trail, improper footwear could lead to injury, whether it be as minor as blisters, or as major as a sprain or broken bone. Before your trip, if your boots are new, ensure you have broken them in. You will also want to waterproof your boots, since some portions of the trail can be quite wet. A waxy waterproofer, such as Dubbin, Biwell or Snoseal, works well on leather, while 3M Scotchguard works surprisingly well on cordura.

You should also find a sock system that works for you. Everyone's feet are different. Some people swear by a two-sock system (a main sock with a lightweight, poly liner); others by a single, heavy sock; still others by no sock at all. A polypropylene sock or liner is highly recommended. It tends to hold moisture away from the foot, minimizing the chance for blisters to develop. Regardless, you will probably want a good blister kit along, just in case! Moleskin, Second Skin and Compeed dressings are three good choices for avoiding or treating blisters.

There are many choices when it comes to footwear on the river. These include river sandals, sneakers and wet suit or reef booties, to name a few. Gore-Tex socks can be used inside any of these types of footwear. It comes down to a personal choice. The Yukon is a cold river, therefore it is important that your feet stay warm. If you are wearing footwear that requires socks, poly or wool socks are recommended, as opposed to materials such as acrylic, nylon or cotton. Wet suit booties will keep your feet the warmest, but may not be comfortable to wear all day, every day (and I can almost guarantee they will start to smell!). River sandals have the advantage that water can drain from them, but this also allows other unwanted items to get into your shoes. When in camp, it's good to have dry socks and footwear to change into. For your camp shoes, a sole with shallow tread is better for the environment than a deep tread.

Handwear

An important consideration, more for the paddling portion, is warm and functional handwear. I have had difficulty finding cold weather handwear that does not hamper my paddling. Wet suit gloves keep hands warm, but I find they make it difficult to grip the paddle, making my hands cramp up. Thinner neoprene gloves are available with fake suede palms, but these do not keep my hands warm.

Canoe pogies protect your hands from the weather and give you a good grip on the paddle.

A sample of canoeing handwear: (top, l-r) Thunderwear neoprene gloves, fingerless gloves, wool mitts, polypropylene glove liners, fleece gloves; (bottom, l-r) Gore-Tex pogies, neoprene pogies, Gore-Tex shell mitts, cycling gloves.

Wool mitts do not work too badly, and can be covered with a Gore-Tex outer liner for wet conditions. Canoe pogies are probably your best option. These neoprene or Gore-Tex "mitts" velcro onto your paddle, so when your hands are slipped inside, they directly contact the paddle. If canoeing, make sure you get canoeing pogies, not kayaking ones.

Gear

Suitable, well-maintained gear is just as important as appropriate clothing. Co-ordinating as a group will ensure that you don't arrive with three sets of pots but no utensils or stove! In addition, you should ensure that all your gear is in good working order, with spare parts where they may be required. Imagine if someone says they'll bring the only stove for the hike, only to find out that they didn't test it and it won't light. Please use the gear checklist on page 258 to get organized.

The gear you need for backpacking is quite different than that for the river. For backpacking, it is essential that you take as little as possible and it must all be practical. Your menu should require minimal fuel and cookware, and your clothes and sleepwear should be very lightweight. For canoeing, you can afford to take a little more weight, for example, more elaborate cookware, more food and supplies, an axe and camp chairs. You don't want to go overboard though (no pun intended!), since you have large, cold lakes to traverse and don't want your boat to be overloaded.

Whatever you do bring, make sure that anything you wish to stay dry is properly waterproofed. An unplanned dumping or even a solid downpour can cause considerable hardship without the proper waterproofing. There are many methods of waterproofing gear, and your method may also depend on whether you are backpacking or canoeing. Again, staff at a good outdoor store are the best resource for current waterproofing methods.

Here is a system that I use which works well for me. For backpacking, placing the most essential gear (clothes and sleeping bag) in plastic garbage bags, then into a stuff sack (to avoid tearing) has proven to be a lightweight and effective method of waterproofing. For added protection, I wear a backpacking poncho or a waterproof pack cover. For canoeing, we put our clothes and food into 60-litre barrel packs, with a harness for portaging if required. (Your only portage will be around the Whitehorse dam.) These barrel packs make an excellent platform on which to rest an upside down canoe as a table. Other items that must be kept dry are kept in watertight "dry bags." The best method to save my camera from both water and bangs is a hard-shell Pelican box. To help keep water out of my boat in downpours, a spray cover is valuable, and it keeps my legs and feet warm on a cold day. A sponge and a bailing bucket are good for taking out rain and spraywater too.

A repair kit for their canoe is one thing that many people don't bring. We always have one with us, having needed it in the past. The Yukon River is relatively gentle with few rocks, so it is unlikely that major damage will be done to your canoe. But a few essentials can go a long way, such as the trusty duct tape; an all-in-one tool; a sewing kit; and spare parts for stove and filter.

All this...

...fits into this!.

One way of setting up a canoe tarp.

I have found that a good-sized tarp is a valuable component of my paddling gear, and many others I know consider it essential. A tarp can provide protection from rain, sun and wind. Over the years, my husband and I have developed what we consider to be a fantastic canoeing shelter, as shown in the photograph above. Using the canoe as a backboard for the tarp gives extra protection and a clean place to store the packs and gear. The sides can be raised or dropped to adjust to changing winds and weather conditions. A second canoe can be used as a table.

■ FOOD

Food is one aspect of outdoor travel that everyone deals with differently. It can be a tough challenge when you bring together people with different nutritional needs and desires. However, there are some basic principles that you may want to consider when drawing up your menu.

- Have balanced, high energy meals, with starches, fruits, vegetables, grains and proteins;
- Remember that you are working hard and will require more food than usual;
- Have liquids available that replace electrolytes (e.g. Gatorade, V8, citrus juice crystals);
- Sort out peoples' allergies and dislikes *before* you head out;
- It is best to share in the food preparation and cleanup — this is a social time;
- Everyone can take responsibility for certain meals; alternate with cleanup chores; and
- Do not rely on fishing or hunting en route for the basics of your menu, as they are unreliable.

In general, when backpacking, you should plan meals that, most importantly, weigh as little as possible, and require minimal fuel and dishes. Meals that require no addition of water, such as boil-in-the-bag meals, mean that you are carrying that water in the food. Simple, freeze dried meals tend to be very well suited for backpacking, since they require little fuel, time or dishes to prepare. Save the gourmet cooking for the canoeing portion!

Canoeing affords a little more flexibility with meal choices because you can carry more. Dehydrated meals are suitable, but there are now many great, inexpensive meal packages that can be bought at your local grocery store. A bonus of travelling on the Yukon River is that, for fresh food or cold beer, you can plan for several stock-up points (grocery stores at Whitehorse and Carmacks, more basic supplies at Carcross and Tagish). You may want to incorporate these into your menu. Just remember that the selection may not be as great as you are used to. Some "fresh" foods, such as cured meats, carrots, potatoes and cheeses, will last quite some time.

Don't forget that you must have everything you need to create your meals on your trip. This includes items such as margarine, oil, sugar, flour, salt, pepper and milk powder. Read the directions of any prepackaged meals to see what other ingredients might be required, and include them in measured quantities where possible. Also, don't forget other staples such as drinks (tea, coffee, hot chocolate), snacks, appetizers and desserts!

Whatever type of food you bring, prepare meals you are familiar with and know are successful, unless you have a real taste for adventure! Unless you have a group with hardy tastebuds, watch the spice levels. A poor meal on a trip is not only a big disappointment, but a meal not eaten doesn't provide the energy required to paddle or hike a full day. That said, I have rarely experienced a meal outdoors I haven't enjoyed; there's something about that fresh air.

There are many good backcountry cooking guides and recipe books on the market, typically sold at outdoor stores. Below are some you might find useful.

- *Dry It — You'll Like It*, by Gen Maniman
- *Good Food for Camp & Trail — All Natural Recipes for Delicious Meals Outdoors*, by Dorcas S. Miller
- *Gorp, Glop and Glue Stew — Favourite Foods from 165 Outdoor Experts*, by Yvonne Prater, Ruth Dyar Mandenhall
- *Recipes for Roaming — Adventure Food for the Canadian Rockies*, by Astrid Blodgett, Brenda McIntyre, Janet Pullan
- *Simple Foods for the Pack*, by Claudia Axcell, Diane Cooke, Vikki Kinmount
- *The Little Cookbook for the Great Outdoors*, by Linda Darling, Suat Tuzlak
- *The NOLS Cookery*, by Sukey Richard, Donna Orr, Claudia Lindholm
- *The One Pan Gourmet — Fresh Food on the Trail*, by Don Jacobson
- *The One Pan Gourmet Cooks Lite — A Low-Fat Guide to Outdoor Cooking*, by Don Jacobson, Don Mauer
- *The Well-Fed Backpacker*, by June Fleming
- *Wanipitei Canoe Tripper's Cookbook; Wilderness Cooking for Fun and Nutrition*, by Carol Hodgins

FINAL TIPS

During and after each trip, I make a list of lessons I've learned from the particular circumstances we've encountered. It's embarrassing how many lessons I seemed to have had to learn more than once! But the list has come in handy many times when I have prepared for an upcoming trip.

Here are the highlights. I hope they can prevent some hardship for you. Remember — these have been learned first hand!

- Make sure all your gear is in good working order.
- Have more than one set of maps.
- Bring more than one water filter for a group of six.
- Do not drink untreated water out of streams (followed by "keep Imodium in the first aid kit").
- Make tea for the thermos in the morning.
- Leave snacks accessible during the day, but pack them away at night.

- Green peppers do not last six days.
- A margarine container does not hold up.
- A conservative guide for white gas is one litre per person per week.
- Double waterproof toilet paper.
- Bring an extra stuff sack for hanging food.
- Bring an extra ground sheet for gear on sandy campsites.
- Mice eat shoelaces and toilet paper.
- Camp within earshot of one another.
- Put up tarps no matter how nice it looks.
- Leave munchies in the car for the end of the trip.
- Always lock the canoes up overnight when they are on the vehicle.
- Have a day to turn yourself around after a trip.
- One never stops learning.
- A bad day on the river, trail or lake is better than a good day at work!

Beaver lodge in bank of Lewes River.

Bruce Bennett

CHAPTER 3...ROUTES & RAPIDS

*T*his chapter describes the complete route from Dyea to Dawson City, including hiking the Chilkoot Trail and canoeing the headwater lakes and the Yukon River. Route descriptions include camping spots (always good to know!), potential hikes in the area, access points, sites of scenic or historical significance and other points of interest. Many of these are shown on the strip maps in Chapter 4 and the specific maps are referenced in the descriptions in this chapter.

The route has been divided into four sections:
- *Chilkoot Trail;*
- *Headwater Lakes, Bennett to Whitehorse;*
- *Yukon River, Whitehorse to Carmacks; and*
- *Yukon River, Carmacks to Dawson City.*

The descriptions are meant to enhance your enjoyment of the route by pointing out aspects that might otherwise be passed by without notice. Of course, there is lots more for you to discover on your own.

A comfortable spot for the night.

■ RATING THE ROUTE

Trail

The Chilkoot Trail is a challenge and a thrill. Luckily, conditions today are not nearly as difficult as 100 years ago. We modern-day travellers have lightweight materials for tents, moisture-wicking materials for clothing, high tech hiking boots and many other items that increase our comfort. We have the pleasure of a quota system that avoids overcrowding by restricting the number of people allowed on the trail at one time. We are not attempting the pass in the winter and we are not required to take in a ton of supplies like the stampeders!

However, this does not mean that it will be easy. The trail rises 1,122 metres from the ocean through a coastal rainforest. Much of this climb is located between Sheep Camp and the summit, rising 817 metres over six kilometres. The crunch is up the Golden Stairs to the summit, a steep steady climb. And as if that was not enough for one day, hikers must travel another six kilometres beyond the summit on rolling, difficult terrain before stopping at Happy Camp. The rest of the trail is of more moderate difficulty. The best preparation is to be in the best physical shape possible for the experience!

Site	Distance (km)	Approximate time (hours)	Terrain and difficulty
Dyea	0		
Finnegan's Point	7.9	2-3	coastal trail; moderate
Canyon City	4.6	1-1½	coastal trail; easy
Pleasant Camp	4.4	1½-2½	coastal trail; moderate
Sheep Camp	4	½	coastal trail; easy
Scales	4.8	3-4	subalpine; rough and difficult
Summit	0.9	1-1½	alpine; steep, difficult footing
Happy Camp	6.4	2½-3½	alpine; rough, difficult footing
Deep Lake	4	1-1½	subalpine; moderate, rolling
Lindeman	4.8	2½-3½	dry sub-boreal spruce; easy
Bare Loon Lake	4.9	1½-2	sub-boreal spruce; moderate
Bennett	6.4	1½-2	sub-boreal spruce, sand dunes; easy
Cut-off trail	9.5	2½-3	easy trail, alongside the railway tracks for much of the way

Lake

The lakes on the Yukon River system, which include Bennett, Tagish, Marsh and Laberge, are all large, cold, northern lakes. Winds are unpredictable in strength and direction. Although a lake may be calm when you first paddle onto it, the wind may suddenly pick up and cause large waves with whitecaps in minutes. Prevailing winds, generally from the south and west, tend to be strongest in the afternoon, dying down in the late afternoon. Yet strong winds can blow from any direction for days at a time. Never go further from shore than you would feel comfortable swimming while fully clothed, and stay close to the other boats in your party. Most importantly, always wear your lifejacket properly.

River

The Yukon River is a gently flowing river for much of its length. There are only four spots with rapids — Miles Canyon, Whitehorse Rapids, Five Finger Rapids and Rink Rapids. All but Whitehorse Rapids can be easily run by canoeists with solid flatwater skills; your challenge is no more than large-volume Class 1 rapids, involving tricky currents with no major obstructions. What remains of Whitehorse Rapids are situated below the Whitehorse dam, and are bypassed with an easy portage.

The International River Grading System was developed to describe the level of difficulty of river rapids. This system is used as a guide only, since nothing can replace a visual inspection of a river and its rapids before running it. The grading system is measured in six levels, with "1" being the easiest, "6" being the hardest, and "3" being the upper limit for open canoes. A "grade" is given to a river as a whole, while a "class" is given to a specific rapid. One should keep in mind that a rapid may change dramatically with varying water levels, thereby changing its rating. In addition, riverbeds may change at any time due to flooding, changing the location of rocks, waves and debris. A large river like the Yukon is constantly changing, shifting gravel bars and channels.

It is advisable to remember that accidents can happen in even the easiest rapids. I have seen canoes wrapped on rocks by experienced paddlers in easy, low volume Class 2 rapids. Always be aware well ahead of the hazards, such as sweepers and log jams, so you can plan in advance. It is advisable to take basic moving water lessons before going on the river, and it is essential to have solid flatwater paddling skills. Not only will this reduce the risk of a mishap, but also increase your enjoyment of the river.

Class 1 rapids	Class 2 rapids	Class 3 rapids
• fast moving water with riffles and small, regular waves	• medium to difficult, with some technical manoeuvring required	• difficult, technical manoeuvring required
• safe route through is obvious, with little to no manoeuvring required	• route easy to recognize	• high irregular waves, breakers, rollers, unstable boils
• obstructions are few and easy to avoid	• easy to medium drop-offs	• clear route through is not immediately obvious, requires scouting from shore
• suitable for open canoes; floatation and spray cover not required	• suitable for open canoes; floatation an asset, spray cover not necessary except in high volume	• difficult drop-offs
		• upper limit for open canoes; floatation and spray cover may be necessary to avoid swamping

If you plan to enter the Yukon River via one of its major tributaries, such as the Teslin, Big Salmon, or Pelly rivers, you may encounter Class 2 or 3 rapids. For these routes, you require solid flatwater and moving water skills. It is suggested that your group members take a local canoeing course to prepare for the more difficult water.

Consistent with standard terminology, river right refers to the right shore or edge of the river when looking downstream. Likewise, river left refers to the left side of the river when facing downstream. These terms will pop up frequently in this chapter.

MSCUA, University of Washington, Hegg photog., 2115b

Those who built their boats at Lindeman had to negotiate the dangerous One Mile Rapids between Lindeman and Bennett lakes.

SKAGWAY

Skagway originated with the Klondike gold rush, although there were a few settlers there before that. Captain William Moore, who had piloted riverboats throughout western Canada, had a premonition that gold would be discovered in the Yukon, that the White Pass was the route in, and that Skagway would become the gateway to the goldfields. He set himself up here with his son J. Bernard, several years before the rush, staking a homestead, building wharves and waiting to cash in when the masses came.

Amazingly enough, his prediction came true and the masses came, but Moore was overrun and came out of the deal with very little. With its good docking facilities and the construction of the White Pass & Yukon Route railway, Skagway boomed. The name Skagway, which was originally Skagua or Skaguay, is said to mean "home of the north wind" in the local Tlingit dialect. After the gold rush, Skagway dwindled, but managed to survive as an ocean port and terminus of the White Pass & Yukon Route railway. Later, cruise ships and the Alaska marine ferry would help sustain the city.

Today, Skagway is a beautiful, cheerful town, catering primarily to tourism through the cruise ship industry. Much of its attraction lies in the fact that it is the only gold rush town that was not destroyed by fire at some time in its history, so many of the buildings date back over 100 years. Another small attraction, lying north of the town, is the gold rush cemetery that contains the graves of famous gold rush characters Frank Reid and Soapy Smith.

Skagway presents a cheerful face to tourists.

DYEA

In its brief heyday, Dyea was a thriving city of 8,000 to 10,000 stampeders, with a short-lived claim as one of the largest towns in Alaska. It's hard to imagine this as you start out your hike in the lush coastal forest. You could easily skip past the site, not realizing its presence.

Dyea grew quickly out of gold rush dreams, and died just as quickly after the White Pass & Yukon Route railway was completed to Bennett in 1899. It had a street grid, and all the typical gold rush businesses to serve and entertain the stampeders during their brief stay.

Located on the west side of the Taiya River, a couple of kilometres south of the trailhead, the Dyea townsite is a worthwhile visit if you have the time. Although the street grid is, for the most part, no longer visible, you can still find some wooden ruins, a building facade, piers of the quays for docking boats, and the Slide Cemetery, where victims of the Palm Sunday avalanche near the Scales were laid to rest.

One of the reasons that Dyea is so far from the ocean today is that the land is still rising after the last ice age over 10,000 years ago. As a matter of fact, the land here is rebounding at approximately 13 millimetres each year. That puts it 1.3 metres higher than it was in 1898!

MSCUA, University of Washington, Special Coll. Division, Hegg #51B

(above) Overlooking Dyea, during the gold rush. (facing page) Townsite plan for Dyea, also during the gold rush period.

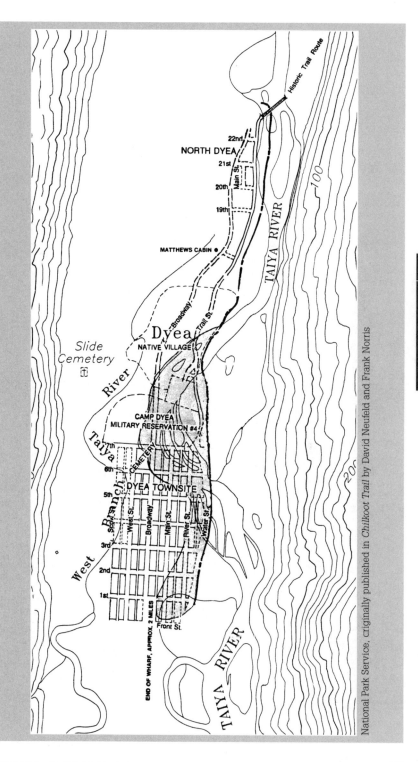

NORTH DYEA

22nd
21st
20th
Main St.
19th

TAIYA RIVER

Historic Trail Route

100

MATTHEWS CABIN ●

Broadway

Trail St.

Dyea

NATIVE VILLAGE

Slide
Cemetery

River

Taiya

CAMP DYEA
MILITARY RESERVATION #4

7th

6th

CEMETERY

5th

DYEA TOWNSITE

West Fork Branch

West St.

Broadway

Main St.

River St.

Water St.

3rd

2nd

1st

END OF WHARF, APPROX. 2 MILES

Front St.

TAIYA RIVER

200

TAIYA RIVER

National Park Service, originally published in *Chilkoot Trail* by David Neufeld and Frank Norris

ROUTES & RAPIDS

3

A boreal forest floor covered with mushrooms after a particularly rainy season.

Chilkoot Trail, Dyea to Bennett

The U.S. National Park Service attempts to maintain the trails to reduce damage and make it easier for hikers.

Distance: 53.1 kilometres
Time to complete: 3 to 6 days, depending on ambitions
Challenges: Rough terrain, steep incline, moist climate
Rewards: Spectacular scenery, passage through history

Maps	page
1 • Skagway	155
2 • Dyea	156
3 • Canyon City	157
4 • Sheep Camp	158
5 • Chilkoot Pass	159
6 • Lindeman	160
7 • Bennett	161
8 • Cut-off trail to Log Cabin	162

Long before you journey north, you must decide how many days it will take to complete your trip on the Chilkoot Trail. The trail is typically done over three to five days. Three days would be pushing it for most groups, with long hard days averaging 18 kilometres. Five days would be a much more relaxed trip, with time to enjoy life in camp, the scenery and the experience. Some groups have completed the full route by trying to run it in a day, however this is heavily frowned upon by the park staff. To decide how much time you need, you must seriously consider the capabilities of your group, meaning the abilities of your weakest member. Failing to do this could result in a frustrating, miserable trip for all. Once you have decided the length, you should call the park staff to pre-register your trip, providing your expected arrival and start/finish dates. It is suggested this be completed as far in advance as possible, to ensure you can get into the campgrounds you want, when you want them.

Once you've arrived in the north, the excitement mounts. All your planning through the winter has finally come to fruition. This is where it all begins! Your journey over the Chilkoot Trail will actually start in **Skagway**, at the Trail Centre, where all hikers passing into Canada over the Chilkoot Trail must register and sign in. The park staff have current information about trail and campground conditions, such as bear sightings, weather and forest fire activity. They will also confirm each campground that you will be staying in, for each night of your journey. (Parties are booked into campgrounds ahead of time to avoid stranded hikers.)

Now that you are registered, you must find a way to the trailhead near Dyea. The most common method is by shuttle service. Contact the Skagway Convention and Visitors Bureau or the Parks Canada Trail Centre to find names of available companies. This is an arrangement that is best made long before your boot soles hit Skagway dirt.

The Saintly Hill is a breathtaking way to begin your trek.

Hosford's sawmill along the Chilkoot Trail, last used in the 1950s.

3
ROUTES & RAPIDS

A tantalizing glimpse of Irene Glacier, from the trail.

The Dyea campground is about 500 metres south of the Dyea trailhead if you wish to spend your first night here. If you have an extra day, it is worth taking a tour of Dyea across the river.

From the trailhead (Map 2, km 0), the trail begins abruptly with an unexpected climb up the side of the valley. Dyea and the original trailhead were placed on the other side of the river because of this bluff, referred to as Saintly Hill, that hikers must now climb. Cold muscles unaccustomed to the brisk workout, and lungs needing more oxygen than they can take in with normal breaths, may make you wonder what you have got yourself into! But don't give up because before long, you will descend back onto the valley bottom where the trail remains flat for quite some time. You will cross several bridges along this flat stretch, the third of which crosses over a salmon-spawning creek. Late summer and fall is a good period in which to witness spawning salmon here.

From here to Sheep Camp is typical coastal rainforest. The dominant tree species are Western hemlock and amabilis fir, but you will also see Western red cedar, Sitka spruce, Douglas fir and vine maples. Receiving an estimated average of 1,400 millimetre of rain each year, the forest is very lush, with mosses, lichens and fungus visually abundant. Due to the plentiful rainfall and mild temperatures, this forest is one of the most productive in North America.

Near a sign that indicates you have travelled 1.6 miles (2.6 kilometres), the trail joins a wider track along flat terrain, allowing easy travel through the forest. This trail is actually an old logging road from the 1950s. The original Chilkoot Trail in this part of the valley followed the river in winter, and the other shore in summer. Shortly after meeting this trail, passing a small cabin on the right side of the trail (actually an old sawmill from the 1950s), you will encounter a sign that reads "Private Property Next 1.4 miles. Stay on trail." The following stretch is quite boggy, but the park staff have put in boardwalks over the worst of it. (It is still a good idea to waterproof your boots before this trip because of areas like this.) After the wet stretch, the trail is in good shape and relatively flat right up to Finnegan's Point (Map 3, km 7.9). This point can be reached in between two and three hours, depending on your pace.

Finnegan's Point was at one time a very small settlement with about 75 tents scattered around the site. Services included a blacksmith shop, restaurant and saloon. The site was set up by Pat Finnegan who, with his sons, built a corduroy bridge and road to transport goldseekers over the Taiya River. At that time, the original trail crossed over the river many times; now it stays on the east side of the valley until after Sheep Camp. When the first people came to this point, they were charged a toll for use of the bridge and road, but before long, the masses simply swept them aside. Today, there is a small shelter, outhouses and room for 15 overnight campers. It is a great place for a lunch for those going to Canyon City for the night. The views across the river to Mount Yeatman and Irene Glacier (on clear days, of course!) are breathtaking.

You will leave the logging road behind after Finnegan's Point. Although the park map shows another 4.6 kilometres to get to Canyon City, it seems less than that along the easy trail. We completed this section in just one and a quarter hours.

The trail meanders up and down amongst the lichens and mosses and an amazing variety of fungus and mushrooms. After a couple of kilometres, the presence of many rounded rocks indicates that the Taiya River likely once flowed here.

Despite a short day, the **Canyon City** campground (Map 3, km 12.5), is a welcome site after your first day with a heavy load. The main monument in the campground is the group shelter, a small, beautiful log structure with a covered veranda out front. (In the Klondike Gold Rush National Historic Park, hikers must cook and wash up at the group shelters. Grey water pits are provided for dishwater and cooking water.) This is one of the larger campgrounds along the Chilkoot, accommodating 60 hikers. Surrounding the shelter are many shady sites, and a number of other sites can be found along the river north (upstream) of the shelter. A bear pole is situated behind the shelter; you must bring your own rope to string up your pack.

A visit to the Canyon City ruins is a must for anyone interested in gold rush history. A few hundred metres upstream from the campsite you can take a side trail that crosses over the Taiya River on a suspension bridge, then proceed upstream about 10 more minutes until you begin to see some clearings and an old stove.

Since Canyon City is situated at the mouth of the Taiya Canyon, the main trail is once again forced up the side of the valley. After leaving the campground, you will travel along a flat trail for about 15 minutes before it rises steeply through a more open forest than before. A half-hour climb takes you well above the rushing river, but the noise of the water can still be heard. After about another half hour of relatively flat hiking (although the side slope is quite steep!), a little side trail takes you to an abrupt escarpment overlooking the valley towards the pass, although the pass is still out of sight. This escarpment drops off sharply and is not for the faint of heart!

This part of the trail follows the route of the telegraph line. If you look up, you may see evidence of the line itself or of old telegraph poles. This telegraph wire was part of a line that went through Bennett, Log Cabin, Skagway, Dyea and back to the summit, allowing easy communication between these communities. If you are alert and lucky, you may also see Rufous hummingbirds, since this area is near the northern limit of their range.

From here, another hour of walking through gentle terrain will bring you to **Pleasant Camp** (Map 4, km 17.5). Although the trail is fairly flat, the river rises to meet it and once again you are serenaded by the sound of the river beside you as you walk. Pleasant Camp park facilities have actually been moved upstream to this point, about half a kilometre from its original position, due to erosion at the original site. In 1897, the old site included a toll bridge and restaurant, and the bridge carrying the stampeders across to the west bank of the Taiya River. Apparently, the area from here to Sheep Camp was almost solid with tents. The current Pleasant Camp has a small shelter and outhouses, and accommodates 27 campers.

The distance from Pleasant Camp to Sheep Camp during the gold rush was about four kilometres. That distance has been shortened to less than two and a half kilometres due to the shifting of Pleasant Camp upstream by 0.6 kilometres, and of Sheep Camp downstream by 1.2 kilometres. Sheep Camp was moved due

3

ROUTES & RAPIDS

The bridge to Canyon City over the swift waters of the Taiya River.

CANYON CITY

Canyon City, aptly named, is situated at the mouth of the canyon on the Taiya River. It was a natural camping site for Chilkat Tlingit First Nations long before the Klondike gold rush (see Chapter 5). It was at this point, just downstream of the narrow, steep canyon, that transporting gear became much more difficult for the stampeders. For this reason, two separate companies established powerhouses to drive overhead trams that transported gear over the canyon and past the summit.

At its peak in the spring of 1898, Canyon City, formally laid out in lots, blocks and streets, boasted a population of 1,500 and many of the typical gold rush establishments. It even had electricity, thanks to the huge boilers for the overhead trams. Although not much is left of the original settlement, you can still see one of the huge boilers, several clearings and some small artifacts. It is hard to imagine this place stripped of trees and complete with a system of streets filled with people, goods and animals, when all you hear now are the rush of the river and the songs of birds in the forest.

Some ruins remain at Canyon City, such as this boiler that once powered the overhead tramways during the gold rush.

A beach at Pleasant Camp lives up to its name.

to shifting of creeks and to enlarge the site. We completed the distance between the two camps in about a half hour. The terrain is relatively flat, with several creek crossings via bridges.

The **Sheep Camp** campground (Map 4, km 19.7) is quite large, accommodating up to 81 campers in many shady sites. The size of the site is enough to justify two group shelters for cooking and eating. Near the river is a large open cobble beach, from which you can see spectacular views up and down the valley. Here, the valley gets narrower and more hemmed in as it rises towards the pass.

All parties backpacking over the pass will stop at Sheep Camp, since the hike from here to Happy Camp, the first opportunity to camp on the far side of the pass, takes most hikers a full day. Some hikers will get to Sheep Camp in one day, about six to seven hours of travel, plus breaks. Giving yourself two days allows more time to admire the views, both far to surrounding glaciers, and near to the details of the forest.

Throughout the summer, the rangers at Sheep Camp put on a fantastic interpretive program at the first shelter. The rangers are a wealth of information, which can enhance your experience on the trail. You will continue on from here armed with information about the trail, weather, history and nature!

You can either take the time to investigate the original Sheep Camp site in the late afternoon after arriving, or on your way through the next day, depending on how

CHILKOOT TRAIL
Dyea to Bennett

HEADWATER LAKES
Bennett to Whitehorse

YUKON RIVER
Whitehorse to Carmacks

YUKON RIVER
Carmacks to Dawson

SHEEP CAMP

Sheep Camp, which began as a base camp for hunters, grew thick with tents in 1898 when traffic was slowed down by winter weather over the pass. At the time, it was called "The City of Tents," and contained 16 hotels, 14 restaurants, 13 supply houses, five doctors or drug merchants, three saloons, two dance halls, two laundries, a hospital, bath house, lumber yard, and a post office. It peaked at 6,000 to 8,000 transients, but was almost abandoned by May 1898, when most had packed over the pass.

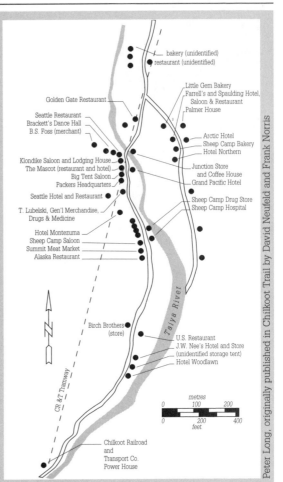

bakery (unidentified)
restaurant (unidentified)

Little Gem Bakery
Farrell's and Spaulding Hotel,
Saloon & Restaurant
Palmer House

Golden Gate Restaurant

Seattle Restaurant
Brackett's Dance Hall
B.S. Foss (merchant)

Arctic Hotel
Sheep Camp Bakery
Hotel Northern

Klondike Saloon and Lodging House
The Mascot (restaurant and hotel)
Big Tent Saloon
Packers Headquarters

Junction Store
and Coffee House
Grand Pacific Hotel

Seattle Hotel and Restaurant

Sheep Camp Drug Store
Sheep Camp Hospital

T. Lubelski, Gen'l Merchandise,
Drugs & Medicine

Hotel Montezuma
Sheep Camp Saloon
Summit Meat Market
Alaska Restaurant

Taiya River

Birch Brothers
(store)

U.S. Restaurant
J.W. Nee's Hotel and Store
(unidentified storage tent)
Hotel Woodlawn

CR &T Tramway

metres
0   100   200

0   200   400
feet

Chilkoot Railroad
and
Transport Co.
Power House

Peter Long, originally published in Chilkoot Trail by David Neufeld and Frank Norris

The shelter at the old Sheep Camp site now houses a fascinating interpretive display.

Shortly after Sheep Camp, the vegetation begins to thin out as you rise towards the alpine.

much you want to explore. The original site is about 1.2 kilometres further along the trail from the Sheep Camp campground. The wardens' station and an interpretive display are located at the original site. If you plan on a quick tour, a half hour in the morning could be afforded. However, if you are a real history buff and wish to poke around a lot, you may not wish to take that much time out of your hike to Happy Camp.

Plan for a long day from Sheep Camp to Happy Camp. Due to the archaeological and ecological sensitivity of the area, no camping is allowed between these two sites. Although the distance travelled is not excessive, the elevation gain of over 800 metres over six kilometres, followed by six kilometres of difficult, rolling terrain makes for a tough day.

The Long Hill was considered by some stampeders to be the most difficult portion of the trail.

The park staff suggest you allow 12 hours to complete it. The breathtaking scenery can be enough to lift your spirits and legs!

Shortly after leaving the campground, the vegetation begins to thin, allowing views to the side walls of the valley, and the many steep creeks flowing down to join the Taiya River. Before you hit the original Sheep Camp, you will pass through an avalanche area, which treats you with an abundance of wildflowers and views. An avalanche here in 1996 caused 130 downed trees and opened up the views to the surrounding peaks.

After Sheep Camp, the trail starts to rise a little more steeply. The section from here to the Scales was dubbed "The Long Hill" by the stampeders, and was considered by many to be the toughest section. Although it is not overly steep, it is deceiving; a steady and long climb, gaining about half the

The Scales, where loads were reweighed for the ascent up the Stairs, was a natural trap for artifacts.

day's elevation. However, as you climb, you will rise out of the thick valley vegetation into a subalpine zone. You will start to see more and more artifacts along the trail, including cables from the tramways, telegraph line, sled runners, wheels and a grave marker. Artifacts should not be removed. This portion also requires careful attention to your footing, since the trail becomes quite rocky. The view back down the valley as you rise above the vegetation is a momentary reward as you work towards the summit.

The Scales (Map 4, km 25.7), marking the end of the Long Hill, was the place where packers reweighed their loads, charging a higher fee for the last ascent up the Golden Stairs. Many stampeders gave up at this point, abandoning their gear. The area is now littered with the remains from these dejected souls — boots, tools, and other items that were far more important to them at the beginning of the journey than at the end. The Scales is now a great place to regroup, rest and have a bite to eat before the final assault to the summit. And to marvel at the types of things stampeders dragged with them to this point.

You may now be wondering why the number of artifacts in the alpine and subalpine area seems so much greater than down in the forested valley. Certain spots were natural traps for discards, such as this area near the Stairs. On the other hand, artifacts below the timberline, such as in the vicinity of Sheep Camp, are often covered by the lush forest that has regrown in the silent years after the rush. Also, in some areas, the trail and much of the activity during the rush were on the opposite side of the river from the current trail. Furthermore, some artifacts have been scavenged.

Don't expect much from the weather on the pass. Typically, because it's the coast, the pass is socked in with clouds. Rain often plagues the south side of the pass, which is why the trees grow so big and thick down in the valley! When we asked the ranger at the summit station about the weather, she told us that this was only the second day in 18 in which she had seen the sun! When you finally stand on the summit, you will likely feel the brisk and relentless winds. (We felt these winds continuously all the way along the headwater lakes to the Yukon River!)

The trail beyond the Scales remains at a moderate pitch for a short distance until the base of the **Golden Stairs**. If you continued straight, you would head over Peterson's Pass, a less successful option for stampeders due to the higher avalanche hazard and unstable boulders. The Stairs are to your left, marked with orange poles. Don't despair at this point as you look up the path ahead, which appears to go straight up. Due to the steep pitch, your climb will likely be over within an hour. The Stairs go up steeply for approximately half an hour. You are quickly rewarded with better and better views down the valley. Don't be surprised to encounter patches of snow on the Stairs, even in the heat of summer. Some years, these patches do not disappear before they are covered by more snow the next winter. Near the top of the Stairs, as you think you are rounding out to the summit, you find yourself in a gully looking at another summit. After a couple more false summits, you will be on the top of the world, with views to a whole new area

3

ROUTES & RAPIDS

Just like many before, two hikers start their ascent up the Golden Stairs.

THE GOLDEN STAIRS

The Golden Stairs is the visual epitome of the gold rush. The most striking images captured during that time were of long queues of people trudging their way up the Stairs, heavy packs on their backs and a look of dogged determination on their faces. Since the Northwest Mounted Police (NWMP), who operated a post at the summit, required each person to have one ton of goods, it took many stampeders up to 30 trips to get their gear over the trail from camp to camp, and the Stairs was the hardest part of all. Those with money went up only once, while their gear was transported by the aerial trams for 7¢ per pound, an amount equivalent to about $10 per kilogram ($5 per pound) today!

You can just hear the groans of the hundreds of people working their way up the Golden Stairs in the winter of 1897–1898. And for all that work, few made it to the Klondike in time to stake any fresh gold-bearing claims. Although the trip up the Stairs would have taken them between two and six hours, with the trip down a very quick slide on a shovel, it was often only possible to take one trip each day due to the mass of humanity trying to complete the same task. They daren't take a step off the trail for fear that an opening would not occur in the queue again for hours.

MSCUA, University of Washington Library, Larson coll., Hegg photog., 105c

The Chilkoot Trail is the line straight up from the tents by The Scales, to the top of the ridge. The route to Peterson's Pass is to the right of the Chilkoot, nearer the head of the valley.

3

ROUTES & RAPIDS

A TON OF GOODS

2 suits heavy knit underwear
6 pair wool socks
1 pair heavy moccasins
2 pairs German stockings
2 heavy flannel overshirts
1 heavy woollen sweater
1 pair overalls
2 pair 12 lb blankets
1 waterproof blanket
1 dozen bandana handkerchiefs
1 stiff brim cowboy hat
1 pair hip rubber boots
1 pair prospectors' high land boots
1 mackinaw
1 pair heavy buck mitts, lined
1 pair unlined leather gloves
1 duck coat, pants, vest
6 towels
1 pocket matchbox, buttons, needles, etc.
1 sleeping bag/medicine chest
pack saddles
flat sleighs
1 pkg tin matches
6 cakes borax
1/2 lb ground ginger
1 lb citric acid
100 lbs navy beans
150 lbs bacon
400 lbs flour
40 lbs rolled oats
20 lbs corn meal
10 lbs rice
25 lbs sugar
10 lbs tea

20 lbs coffee
10 lbs baking powder
20 lbs salt
1 lb pepper
2 lbs baking soda
1/2 lb mustard
1 lb vinegar
2 dozen condensed milk
20 lb evaporated potatoes
5 lbs evaporated onions
6 tins/4 oz extract beef
75 lbs evaporated fruit
4 pkgs yeast cakes
20 lbs candles
6 lbs laundry soap
25 lbs hard tack
2 bottles Jamaica ginger

N. W. M. P.

DAWSON, Nov. 18, 1898.

THE Commissioner of the Yukon Territory orders that no person will be permitted to enter the Territory without satisfying the N. W. M. Police Officers at Tagish and White Horse Rapids that they have with them two months' assorted provisions and at least $500 in cash, or six months' assorted provisions and not less than $200 in cash, over and above the money required to pay expenses from the border to Dawson.

N. B.—This order will not apply to residents of the Yukon Territory returning, if they are identified and prove their competence to pay their way into the country.

By order,

(Signed), **S. B. STEELE,** Supt.,
Commanding N.W.M. Police, Yukon Territory.

Yukon Archives pamphlet 1978-1C

Sam Steele's order (above right) translated into "a ton of goods," such as this typical outfit.

3

ROUTES & RAPIDS

MSCUA, University of Washington, Hegg photog., 97

Packers form a nearly continuous line up to Chilkoot Pass. Dugouts for resting are to the left of the line, beginning about halfway up in the photo. Chutes for sliding to the bottom fan out to the right.

University of Alaska Fairbanks, Blankenberg photog., 57-1041-3

The Chilkoot Pass was a repository for an amazing assortment of gear and people in 1898.

in British Columbia! On your way up to the summit, you will see evidence of the wooden towers used for the aerial tram, as well as some of the equipment.

There are great opportunities to explore at the **Summit**, if you wish to set down your load and take a break. Peaks on either side of the trail improve your view (and you thought that was impossible by this point!), and give you insight into life up here 100 years ago. Not far from the summit, on the west side of the trail, lies the foundation of one of the NWMP post buildings. Past this spot you will find a warming hut and the wardens' station for Parks Canada. To the east and south of the trail summit lies a stash of folding canvas boats that are in great shape considering they were abandoned more than 100 years ago. It is believed that these boats were brought in by American entrepreneurs who thought Lindeman Lake was in Alaska. After being asked to remove their operation by the NWMP, the boats were abandoned here.

3

ROUTES & RAPIDS

(above) Several false summits fool unwary hikers near the Chilkoot Summit.
(below) On a clear day, the summit affords fantastic views to the north and south.

CHILKOOT TRAIL
Dyea to Bennett

HEADWATER LAKES
Bennett to Whitehorse

YUKON RIVER
Whitehorse to Carmacks

YUKON RIVER
Carmacks to Dawson

3

ROUTES & RAPIDS

A stash of folding boats has sat for 100 years, waiting for someone to take them down the Yukon River.

It will probably have taken your group between three and five hours to come from Sheep Camp to this point, not counting any breaks you may have taken. Now you face the same amount of time to cover less steep but nonetheless difficult terrain. The next six kilometres to Happy Camp involve a net loss in elevation, but the trail goes up and down over ridges and moraines. It will take about two and a half to three hours of solid hiking.

The scenery here is much different than on the south side of the pass. Much of the moisture from the clouds was released on its way up the Taiya River valley. You are now in a drier zone, and will remain in the alpine until shortly between Happy Camp and Deep Lake. The vegetation is typical of alpine or arctic environments, with heathers, mosses and small, hardy tree species that grow close to the ground. Wildflowers abound in July and August.

The trail from the summit first descends towards Crater Lake, a beautiful azure lake reflecting the sky and mountains that surround it. Partway down, you will find the **Stone Crib**, the remains of the terminus of the Chilkoot Railroad and Transport Company tram that ran from Canyon City to here. With this aerial tramway, a wagon system and boats on the upper lakes, stampeders could have their goods shipped to Lindeman with little effort on their part. The tramway was purchased and dismantled by the White Pass & Yukon Route in early 1900, in order to eliminate any competition to the railway. Now, the remains consist of a pile of stones, wood and machinery.

As you descend to **Crater Lake**, try to imagine up to 150 horses and mules stabled in the meadows beside the lake. These steeds hauled wagons over rough trails, transporting gear northwards from the end of the trams to Bennett or Lindeman. By keeping a watchful eye, you will see evidence of these operations.

3

ROUTES & RAPIDS

The British Columbia side of the Coast Mountains show a soft side.

Once at the level of Crater Lake, your trail leads up over rough moraines, and back down over flatter outwashes. Depending on the time of year, there may be quite a bit of snow in this stretch. Finally, there is **Happy Camp** (Map 5, km 33.0), a very happy sight indeed! This campground is nestled among sparse subalpine firs, on a meadowy slope that reaches down to Coltsfoot Creek, one of the many rivulets that ultimately feeds the Yukon River. The stunted trees give some shelter from the incessant winds coming down from the pass. The beautiful campsites and single group shelter serve the maximum 50 people who are allowed to cross the summit in a single day. By this time, you will likely be recognizing groups you have been travelling alongside for two to three days.

There are some people, with few vacation days from work, who hike out from Happy Camp in one day. It is about 20 kilometres to Bennett, and more to Log Cabin, over moderate, rolling terrain. So it is possible, but if you have the time, why would you want to rush this most beautiful part of the trail? The climate is typically dry (though there are no guarantees!) and the scenery is wonderful.

Fog envelopes a hiker on their way over Long Lake Ridge.

Even better for those with extra time on their hands, a layover day may be possible depending on campsite bookings, or you could go out in three to four days, staying at Deep Lake, Lindeman and Bare Loon Lake. This makes for a much more relaxed hike, giving you time to look around more, or to just hang back! Most people hike out in two days with an overnight at Lindeman.

Leaving Happy Camp, the trail follows the shore of Coltsfoot Creek for a while before rising up to a high bluff over Long Lake. The footing is rough and unstable over loose rock. The trail stays high over rounded, rocky ridges until the north end of the lake, where it descends to a bridge over the torrent between Long and Deep lakes before reaching the **Deep Lake** campground (Map 6, km 37.0). It is a small campground, accommodating 20 hikers. Here you can imagine boats taking stampeders' gear along the length of Long Lake, unloading it onto wagons on quays at the north end of the lake. From here, a wagon trail led to Lindeman.

Around Deep Lake, you enter the subalpine boreal forest zone, leaving the stunted subalpine vegetation behind. This zone is characterized by a more moderate climate than the alpine zone, providing habitat for thicker and more continuous stands of Engelmann spruce, subalpine fir and lodgepole pine.

After leaving the lake, Moose Creek drops into a deep gorge named Moose Creek Canyon. At one point, the river drops over a series of cascades. A short spur in the trail takes you to the brink of the falls.

As the trail turns slightly left towards Lindeman Lake, you suddenly find yourself in a dry forest dominated by stands of tall lodgepole pine. The trail is well worn here and the going is easy. As the trail slowly descends to the lake, you can catch glimpses of the magnificent green waters of Lindeman Lake through the trees. You can also now see the mountains surrounding the chain of lakes that works northwards towards Carcross.

Lindeman (Map 6, km 41.8) is a large site, divided into two campgrounds, the upper and the lower. The upper campground is situated on the shores of Lindeman with a view to the south up Lindeman Creek. The lower campground is situated where Moose Creek spills into the lake, providing a supply of fresh clear water. In total, the two spots will accommodate up to 60 campers. Artifacts are visible throughout the campground and you are expected to leave things where you find them. A wardens' station and interpretive centre are located at the lower camp. The interpretive centre is worth a lengthy visit. No matter what your interest, you are likely to find it here. There are field guides, historical books, diaries of stampeders, historical photos and certificates for hikers indicating they have hiked the Chilkoot Trail.

Between the two campgrounds lies a small graveyard on a hillside overlooking Mount Harvey across the lake. In it lie the bodies of eleven people who died in the days of the gold rush — some by scurvy, some by hypothermia or starvation, and some by drowning in Lindeman Rapids between Lindeman and Bennett lakes. The graves are marked in the way of the north, with fences around each site to keep out the "savage" wilderness. A monument has been placed here in more recent times, remembering Bruce Harvey, one-time Superintendent of Historic Sites for Parks Canada.

3

ROUTES & RAPIDS

The trail leaving Lindeman crosses two creeks, including Moose Creek, before rising to the top of the ridge between Lindeman and Bare Loon lakes. The trail leads along the spine of the ridge for some distance, through an open pine forest with frequent bedrock outcrops. Before dipping down towards Bare Loon Lake, you will pass a spectacular lookout over the north end of Lindeman Lake towards Bennett Lake.

If you've set your sights on Bare Loon Lake, don't be fooled by a small lake encountered shortly after descending from the ridge. This is Dan Johnson Lake,

LINDEMAN

As with many of the gold rush towns, Lindeman went quickly from boom to bust. To the backdrop of thousands of tents in the spring of 1898, the city rang with the sounds of whipsaws as stampeders scrambled to get seaworthy boats made before the spring break-up. All the trees within hauling distance were stripped for one of three things; boats, fuel or shelter. Lindeman, which peaked at about 400 souls, was considerably smaller than Bennett, since boats built here had to be taken through or around the mighty rapids between Lindeman and Bennett lakes. For those who passed through later in the season, steamers and barges transported passengers and freight across the lake.

Similar to other settlements along the Chilkoot, Lindeman was deserted by the fall of 1899, with the completion of the WP&YR railway.

A modern-day view of Lindeman.

3

ROUTES & RAPIDS

CHILKOOT TRAIL
Dyea to Bennett

HEADWATER LAKES
Bennett to Whitehorse

YUKON RIVER
Whitehorse to Carmacks

YUKON RIVER
Carmacks to Dawson

Moose Creek falls swiftly out of Deep Lake.

3

ROUTES & RAPIDS

Bare Loon Lake is a wonderful place for a bath or a swim.

which is followed shortly by Bare Loon Lake at km 46.8. The **Bare Loon Lake** campground (Map 7) is small, but beautiful, taking 30 hikers. It is a more primitive site than most, with a small outhouse being the only facility. The open, terraced site overlooking the lake is spattered with tall pines. The swimming in the lake is brisk but refreshing after the short day on the trail! Many hikers come through the site, but most press on to Bennett for the night. We wondered at first if "bare loon" referred to the seagulls (loons without the jackets!), since the lake seemed empty of loons. But then, as evening set in, we heard and saw the magnificent loons.

Shortly after leaving Bare Loon Lake, hikers will come across the cut-off trail to **Log Cabin** (Map 8). For those who go on to Bennett, there are five ways out from Bennett. The first is to continue on by canoe through Bennett Lake and down the Yukon River, for which you must make arrangements in advance. The second is by a water taxi to Carcross, which also must be pre-arranged. The third is to hike out via the WP&YR tracks to the Klondike Highway at Log Cabin, taking a pre-arranged ride from there. A fourth is to continue hiking along the tracks to Carcross, and getting a ride out from there. The fifth is to take the WP&YR train back to Fraser or Skagway. This, too, must be booked well in advance. As of summer 2000, hikers could take the train back to Skagway from Bennett five days a week, or a speeder train to Fraser twice daily, five days a week. It is possible that future train service will be provided regularly to Carcross and perhaps Whitehorse.

Continuing from the cut off trail on towards Bennett, you find yourself once more along the ridge next to Lindeman Lake, with occasional views over the lake. Towards the north end of Lindeman, the typically rocky terrain becomes very sandy, sometimes quite difficult to walk through. The sand is caused by erosion from the strong winds that persist down Lindeman Lake. The trail passes by an active trapper's cabin, with the peak of the roof less than six feet high. (Please respect this and all other private property you may encounter.)

Bennett (Map 7, km 53.1) is situated on a hillside at the very south end of Bennett Lake, next to Lindeman Creek. The trail meets the townsite at its upper end, near the only remaining wooden structure, St. Andrews Presbyterian Church. The campground is large, but due to the amount of ground that is archaeologically significant, Parks Canada has dedicated space for only 32 campers. The overflow must stay at Bare Loon Lake. The tent sites are scattered in amongst visible ruins from the gold rush days — hollows where tents and structures stood, piles of refuse or artifacts. The wardens want as little disturbance as possible at the townsite.

To the east of the town is the train station for the WP&YR. Most of the open portion of the train station is used now as an interpretive centre, unfortunately with limited hours. The outside of the station has been beautifully restored to its former glory.

Dunes make for difficult travel near the south end of Lindeman Lake.

3

ROUTES & RAPIDS

BENNETT

Bennett was large in its short life, taking stampeders from both the White and Chilkoot passes. It is estimated by some that approximately 20,000 spent the winter of 1897–1898 building boats and waiting out the ice. There was no lack of things to while away the time — entrepreneurs made sure of that, milking the stampeders for all they

The WP&YR train pulls up at Bennett Station.

could. After the long winter, May 29, 1898 resounded with the crunch of the lake ice breaking up. In the next week, more than 7,000 boats began the long journey down the mighty Yukon River towards Dawson City.

Bennett is one town that did not die immediately with the passing of the rush of the people on to Dawson. The town flourished with WP&YR in 1899. It wasn't until the railway reached Whitehorse in 1900 that the town lost its purpose.

The town was quite something to see, overlooking Bennett Lake, with its system of streets, hotels, stores, warehouses, and shipping offices. The St. Andrews Church was built in 1899 by public subscription and volunteer labour — it is now the only gold rush building still standing in Bennett. Artifacts abound, mostly items discarded by the transient population.

St. Andrews Presbyterian Church stands tall on the hill overlooking Bennett Lake.

3

ROUTES & RAPIDS

Yukon Archives, Vogee Coll., 45

A view of Bennett during the stampede, looking southwest.

3

ROUTES & RAPIDS

CHILKOOT TRAIL
Dyea to Bennett

HEADWATER LAKES
Bennett to Whitehorse

YUKON RIVER
Whitehorse to Carmacks

YUKON RIVER
Carmacks to Dawson

3

ROUTES & RAPIDS

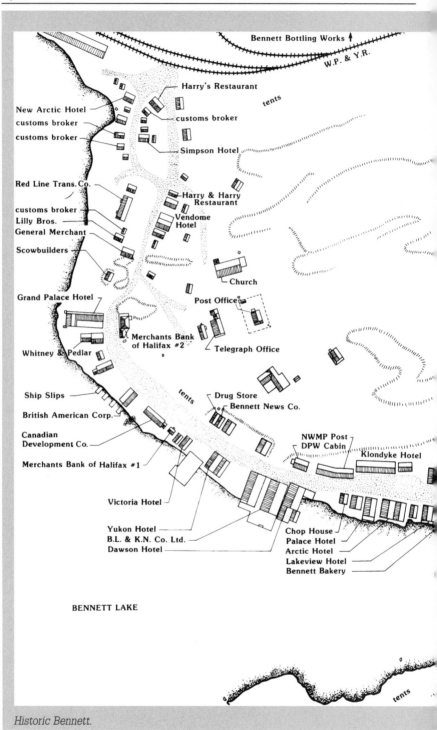

Bennett Bottling Works

W.P. & Y.R.

tents

Harry's Restaurant

New Arctic Hotel

customs broker

customs broker

customs broker

Simpson Hotel

Red Line Trans. Co.

Harry & Harry
Restaurant

customs broker

Vendome
Hotel

Lilly Bros.

General Merchant

Scowbuilders

Church

Grand Palace Hotel

Post Office

Merchants Bank
of Halifax #2

Whitney & Pedlar

Telegraph Office

Ship Slips

tents

Drug Store

Bennett News Co.

British American Corp.

Canadian
Development Co.

NWMP Post

DPW Cabin

Klondyke Hotel

Merchants Bank of Halifax #1

Victoria Hotel

Yukon Hotel

B.L. & K.N. Co. Ltd.

Dawson Hotel

Chop House

Palace Hotel

Arctic Hotel

Lakeview Hotel

Bennett Bakery

BENNETT LAKE

tents

Historic Bennett.

CHILKOOT TRAIL
Dyea to Bennett

HEADWATER LAKES
Bennett to Whitehorse

YUKON RIVER
Whitehorse to Carmacks

YUKON RIVER
Carmacks to Dawson

3
ROUTES & RAPIDS

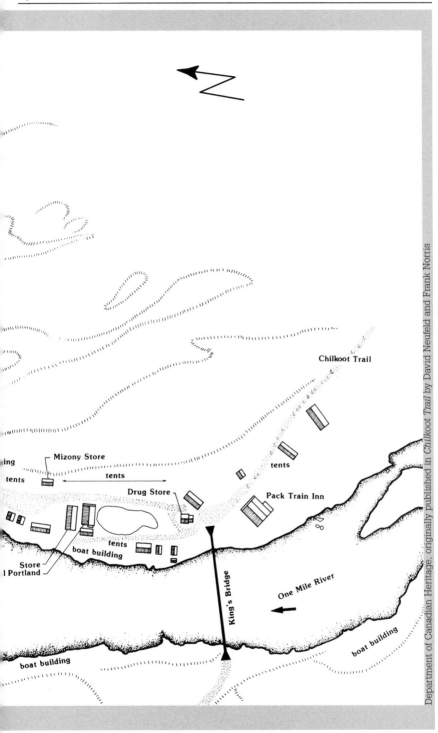

Chilkoot Trail

Mizony Store

tents

tents

ing

tents

Drug Store

Pack Train Inn

Store
l Portland

Drug Store

tents

boat building

King's Bridge

One Mile River

boat building

boat building

Department of Canadian Heritage, originally published in *Chilkoot Trail* by David Neufeld and Frank Norris

CUT-OFF TRAIL TO LOG CABIN

Given the increased rail service from Bennett over the last few years, fewer people are taking the cut-off trail between the Chilkoot Trail and Log Cabin. Mostly those with limited time or funds hike out this way. However, if your arrangements for pick-up are at Log Cabin, and not Fraser or Skagway, you may have to hike out this way.

The cut-off trail is shown on Map 8. This marked trail is encountered shortly after leaving Bare Loon Lake. The first one and a half kilometres are on a trail, after which you travel along the WP&YR right-of-way for about eight kilometres. There is very little elevation gain or loss along the way, making for fairly easy walking. There is a trail beside the ties along much of the railway, however, it is occasionally interrupted by washouts or rail maintenance. You should budget about two and a half to three hours between Bare Loon Lake and Log Cabin.

The settlement of Log Cabin existed briefly during the gold rush. It has for a longer time been a traditional berry-picking area for the Carcross-Tagish people in late summer (see Chapter 5). Many of the stampeders who travelled the White Pass stopped to rest along the way at Log Cabin. The settlement was not ideally situated, and in the spring became a quagmire of mud. The village hosted a NWMP post and many hotels and saloons.

Hikers on the cut-off trail anticipate their arrival at Log Cabin.

ROUTES & RAPIDS

3

Canoeists anxious to get underway on Bennett Lake.

Distance: 164 kilometres
Time to complete: 6 to 8 days, plus layover days
Challenges: Heavy winds, large waves
Rewards: Great potential canoe sailing, fantastic views
of the Coast Mountains and Teslin Plateau
River gradient: 0.3 metres per kilometre

Maps	page
9 • Pennington	163
10 • Border	164
11 • Carcross	165
12 • Tagish Lake	166
13 • Tagish	167
14 • Marsh Lake	168
15 • M'Clintock River	169
16 • Lewes River Bridge	170
17 • Whitehorse	171

Unlike many who are ending their trip at Bennett, your adventure is just beginning! How exciting to follow the path of the stampeders on the next leg of their journey. This next section to Whitehorse should take approximately one week, but times will vary depending on weather. The winds on the lake can be incredibly strong, and can come up suddenly, whipping the lake into a brew of whitecaps in short order. It is advisable to stay close to shore at all times when on these large lakes. Your fate will be decided by the direction of the winds as you could become windbound at any time. Luckily, the prevailing winds are from the southwest, at your back for much of the journey. Even so, there are sections, such as the beginning of Tagish Lake and the end of Marsh Lake that often have headwinds. And prevailing winds sometimes lose out to storm-related winds, causing headwinds along much of your journey.

Hopefully your arrangements to get your canoes and gear to Bennett were successful and your gear is waiting for you. (Methods to get your gear dropped here are discussed in Chapter 1.)

Our trimaran vessel on one of the fine beaches of Bennett Lake.

Your launch will likely be accompanied by moderate tailwinds. A headwind would be a serious challenge on these long, narrow, steep-sided lakes. We completed the entire lakes portion with three canoes roped together with two logs, creating a stable raft to assist in riding the waves when paddling or sailing. For those who have not tried canoe sailing, you don't know what you're missing. Some previous sailing experience would be an asset, but is not essential.

The easiest way to sail is to lash together two to three canoes, preferably with two long logs, each crossways, near the front and back of the canoes to

One way to rig up canoes for sailing.

3

ROUTES & RAPIDS

keep the platform stable. Less water will splash into the boats if the canoes are about a foot apart at their beam. Tie two adjacent corners of a tent fly or small tarp (1.2 metres by 1.8 metres or 1.8 metres by 2.4 metres depending on winds) to the tops of two paddles or strong poles. Tie separate ropes, about five metres long to each of the other two corners. Stand each pole at the bow seat of the two outside canoes, held by the bow person or tied in place with guy lines. One of the stern people can control how the sail catches the wind by pulling in or letting out the ropes tied to the sail. There you have it! The wind should be no more than 30 degrees off your stern. Make sure you have at least one bailer for each canoe in case the waves are big enough to spill into the boat.

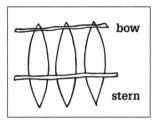

An alternative to a mast-mounted fly is a large hydrofoil or parasail to catch the stronger winds higher up.

Bennett Lake is 43 kilometres long, from one to five kilometres wide and sandwiched by the mountains. On the west shore are the Bennett Range of the Coast Mountains. The mountains on the right shore are part of an unnamed range. At a typical flatwater paddling pace of four kilometres per hour, winds not being a factor, it would take 11 to 12 hours plus breaks to canoe from Bennett to Carcross. With a very strong wind at our backs, sailing and surfing all of the way, it took us about seven hours, plus breaks.

As you start down the lake, you will notice the WP&YR rail grade to your right, which closely follows the shore along much of the length of Bennett Lake.

3

ROUTES & RAPIDS

Sailing under heavy winds, with the beautiful Bennett Range in the background.

Historical buildings in Carcross make a nice backdrop for the little Duchess engine that once ran between Taku Arm on Tagish Lake and Atlin Lake.

CARCROSS

The Carcross area was used as a seasonal site by the Tagish Indians long before the Klondike gold rush (see Chapter 5). It was known to them as *Todezaane*. The current name is a shortening of "Caribou Crossing," the name it was given by early outside visitors for the herds of caribou that used to cross in the narrows of Nares River. Sadly, these large herds of caribou have not been seen in the area for many years, although local efforts are being made to rebuild their numbers.

Although the Tagish people used this spot for seasonal camping, Carcross did not become a permanent settlement until after the gold rush. In 1898, the Northwest Mounted Police established a cabin here to use when hauling supplies down the lake. Then, for several decades after 1900, with the completion of the White Pass & Yukon Route railway and the discovery of gold and silver in the area, the town experienced a boom. Fur farming became important in the 1920s and 1930s until the construction of the Alaska Highway in 1942 caused another short boom time for Carcross.

Today, Carcross is a quaint community of 300 souls and the home of the Carcross-Tagish First Nation. It serves mainly as a tourist stop for highway travellers and cruise ship-bus passengers on excursions from Skagway. The main buildings include the Matthew Watson store, the Caribou Hotel, and the visitors centre, which was once the WP&YR train station. These buildings were all rebuilt after a fire destroyed the original buildings in 1909. Another attraction is the small steam engine, the Duchess, which served to move tourists on a short land link between Tagish and Atlin lakes from 1900 to 1919. The remains of the *S.S. Tutshi* rest on the banks on the Nares River; the steamer was, unfortunately, destroyed by fire in 1990.

The left shore is untouched, for the most part, with the occasional sand beach for lunching or camping. However, if you wish to stay close to shore and avoid long crossings of open water (highly recommended), then it is best to follow the right shore to Carcross.

The first visible historic marker is **Pennington** Station, about 18 kilometres from Bennett along the right shore. A mere one and a half kilometres past this point, you will pass from British Columbia into the Yukon. Now, you're one step closer to the goldfields!

The views are incredible from this point. Looking ahead, you can see a large, rocky island at km 20. Beyond this island, you will start to see Mount Gray, separating the Watson River and the Klondike Highway from the Wheaton River to the west. Ahead to your right, you can see beautiful Montana Mountain, hiding Carcross from your view. And to the left is the Bennett Range, behind which is the **West Arm** of Bennett Lake. As you continue down the lake, you will ultimately see the sand dunes at the mouth of the Wheaton River, and later you can look slightly back to your left and see far down the West Arm. By this time, you should certainly be on the right shore to avoid a long crossing of the West Arm.

Carcross, at km 43 (Map 11), is an opportunity to stock up on some fresh items if you desire. Depending on your timing in relation to cruise ship-bus excursions from Skagway, the town may be quiet, or it may be bustling. The visitor reception centre will provide you with information about the history of the town. Across the street from this is a small store. Here, you can get many things you haven't had in a while, such as ice cream or beer!

When passing through Carcross, you will go under three bridges: a pedestrian bridge, the railway bridge and the Klondike Highway bridge. Depending on water levels and whether you are sailing, you may have to let your sailing rigging down to pass underneath, or you may even need to portage. Your best place to take out is at the beach just upstream of the second bridge, on river left. This also gives you the best access to the town's services.

If you have time to spend in the Carcross area, there is hiking available. The most accessible from the town is at the Carcross Desert, reached from the north end of the waterfront road along Bennett Lake. If someone can give you a ride, you can access great hiking up on Montana Mountain and Caribou Mountain. (The book *Whitehorse & Area Hikes & Bikes* has more detail about area hikes.)

Heading on from Carcross, you will pass through the very short **Nares River**, then into **Nares Lake**. There are no real camping opportunities on Nares Lake, or in the first several kilometres of Tagish Lake, so plan your timing accordingly. **Tagish Lake** starts at Ten Mile Point (Map 11, km 49), where it quickly opens out to about two kilometres wide. You should take note that until you hit Windy Arm, about seven kilometres into Tagish Lake, you are heading slightly south. This means that the prevailing winds will likely be in your face, making progress difficult. If the winds are up, save your travel for early morning or early evening, when the winds may be a little less severe.

The portion of Tagish Lake that you will travel is 35 kilometres long (its full length, including all its arms, is approximately 185 kilometres). Given the typical

3

ROUTES & RAPIDS

paddling pace, it should take about nine hours to get to the far end of the lake. This is approximately how long it took us. However, we experienced intense headwinds in the first leg that restricted our travel pace to four kilometres in two and a half hours! We had severe difficulties crossing Windy Arm (which was very windy!), and heavy cross waves at Taku Arm. But we sailed quickly down the last, northward arm of Tagish Lake. The most dangerous points along the lake are where Windy Arm and Taku Arm enter the main lake, causing tricky winds and swells. It is safest to wait for calm weather and stay to the left shore along the length of the lake, avoiding open crossings.

Camping opportunities are minimal on the lake, with very few sites on the left shore, where it is safest to travel. Unless you are travelling on the right shore and doing at least two, ill-advised open water crossings, you may want to attempt to traverse the entire lake in a day.

Montana Mountain, which towers over the lake to the west, has been the site of gold and silver mining since the early 1900s. With the use of binoculars, you may be able to see tram towers that still lead up the mountain and were used to haul ore down the mountain. These tower remains are also visible from the Klondike Highway between Carcross and Skagway.

There are some camping sites on Tagish Lake on the south shore just before **Windy Arm.** It would be good planning to overnight there so you can cross Windy Arm early the next day before the winds come up and while you are fresh. When the winds are up, it is difficult to avoid the gales coming down the arm. You could either go down the left side of the lake close to shore, facing cross winds and waves from the arm, or go down the right side, facing a long open crossing. It would be prudent to travel down the left shore, since you can stay close to shore and, therefore, safety. The drawback of having severe side winds along the left shore helped us choose to hopscotch across the open arm, using **Bove Island** (Map 12, km 55) and the smaller islands at the mouth of the arm as resting spots. It was a very difficult and scary crossing for us due to a wind storm that did not let up at

The pale rocks of Lime Mountain contain fossils that are only found otherwise in Asia.

3

ROUTES & RAPIDS

3

ROUTES & RAPIDS

Bove Island suffers constant winds out of Windy Arm.

any predictable time of the day. Due to time pressure, we were forced to cross at a less than ideal time, facing three- to four-foot breaking swells. We would never have chosen to cross this way were we not solidly rafted together. Regardless of the crossing you choose, great caution is advised. The water is very cold, and a dumping anywhere more than a few metres from shore could end with trouble.

Bove Island was one of the many natural features of the Yukon named by American explorer Frederick Schwatka, on a survey mission of the Yukon River

in 1883. Ignoring the common usage of the name Tagish, he named both the island and the lake after a lieutenant in the Italian navy. The traditional name Tagish was reinstated for the lake in 1887 by geologist and explorer George Dawson, but the name Bove stuck for the island. The island and some surrounding peaks, such as Lime Mountain, are formed of a light grey dolostone and an "exotic" limestone which contains fossils usually found only in Asia. It is believed that this and the surrounding mountains were a part of the earth's crust that joined North America to Asia about 180 million years ago.

Storms can come out of nowhere, whipping up big waves on the large lakes.

After crossing Windy Arm, there are about eight kilometres of narrows to traverse before hitting Taku Arm. If your timing is such, there are a couple of good camping spots on the south shore of these narrows, which are also good landings for lunch. Note the striking mountains on the south shore, and the guardian of Taku Arm, Lime Mountain.

The prevailing winds along the Tagish Lake Narrows here are from the west. Along **Taku Arm**, the winds typically come from the south. Where these two winds meet, interesting things can happen. Despite generally stormy winds, we found great windless spots at the intersection of these waterways, with large swells coming from multiple directions. Anyone susceptible to motion sickness could have a hard time here. It is safe to stay close to the left shore rounding the corner to the north.

Camps along this last stretch of Tagish Lake are minimal due to unsuitable shores on the right and cottage development on the left. In this more populated region be sure to camp on public land. If there is a cabin nearby, ask permission before setting up your tent. If no one is there, move on. If you are unable to move on, leave the site in pristine condition when you leave.

The **Tagish River**, known locally as the Six Mile River, is a short, lazy, eight-kilometre stretch (Map 13, km 78). Cottages line both sides of the river. There is an organized, government campground on river right just upstream of the bridge at Tagish for those who wish more "civilized" camping It is actually a very nice campground with outhouses, grey water pits and dry firewood. Showers are even available to the south of the campground, a 15-minute walk away. Given that it is a territorial campground, a fee is required. Signs in the campground tell you how to go about purchasing a permit for camping.

This is the traditional territory of the Tagish people. Outside contact was minimal until the gold rush in 1897. In 1898, a NWMP post was established a few kilometres upstream of the campground. The police post acted as a post office, customs station and mining recorder's office, but its main purpose was as a checkpost for the many stampeders heading down the Yukon River. Every party had to check in at the post, and the failure of a party to arrive here or downstream on schedule resulted in the dispatch of a search party. Present-day Tagish is a small settlement on the west side of the river along the highway.

Please note that a sign at the Tagish campground in 1999 warned against overfishing in the Six Mile River. Possession limits can be checked with Tourism Yukon prior to your trip.

Once under the highway bridge near Tagish, you enter **Marsh Lake** (Maps 13 through 15). Interestingly, Marsh Lake was not so named for its sometimes marshy shores, but was named by Frederick Schwatka after O.C. Marsh, a paleontologist at Yale University. Originally, the lake was named Mud Lake for the shallow silty bottom that made navigation a challenge. Marsh Lake is about 33 kilometres long, which, under ideal conditions, should take about eight hours. It took us about nine hours with a combination of good tailwinds and severe headwinds.

Fortunately, prevailing winds on much of Marsh Lake are from the south. However, once the lake starts to turn westward in its northern half, you may be faced with headwinds. The left shore is undeveloped, and in the southern half, there are many sand beaches that make for good camping. But, once you round the bend to the west, there is virtually no opportunity for camping. The right shore is undeveloped for the first half until near the point at which the highway nears the lake. From here to the outlet, the right shore is quite heavily developed. Marsh Lake campground is situated on the right shore near the west end of the lake, with suitable tent sites near the shore. However, taking the right shore increases the distance to travel by about seven kilometres. (On the maps, kilometre markings on the right shore are marked with a "B.")

The large island near the north end of the lake has some opportunities for camping, however an open water crossing is obviously required. Exercise extreme caution if choosing this option.

One way to access the Yukon River as close to its source as possible while avoiding travel on the lakes is to put in where the Alaska Highway crosses the **M'Clintock River** at the very northeast corner of the lake (Map 15, near km 123B). This river was yet another Yukon feature named by Frederick Schwatka, after the Arctic explorer Sir Francis McClintock. A boat ramp is situated at the west end of the bridge, to the south (left after the bridge when driving west), with a very short paddle to the lake.

Near the M'Clintock access point is Swan Haven, an interpretive centre based around the spring swan migration. Both tundra and trumpeter swans visit here by the thousands, usually in late April.

Marsh Lake has some beautiful beaches along the west shore, southern half.

Once you leave Marsh Lake at km 118, you are at long last on the **Yukon River**. For those used to river travel, you will welcome the familiar tug of the current on your boat's hull. Mmmmm, what a feeling! The distance to Whitehorse is about 46 kilometres with a very mild current. Theoretically, this should take from six to eight hours to complete. However, if head winds are strong, they can stall progress. And, starting here, there are more things to look at, so your progress will depend on your schedule and your desire to explore. As you leave Marsh Lake, you have between you and Whitehorse the remnants of the telegraph line, the Lewes River Bridge, a flood control structure with locks to pass through, historic Canyon City, Miles Canyon, and the Whitehorse dam.

The stretch of the Yukon River from Marsh Lake down to Lake Laberge is also sometimes referred to as "The 50 Mile," so named for its approximate length.

The first 12 kilometres along the Yukon River to the Alaska Highway (Lewes River) bridge have no appreciable current due mostly to the control structure just below the bridge. The river is in a wide valley, with large back eddy ponds and wetlands. It has great potential for birders, who can see many species of waterfowl as well as eagles and other raptors.

Another interesting feature that you will start to see more frequently is the remnant telegraph line. This line was installed in 1899 to improve communications between Bennett and Dawson City. The final link to the south via the Teslin Trail was made in 1901. At this point of the journey, the line is on river left. A little bit of poking about will usually result in a find, often the telegraph cable itself or one of the insulators. The line was strung along trees rather than poles and has remained there ever since.

On the river at last!

3

ROUTES & RAPIDS

The only place where the Alaska Highway crosses the Yukon River is the Lewes River bridge.

Due to the marshy nature of the river, camping along the stretch from km 118 to 130 is...well...pitiful. Of course the desperate and the less picky of us can eke out a campsite anywhere, but...

The next public access to the river is at the pullout next to the **Lewes River Bridge** (Map 16, km 130), where the Alaska Highway crosses the river. Here you will find a sign that explains the workings of the **Marsh Lake Control Structure** just downstream. The first structure here was a wooden dam built by WP&YR in 1924. The purpose of the dam was to flush out the river system in the spring, floating the large riverboats over shallow stretches and flushing out the ice on Lake Laberge. The dam was

The Marsh Lake Control Structure was originally built to help flush ice out of Lake Laberge in the spring. It now holds back water for the Yukon's power generation system.

3

ROUTES & RAPIDS

Paddling through locks makes for a unique experience on a canoe trip.

replaced in 1952, then again in 1975 by the Northern Canada Power Commission, with the existing steel structure being built to aid in water supply for the Whitehorse Rapids hydro facility. The footings of the original two structures remain downstream of the present dam, to aid in bank stabilization. This seemingly small structure holds back an amazing amount of water, determining the water level in all the headwater lakes.

During the paddling season, the drop through the flood control structure is minimal, but for the ease of boat travel, a set of locks was built on river right. The locks are manually controlled, with detailed instructions to help out those less mechanically inclined. The current is tricky immediately downstream of the dam, so caution is advised when leaving the eddy below the lock.

The river from here down to Canyon City, about 25 kilometres, is beautiful and meandering, with a slow current. It is characterized by high, pale, silty cutbanks rising from the water. They provide stark contrast to the dark green vegetation and blue water. Beaver activity is evident. Camping is plentiful in this stretch. You will be able to see some of the peaks around Whitehorse, such as Golden Horn Mountain and Grey (also known as Canyon) Mountain. You will also start to hear and see many of the planes going in and out of the Whitehorse airport and the float plane base on Schwatka Lake.

The silty cutbanks that characterize this section of the Yukon are known locally as the "clay cliffs." Between 8,000 and 12,000 years ago, the valley was filled with the large Glacial Lake Champagne. During the retreat of the McConnell continental ice sheet, the meltwater was prohibited from draining down the old channel to the south (now the Takhini valley) due to a build-up of ice in the St. Elias Mountains.

3

ROUTES & RAPIDS

The lake built up to a level of 500 metres above the valley floor before it cut a new channel, the existing Yukon River, to the north and west. During this time, silt from the ice sheet settled to the bottom of the lake, creating the layers that are now exposed due to the action of the river.

At about km 144 (Map 17), you will pass through the southern border of the City of Whitehorse. The northern boundary is not encountered until near the Takhini River, approximately 40 kilometres downstream.

You will know you are nearing **Canyon City** (Map 17, km 155) when you see the remains of a pumphouse on river left. From here, it is about one kilometre to Canyon City. The remains of the settlement are situated on river right on a low bench at a sharp left bend in the river. It is a great place to stop, rest and look around, although camping is not permitted given its archaeological significance. From the site, you can walk about 20 to 30 minutes downstream to Miles Canyon, along the old tram line or one of several other trails along the shore. Downstream, trails on both sides of the river will lead you as far as the Robert Campbell Bridge in Whitehorse. (Yukon Energy Corporation publishes a free brochure, "Enjoying Whitehorse Trails" on the hiking trails in this area.) You can also take a trail leading upstream that goes as far as Marsh Lake.

Shortly downstream of Canyon City is the reason for its existence — **Miles Canyon.** In its day, Miles Canyon was a fearsome sight with its raging rapids between high vertical walls, and a drop over its length of 32 feet. Today, although impressive, it is nowhere near as dangerous, since it has been partly flooded

Paddlers can't help but think of a historical image of raging waters while passing through Miles Canyon. (inset) Miles Canyon posed a significant hazard during the rush.

CANYON CITY & MILES CANYON

Canyon City and Miles Canyon are a natural pair; without the raging and boat-swamping waters of Miles Canyon, seven kilometres upstream of Whitehorse, Canyon City would not exist. It was here that steamers and many handmade boats on the upper river transferred their loads and passengers to rudimentary, horse-drawn trams to be transported around the canyon. The NWMP was stationed here to ensure that boats that went through the rapids were piloted safely by competent boat pilots. Two separate companies built tramways on either side of the river in the winter of 1897–1898, bypassing both Miles Canyon and Whitehorse Rapids. Both companies charged three cents per pound and $25 per boat. Before long, a buy-out allowed the concentration of efforts on the right shore, and Canyon City subsequently thrived, albeit for a short time. Once the WP&YR railway reached Whitehorse in 1900, the wooden structures that stood here were dismantled and used to fire the steamboats, among other things.

The Yukon Government Heritage Branch, in partnership with First Nations, is conducting ongoing archaeological work at the site. You can still see the outlines of old tents and buildings, such as the NWMP post, the Canyon and White Horse Tramway Company offices and the Canyon Hotel and Saloon. A sign will guide you to the various sites.

Miles Canyon can be reached from Canyon City via a short paddle or by a 1.7-kilometre foot path that follows the old tram line. The canyon is a natural wonder, seen close up as you pass between its impressive walls. The vertical columns of

Approaching the rapids, 1898. Tramway visible on far shore.

Yukon Archives, Vancouver Public Library Coll. #2229

CHILKOOT TRAIL
Dyea to Bennett

HEADWATER LAKES
Bennett to Whitehorse

YUKON RIVER
Whitehorse to Carmacks

YUKON RIVER
Carmacks to Dawson

rock that frame the canyon were formed of quick-cooling olivine basalt from volcanic flows. It is believed the lava came in a series of two to 10-metre thick flows from a cinder cone several hundred metres southwest of McRae (near km 152). The cinder cone is no longer visible, as it was since covered in glacial drift. The basalt was laid down between 8.3 and 8.8 million years ago.

Yukon Archives, MacBride Museum Coll. #3609

3
ROUTES & RAPIDS

Canyon City: (above) at its peak during the gold rush and (below) in modern times.

An example of the clay cliffs before Whitehorse.

out by the Whitehorse dam. But don't be lulled into a false sense of security. There are still tricky currents through the corrugated walls of the canyon, especially in high water. Watch out for motor traffic on the river here, including the tour boat *S.S. Schwatka.* While a canoe technically has the right of way, it's wise to head for safety near shore in the narrows of the canyon, pointing your canoe at the waves that will come.

Once you have spilled out of Miles Canyon, you are already technically in the reservoir of **Schwatka Lake,** from which the water used by Whitehorse residents is drawn. The lake is about three kilometres long and lined with float plane docks, since the lake is the float plane base for the region. Take care that you stay close to shore so as not to interfere with float planes landing and taking off.

Schwatka Lake is controlled by Yukon Energy Corporation's **Whitehorse dam**. This dam was constructed in 1958 to supply power to Whitehorse, and the resulting reservoir, Schwatka Lake, calmed the waters of Miles Canyon and the Whitehorse Rapids.

You may be wondering how to plan your passage through downtown Whitehorse. Depending on your timing, you could camp nearby, or press on to camp well downstream. The only place to camp near the downtown area is at Robert Service Campground, located on river left shortly downstream of the dam and the Yukon Energy Corporation building site. This is a tenting-only campground, with 68 walk-in sites from which to choose. However, first you must get past the dam, the only portage that you will encounter on the route to Dawson.

One way is to pull out on the left shore of Schwatka Lake, either at the parking area near the south end, or near the float plane base and tour boat operators at the north end. From these points, you can either portage or arrange a short ride along the Miles Canyon Road to the Robert Service Campground, just past the dam.

Alternately, you may portage around the dam on river right, as do most groups travelling through. A road to the right of the dam makes this portage easier. You will find a small beach on the right from which you can access the road that parallels the fish ladder. Follow the road past the dam, head onto a shoreline trail, then lower your gear down the slope to the river below the rapids, near the point at which the hydro lines cross the river. If you want to stop at the campground on river left, ferry quickly across the river and then follow the left shore until you come to the small bridge connecting an island to the mainland, pulling out on the left, upstream of the bridge and within the campground. The length of the portage is about 700 metres.

The river between the dam and Whitehorse braids into three main channels. All three will get you into the downtown area. The rightmost channel has some large waves at the top that you may wish to avoid. Some locals spend their spare time surfing here in their unloaded canoes or kayaks. You may be taken aback by the strong current here. This is what allows paddling parties to make great distances on the river downstream, with little effort.

As you reach downtown **Whitehorse** (Map 17, km 164), your first highly visible marker will be the riverboat *S.S. Klondike* on display on river left. Just downstream from that is the Robert Campbell bridge, the only crossing of the Yukon River in Whitehorse. Your first good takeout is downstream of the bridge on river left. At the downstream end of the Rotary Peace Park, there is a boat ramp that provides excellent access to the city. Downstream of the ramp are pilings along the left shore, remnants of the extensive steamboat docks. The last place to pull out is just upstream of the Kanoe People building, near the end of the bank along the left shore. This is closer to laundromats and grocery stores than the park. Downstream of the Kanoe People, one moves into an industrial area away from the city's services. It is possible, but less pleasant, to stop here.

What is left of Whitehorse Rapids is below the dam.

3

ROUTES & RAPIDS

WHITEHORSE

In the late 1800s, just above what is now the City of Whitehorse, lay a set of raging rapids. The resemblance of the foaming, white-crested waves to the manes of white horses resulted in the name Whitehorse Rapids. Named after these wild rapids that have since been drowned by the dam upstream of the city, Whitehorse developed as a result of construction of the White Pass & Yukon Route railway. The rail line from Skagway ended in a logical location, just below the wild rapids that were considered the greatest impediment to the movement of goods along the Trail of '98. The town sprung up as a result of the connection of rail service to the south and riverboat traffic to the north. From this point, there was no turning back. An airport came in 1920, the Alaska Highway in 1942, incorporation as a city in 1950, and, in 1953, designation as the territory's capital.

Whitehorse is now a major centre for government, and provides services and communications for the region, including the Yukon, northern British Columbia and parts of Alaska. With its population exceeding 23,000, Whitehorse is a modern community in terms of its services, but maintains the feeling of a small, quaint, frontier town. This is despite a vast land area of 421 square kilometres, increased in 1974 from its original 6.9 square kilometres when the city acquired large tracts of surrounding land.

Whitehorse is well worth a lengthy visit, with a range of activities in which to partake. For the tourist, there are many historical buildings and museums to visit, including the MacBride Museum, the White Pass Train Depot, the Transportation Museum, the Beringia Interpretive Centre, the Old Log Church, the log skyscraper, the visitor reception centre, and the *S.S. Klondike*. A trolley car now runs along the waterfront, giving rides to tourists. For those wishing to stretch their legs, there are many short and long hikes around Whitehorse. *Whitehorse & Area Hikes & Bikes*, a book put out by the Yukon Conservation Society, is a great resource for hikers and bikers. Of course, there is always the essential laundry, food shopping and making the necessary phone calls!

Yukon Archives, Vancouver Public Library Coll., 2273

Traffic on the Yukon River, at Whitehorse, early in the 1900s.

3

ROUTES & RAPIDS

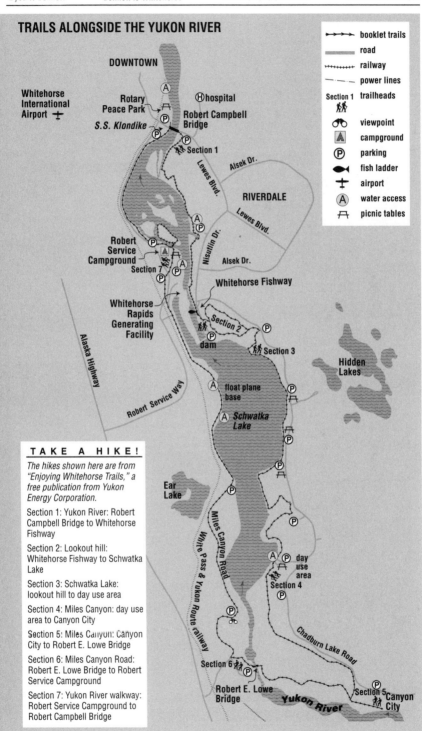

TRAILS ALONGSIDE THE YUKON RIVER

Legend:
- →→→→ booklet trails
- —— road
- ++++++ railway
- —·—·— power lines
- Section 1 trailheads 𝕜𝕜
- 👁 viewpoint
- Ⓐ campground
- Ⓟ parking
- 🐟 fish ladder
- ✈ airport
- Ⓐ water access
- 🪑 picnic tables

3
ROUTES & RAPIDS

TAKE A HIKE!

The hikes shown here are from "Enjoying Whitehorse Trails," a free publication from Yukon Energy Corporation.

Section 1: Yukon River: Robert Campbell Bridge to Whitehorse Fishway

Section 2: Lookout hill: Whitehorse Fishway to Schwatka Lake

Section 3: Schwatka Lake: lookout hill to day use area

Section 4: Miles Canyon: day use area to Canyon City

Section 5: Miles Canyon: Canyon City to Robert E. Lowe Bridge

Section 6: Miles Canyon Road: Robert E. Lowe Bridge to Robert Service Campground

Section 7: Yukon River walkway: Robert Service Campground to Robert Campbell Bridge

3

ROUTES & RAPIDS

Yukon Archives, Galigan Coll.

View of the shipyards in Whitehorse at midnight, no date.

Bruce Bennett

The Yukon River as it flows through the City of Whitehorse.

The S.S. Klondike, letting you know you have reached Whitehorse.

Distance: 313 kilometres
Time to complete: approximately 5-9 days, plus layover days (depends on winds on Lake Laberge, length of day)
Challenges: Possible heavy wind and waves on Lake Laberge
Rewards: Lots of history, swift current
River gradient: 1.3 metres per kilometre

Maps	page
17 • Whitehorse	171
18 • Takhini River	172
19 • Upper Laberge	173
20 • Richthofen Island	174
21 • Hancock Hills	175
22 • Lower Laberge	176
23 • Thirty Mile	177
24 • Hootalinqua	178
25 • Semenof Hills	179
26 • Big Salmon	180
27 • Dutch Bluff	181
28 • Twin Creek	182
29 • Little Salmon	183
30 • Columbia Slough	184
31 • Carmacks	185

This portion of the Yukon River has several markedly different stretches. The piece from Whitehorse down to Lake Laberge is easy, with moderate current. Lake Laberge is a large, wide lake; its typical challenges are winds and cold water. The lake is followed by a stretch of the Yukon River down to Hootalinqua at the Teslin River confluence called "The Thirty Mile." This section, a designated Canadian Heritage River, is characterized by clear, swift water and many bends. From Hootalinqua to Carmacks, the water is somewhat more silty, with a fair current.

The rate at which people travel on this stretch and down to Dawson depends on paddling philosophy. Some guides will tell you that you can travel from

Kanoe People's central location is also a nice place from which to depart Whitehorse.

Whitehorse to Dawson in seven to ten days. This is possible, but with a distance of 720 kilometres to go (including a crossing of Lake Laberge), this would mean from 72 to 103 kilometres per day. Not my idea of fun! Mind you, the current is swift, but I would guess that many groups who take this short amount of time are paddling some very long days, and maybe nights. We took a full two weeks to go from Whitehorse to Dawson, and although we had two half-day layovers, we were pushing long days the rest of the time. After a hard crossing of Lake Laberge, we still had to go 59 kilometres each day just to make it to Dawson by our target — 72 kilometres each day to get our two half-days off. But everyone has their own way of approaching things.

Although this stretch of the Yukon River is not very developed at this time, it was quite busy in the first half of the 20th century with steamboats plying its waters. Almost every bend in the river has a name that relates to an incident with a steamboat. Today, you will encounter several modern settlements, many abandoned posts and wood lots for the steamboats, a few First Nation settlements, an old shipyard, and some old equipment, such as gold dredges.

Your travels start with the slow transition from "urban" Whitehorse, to outlying settled areas, to relative solitude. Development continues sporadically to the Takhini River, after which it virtually disappears. Don't count on camping until you are well downstream of downtown Whitehorse, to get away from private land.

Until McIntyre Creek, at km 170, the river braids around many lush islands. This area is great for viewing eagles and many types of waterfowl. When the river narrows below McIntyre Creek (named after the founder of the rich Copper King deposits), the current picks up a bit. There are a few cabins and fish camps along the shores, but the area is mostly uninhabited. At a sharp left bend at km 175 (Whistle Bend, so named for the warning blast given by steamers when

ROUTES & RAPIDS

3

entering the bend, due to the tight confines), you will have the City of Whitehorse wastewater treatment facility on river right. This facility is a series of lagoons that are discharged once per year into a nearby pothole lake, to filter through the ground into the Yukon River. This facility is followed shortly by the location of the old wastewater outlet pipe, and a sign saying "CITY OF WHITEHORSE SEWER OUTPOUR BEWARE!" The old outfall is no longer used, and the filtered discharge from the new facility is likely of good quality. However, from here until at least partway down Lake Laberge, you should have a reliable method of water purification, or use fresh drinking water brought from Whitehorse.

Not far upstream of the Takhini River is **Little Takhini Creek**, which looks just like a quiet backwater. This is a potential camp spot, and is apparently a favourite place for Northern Pike. The **Takhini River** flows from the left into the Yukon River at km 183 (Map 18). Looking up this tributary, you can see the Klondike Highway bridge, which provides another good access point to the river for either putting in or taking out. Ancient records indicate that a trail once led from the Chilkat Pass to the Yukon River along the Takhini River. It is possible that the name Takhini is derived from a First Nation word referring to the mosquitos that can inhabit this area (from the Tagish words *tahk*, meaning mosquito, and *heena*, meaning river). It is theorized that the Yukon River once flowed through this valley.

The Takhini River joins the Yukon River, about 20 kilometres downstream of downtown Whitehorse. This portion of the Yukon River can be travelled in three to four hours, depending on conditions. From the Takhini River to the entry to Lake Laberge is about 22 kilometres, which can be travelled in a further two and a half to three and a half hours. You may find progress slows somewhat as you reach Lake Laberge, due to the backwater effect of the lake.

About two kilometres below the Takhini River is Egg Island, a good place to stop for the night. A nice flat area for camping is accompanied by picnic tables, shelters and outhouses. Further on, at km 192 (Map 19), on the outside bend, you will see Raymond's Landing. There are modern farm buildings at this location. Shortly after, you come to **Steamboat Slough**, a very wide, almost 270-degree bend in the river starting at km 196. The main river now goes through the inside channel, and you can find a great, high water camping spot on river right along this channel. The best part about camping in this location is the exploration you can do through the marshy backwaters behind your tent. It is also the last campsite before entering the lake, so you can rest up here in preparation for a potentially difficult day.

Jim Boss cut-off is a place where the trail and telegraph line cut across the point of land here at Steamboat Slough. The feature was named after a local First Nation chief who was influential in the early treaty process.

At km 200, only a couple of kilometres before the river widens into the lake, you will pass by **Upper Laberge**, the site of a NWMP post built in 1899. This is also referred to as Policemen's Point. If you venture up the bank, you will be able to pick out the outlines of a couple of buildings that once belonged to the post. This was an important post from the gold rush on, ultimately replacing the Tagish post when it was shut down. This is also an access point to the river, via Policeman's

3

ROUTES & RAPIDS

PREHISTORICAL FLOW OF THE YUKON RIVER

The Yukon River did not always flow in the direction and channels that it now does. As a matter of fact, it is very likely that the river flowed to the south before the latest ice age changed its direction northwards. Before the uplift of the St. Elias and Pelly mountains, it is likely that the southern Yukon had relatively low relief. There is evidence that during this time, water may have drained to the south directly into the Pacific Ocean. This hypothesis would explain inconsistencies in the size of some valleys in relation to the rivers that flow through them. The Takhini and Dezadeash valleys are quite large in comparison with the streams that now occupy them. This indicates that a single large river created this valley, likely the outlet of the Yukon River flow to the Pacific. In contrast, the valleys of the Stewart and Yukon rivers within the Klondike Plateau are small for their current streams, indicating that these large streams have only recently occupied the valleys. This region may be the original headwaters of the south-flowing Yukon River. Other evidence points to a south-flowing drainage, such as the slopes of subsurface gravels from previous drainage.

Although the St. Elias Mountains were rapidly uplifted in comparison with the rest of southern Yukon, it is believed that for a time the south-flowing drainage cut downwards at a similar rate. The reversal of flow patterns is believed to have occurred during the Pleistocene ice age. During the successive advances and retreats of the great ice sheets, ice remained along the coastal strip longer than in the interior, creating a barrier to southern drainage. This huge ice dam caused a glacial lake to form over a vast area centred over Whitehorse. Ultimately and in several stages, the water found the only way it could to drain to the ocean — northwest down the current route of the Yukon River.

The maps below show two hypothesized routes of the prehistoric Yukon River.

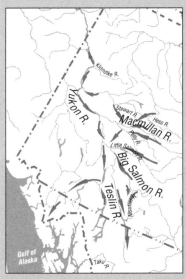

Adapted from "Evolution of physiography and drainage in southern Yukon," by Dirk Templeman-Kluit.

Canoeists put in at the mouth of the Takhini River, by the Klondike Highway bridge.

3

ROUTES & RAPIDS

Point Road off the Klondike Highway. Respect the private dwellings in the vicinity of the launch area.

As the river begins to widen and slow before the lake, you will notice a double row of pilings. At the height of the gold rush, these pilings were constructed to direct the Yukon River flow directly into the lake. Before they were built, a large, shallow sand bar lay across the entry to the lake, with flow split down either side. By keeping the flow contained, it was hoped that the water would scour out a channel passable by steamboats. The system never worked well, and within a couple of years, with damage to the piles by ice, the river reverted to its rightmost channel. About ten years later, the river returned to the central channel, and was maintained through blasting and dredging. Now the pilings provide roosting spots for passing gulls.

Lake Laberge is over 50 kilometres long (52 kilometres along the east shore, 55 kilometres along the west), and up to seven kilometres wide. Winds can develop quickly, and within minutes turn a calm placid pond to an ocean of waves. Although prevailing winds are from the south, they can also change direction very quickly, at any time without notice. As you enter the lake, you have a decision to make — the left (west) or right (east) shore. Once you decide, you would be ill-advised to cross to the other side. The right shore is a more direct route, although there are fewer bays for shelter from bad weather. The left requires more paddling into bays, but the bays provide shelter and some incredible campsites. The danger with the left shore is that most canoeists will cut across the mouths of most bays, increasing their distance from shore and thus exposure to winds. If you anticipate doing this, you may be better off heading up the right shore. There are good but spotty camping opportunities up both sides. Both shores also each have a long, exposed stretch with little opportunity for shelter.

WHITE RIVER ASH

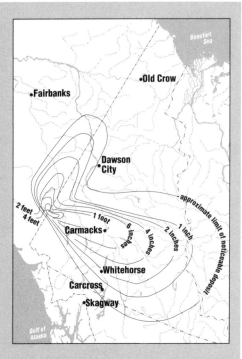

You may notice a thin white layer in the sediments near the top of the riverbank. This "White River Ash," which covers an amazing 325,000 square kilometres or one third of southern Yukon, is a result of a volcanic explosion in the St. Elias Range near the Yukon-Alaska border about 1,300 years ago. Sources are inconclusive about the exact location of the blast, but some experts believe it to be under the Klutlan Glacier in eastern Alaska, near the headwaters of the White River. The thickness of the layer varies from a few centimetres to a few metres. A particularly thick deposit, labelled Sam McGee's ashes (Map 33), can be seen just upstream of Yukon Crossing (km 530) on river right. You will see the White River Ash intermittently until around Minto. This ash layer is used as a simple dating tool, since all layers above the ash were laid down more recently than the volcanic event that caused it. The small amount of soil above the White River Ash is an indicator of how slowly soil is created in the north.

The thin white line of the White River Ash (marked by arrow) can be seen along much of the length of the Upper Yukon River.

Yukon Archives, Greenbank Coll., 89/12, pho 371, 12

On the many large lakes, such as Lake Laberge shown here in 1898, goldseekers hoped for favourable winds.

It has been reported that the Tagish knew the lake as *Kluk-tas-si*, while the Tlingit knew it as *Tahini-wud*.

Lake Laberge was a trouble spot to steamers early in the season, since it was one of the last stretches of water to lose its ice. Several tactics were employed to break the ice in the spring, including the control dam below Marsh Lake, which allowed a gush of water to be released in the spring to break up the ice. Another method was to spread discarded crankcase oil along the length of the lake,

Piers at the head of Lake Laberge provide roosting spots for passing gulls.

3

ROUTES & RAPIDS

amplifying the heat of the sun to warm and melt the ice. This technique would certainly be frowned upon today!

Please note that in 1999, a sign at the Lake Laberge campground advised limiting lake trout to two meals per month, and warned against consuming burbot livers, due to contamination. It also cautioned travellers to boil water before consumption, something recommended throughout the Yukon.

In times of low water, you may have difficulty finding the channel into the lake. Shifting silt and sand cause the channel to change from year to year. The main channel entering the lake is to the left of the row of pilings, but the mud flats extend far beyond the pilings.

As you enter the lake, to the left you will see the Miners Range, a series of forested, dome-shaped mountains and high ridges. Pilot Mountain is the most prominent of these, guarding the southern end of the lake. Explorer and geologist George Dawson named these for the miners he met on his journeys to survey the territory. On the right are higher, more prominent mountains near the south end of the lake. This is part of a range that, according to geological sources, is unnamed. The most prominent of these mountains is Teslin Mountain. North of Teslin Mountain are lower hills referred to on some maps as Hancock Hills.

Those familiar with Robert Service and his poems about the north may find a certain rhyme going through their heads now:

"There are strange things done in the midnight sun
By the men who moil for gold;
The Arctic trails have their secret tales
That would make your blood run cold;
The Northern Lights have seen queer sights,
But the queerest they ever did see
Was the night on the marge of Lake Lebarge
I cremated Sam McGee."

Entering Lake Laberge on a calm day is a special treat.

West (left) shore of Lake Laberge

If you are travelling along the west shore, you will remain fairly exposed until **Jackfish Bay**, at km 209 (Map 20), about seven kilometres into the lake. You will see a few small cabins near the very south end, followed by some beaches separated by rocky points. Watch for private property from the south end of the lake through Jackfish Bay. The point you round to enter Jackfish Bay has a number of houses and cottages on it. Luckily, an island at the mouth of the bay makes crossing much safer. This island also provides camping for those whose timing is right. Camping sites can also be found along the shore north of Jackfish Bay.

Richthofen Island should be visible from the head of the lake. At first sight it is 12 kilometres away, and may appear quite small, but looms larger as you near it. As you travel north of Jackfish Bay, you will encounter many more small bays. If your weather is favourable, you may want to make the two-kilometre crossing to the south end of Richthofen Island and work up its west shoreline, although camping opportunities on this side of the island are fewer. Its north end requires only a half-kilometre crossing back to the west shore of the lake.

The one public access point on Lake Laberge is by Deep Creek at the Lake Laberge campground boat launch on the west shore (Map 20, km 216), about even in latitude with the south end of Richthofen Island. Many groups who do not want to travel the full length of Lake Laberge or who have less time, will put in at this point, leaving about 35 kilometres of lake to travel. The next access is not encountered until Little Salmon (and you must drive through Carmacks, even farther down the river, to get to Little Salmon). The Lake Laberge campground also provides civilized camping for those passing through on their journey (no showers, though!). North of the campground, at about km 217, is a place locally

Rocky shores along Lake Laberge.

3

ROUTES & RAPIDS

Several wrecks, such as this one, can be found on the west shore of Lake Laberge.

known as Fossil Point, where some searching may show you a fossil embedded in a rocky outcrop.

North of Richthofen Island, the shoreline straightens out considerably, making shelter a little harder to find. There are still a few beaches to be found, but mostly with rounded pebbles instead of sand. The first nice camping spot can be found

One of the sheltered bays on the west shore of Lake Laberge.

at km 230, with a number of beaches between here and **Ptarmigan Point**. Some
of the rocky points between beaches may provide high water camps, but could
be exposed to the winds. If your timing is right to camp along here, there are a
number of sites to choose from near the north end of the lake. A large stretch
of the north end of the west shoreline was burned in the Fox Lake fire of 1998
(see mark on maps).

East (right) shore of Lake Laberge

(Kilometres are indicated along the east shore for reference, but the kilometre
markers below Lower Laberge are continued from those along the west shore.)

The east shore is a shorter route by about three kilometres, since there are
fewer bays. This makes shelter harder to find if the wind picks up. However, there
are still small bays and rocky points that provide some shelter and camping areas.
The first point of interest on your jaunt down the east side is the abandoned First
Nation village of **Upper Laberge**, located at km 205B near Joe Creek. There are
still a few buildings there that are occasionally used by trappers. On the hill behind
the village stands a graveyard. Please respect this sacred site.

The mountains along the eastern border of the lake are quite beautiful. Some
of the peaks reach over 1,500 metres. As you enter the lake, Joe Mountain can be
seen at about four o'clock. (Twelve o'clock is straight ahead). At about two o'clock
are Mount Laurier and Lime Peak. Looming behind and in between these mountains
is the magnificent **Teslin Mountain**, at 1,953 metres. Farther down the lake, the
Hancock Hills are more subdued. A common characteristic of these hills lining Lake
Laberge is the white limestone bedrock that you see in the many outcrops. These
rocks were laid down under a warm ocean between 245 and 208 million years ago.
Due to the susceptibility of limestone to erosion when it comes in contact with
water, you will also see a number of caves along and above the shoreline.

3

ROUTES & RAPIDS

Upper Laberge Indian village is still used as a base for fishing and hunting.

3

ROUTES & RAPIDS

Hancock Hills on the east shore of Lake Laberge.

Laurier Creek is found on the east shore, even with the north end of Richthofen Island. There is limited camping at the mouth of the creek, but good grayling fishing. The Livingstone Trail once came through here from Whitehorse, up the Laurier valley to the base of Mount Laurier, then over to the Teslin River and on to the south fork of the Big Salmon River where the mining town of Livingstone was located. A winter trail now, parts of it are impassable in the summer. In more recent times, the trail has been used again to haul equipment into mining operations, but it has been significantly rerouted from its original path. If you camp here, be mindful of private property, as there are a number of cabins in the area.

There are enough good camping locations along the east shore. With a bit of planning and some luck with weather, you shouldn't have too much difficulty finding a place for the night. There is a concentration of sites a few kilometres north of Richthofen Island, which would put you about halfway down the lake. However, there are other, moderately spaced sites between there and the outlet. The last half of the lake has rocky bluffs and a straight shoreline, making it quite exposed, so sites are smaller and less ideal than in the south half. Most of the sites are at the outlets of small creeks.

You will pass **Goddard Point** about five kilometres from the outlet, named after a small steamboat, the *A.J. Goddard*, wrecked here in 1899. The boat had been in service barely over a year, taking four crew members down with it. It was actually the first steamer to complete the full trip between Bennett and Dawson City. The hardships of this unprecedented trip through the headwater lakes, Miles Canyon and Whitehorse Rapids resulted in a 23-day journey. Later, steamer trips between Whitehorse and Dawson City took only about five days.

Near the end of Lake Laberge, in the northwest corner, is the Ogilvie Valley, containing the tiny Ogilvie Creek. This wide valley seems far too large for such a tiny stream. It is possible that this valley once held the ancient Yukon River, draining a huge area to the north, through Lake Laberge and the Takhini, Dezadeash and Alsek valleys.

The end of the lake (km 258, Map 22) is marked by **Lower Laberge**, a community of about 20 or so cabins that was based around the transportation industry until the 1950s, when the steamers stopped running. Wood camps were situated on both shores, and the remains of wood roads can still be seen. A NWMP post was established here, first on the left shore, but more recently and prominently on river right. A telegraph office and roadhouse can still be found at the village. A rusted old truck on the site was once used to haul in wood for the steamers from active cut areas. On the shore lie the remains of the hull of the *S.S.Casca #1*. After the original *Casca* was dismantled in Whitehorse, the hull was towed to Lower Laberge to serve as a landing dock. The superstructure and machinery were removed for use on the *Casca #2*. On the left shore, upstream of the village, lie the remains of a NWMP post.

Camping facilities have been developed at Lower Laberge, including picnic tables, shelter and outhouses. Just downstream of Lower Laberge, the telegraph line once crossed from river left to river right. With some effort, you will be able to see wire on the right from here until it crosses back to the left just upstream of Hootalinqua, by the confluence of the Teslin River.

Between here and Minto, you will pass through an area that is referred to as the **Whitehorse Trough**. Between approximately 240 and 140 million years ago, volcanic flows, alluvial fans and lagoonal sediment accumulated in the trough.

Lower Laberge was a wood camp, NWMP post and telegraph station.

These were then subsequently folded and faulted. Primary rock groups include sandstone, conglomerate and shale. Prominent rock types are red-brown weathering volcanic flows and white-weathering limestone.

When you leave Lower Laberge, you are entering one of the most beautiful stretches of the Yukon River — **The Thirty Mile**. So named for its length, from Lake Laberge to Hootalinqua at the Teslin River confluence, The Thirty Mile caused fear among early river travellers due to its fast current and sharp corners, resulting in a great many wrecks. For modern day travellers, the swift current and crystal clear water combine to make a pleasant paddling experience, with a more wilderness feeling. As indicated on a sign at Lower Laberge, The Thirty Mile has been designated a Canadian Heritage River, and is jointly managed by the Yukon government, the Ta'an Kwach'an Council (a local First Nation), the Council of Yukon First Nations and the Department of Indian Affairs and Northern Development. This joint management is resulting in more camping facilities to increase enjoyment of river travellers and lessen the impact on the river. These camping facilities are free. Water quality is monitored on a regular basis in this stretch.

About 10 kilometres below Lower Laberge at km 270 (Map 23), **U.S. Bend** rears its head, a series of two hairpin turns, of which the first completes almost a full circle. There is great camping on both the head and tail of the island at the second, left bend. Another kilometre downstream, **Domville Creek** (spelled Donvill on some old steamer charts) empties into the Yukon on river right. This is the site of the wreck of the steamer *S.S. James Domville*. It was possible to see the wreck for many years, but it is now so silted and overgrown that it cannot be seen. The creek makes for a great rest spot, though, and a good opportunity to see the telegraph line. Camping here is marginal.

Within a couple of kilometres (about km 273), you should be able to see the bluffs of Maunoir Butte ahead. As you near it (about km 279), you will start to see another bluff on river left, stained with the red of iron oxide. Keep your eyes peeled also on the river banks for the White River Ash.

There were many woodyards along the Yukon River during the steamboat era from the early 1900s to the 1950s. The boats' appetite for wood was tremendous, with larger steamers burning one cord per hour. Many woodyards had roads which reached 10 to 20 kilometres into the bush before they simply ran out of available wood, closed, and were replaced by another woodlot at another location. At about km 285 is the site of Wickstrom Woodyard, where there are still piles of cordwood to be seen. Just downstream on river left you will see the Government of the Yukon sign indicating **Seventeen Mile Woodyard**. The Seventeen Mile Woodyard, so named because of its distance below Lower Laberge, was a particularly large yard in its day. The remains of several cabins, wagons and other artifacts still lie on the site today. The remains of wood roads beckon as they reach back into the woods. Across from the Seventeen Mile Woodyard is Casca Reef, one of the many sites where a *Casca* steamer went down. On this particular occasion around 1910, the *S.S. Casca #1* was refloated.

Old equipment lies in a clearing at Seventeen Mile Woodyard along The Thirty Mile.

3

ROUTES & RAPIDS

From here, it is about 20 kilometres to Hootalinqua at the confluence of the Teslin River. This stretch is enjoyable; swift current, clear water, mild bends. Five kilometres before Hootalinqua, the telegraph line once crossed the river from the right to the left shore. The route of the telegraph line stays on the left shore now until near Ogilvie Island by the Sixty Mile River, km 808. There are a few fine camping spots along this stretch to Hootalinqua, the nicest being an organized campground at km 296 (Map 24). It is a beautiful grassy bench with tall, open stands of aspen. A few picnic tables and an outhouse are the extent of the facilities. The next camping is not until the developed site at Hootalinqua.

Just above the Teslin River confluence is Crawford Island. It was named after Jack Crawford, the assistant general manager for the Klondike, Yukon and Copper River Company. In 1898, Crawford brought in a bunch of men and equipment to dredge the Teslin River. When operations failed shortly after, the men pulled out. In the meantime, there was a small settlement known as **Crawfordsville**. One source puts it on river right by this island, where no evidence can be found, while others point to it being across the river from Hootalinqua, where the remains of old buildings lie.

The **Teslin River** flows in from the right at km 305 (Map 24), slightly silty compared with the clear waters of The Thirty Mile. In the relatively short time that there have been people on the river, it has had many names, including Tes-s'l-Heena, Delin Chu, Iyon, Hootalinqua, Newberry, and Teslin-Tuh. It flows 160 kilometres from Teslin Lake, which straddles the B.C./Yukon border. This river

TESLIN RIVER

The Teslin River is a fairly popular way to access the Yukon River. Most parties put in at Johnson's Crossing, with 184 kilometres to get to the Yukon River at Hootalinqua, which takes four to six days. For those who wish to add an extra day or more and enjoy lake paddling, a launch at the Teslin Lake Yukon government campground adds about 37 kilometres. You can terminate your trip at Hootalinqua by arranging to be towed by boat back to Whitehorse, or continue on down the Yukon River, which is what most people do. The distance from Hootalinqua to Carmacks, one common take-out spot, is another 172 kilometres, completed in another two and a half to four days. This makes a total trip of one to one and a half weeks, or more if you want to really enjoy it. Just so you are prepared, the Teslin has some minor rapids that do require manoeuvring and knowledge of moving water. You should be aware of fast currents and occasional obstructions such as sweepers.

The put-in is at the north end of the Alaska Highway bridge over the Teslin River, at Johnson's Crossing. The river is slow and marshy for the first while, with few opportunities for camping. Squanga Creek (so named for a First Nation word for a type of whitefish found here) or sites near 100 Mile Crossing are your first chances for camping. Below this point, the wide valley closes in, the camping sites become somewhat more plentiful and the current picks up.

Below Indian River, the river once again changes. The river broadens with extra flow, and braids around islands. The river valley once again widens out. Shortly downstream of the Indian River is Roaring Bull Rapids, which don't live up to their name and are fairly straightforward. They are still worth a look first if you are uncertain. The increase in islands makes for more numerous camping spots.

Mason's Landing was once considered the head of navigation on the Teslin, due to the shallows upstream. From here down to Hootalinqua, the river picks up speed, preparing to meet the Yukon River. For more information, pick up Gus Karpes' guide, *The Teslin River — Johnson's Crossing to Hootalinqua Yukon, Canada.*

was part of the "All-Canadian route" to the Klondike goldfields, which started in Ashcroft, British Columbia, passing through Telegraph Creek on the Stikine River. This route proved to be at least as miserable and unsuccessful as any of the other routes at the time, due to the gruelling land portion. For many years, the Teslin River was used as a transportation route to access the Yukon River and the gold diggings on Livingstone Creek (a tributary of the Big Salmon River). Although the river has been heavily prospected, gold has only been found in minute quantities.

Some paddling parties, in order to avoid windy Lake Laberge, canoe down the Teslin River from Johnson's Crossing on the Alaska Highway, to meet the Yukon at Hootalinqua. In doing this though, they miss the most spectacular part of The Thirty Mile.

The name **Hootalinqua** (km 306, Map 24) was an approximation of the First Nation word for the Teslin River, meaning "running against the mountain" in Northern Tutchone. The village was established just downstream of the Teslin River on river left in the mid-1890s in response to findings of fine gold on the Teslin and Yukon rivers. Within a few years, a NWMP post, a telegraph office and a Taylor & Drury store had been established here. Despite this, and a shipyard on Hootalinqua Island, the settlement never thrived. The roadhouse, telegraph office and a small trapper's cabin are still standing on the site. Organized camping is offered here, with outhouses and picnic tables.

For those interested in steamboat history, a stop at **Shipyard Island** (also known as Hootalinqua Island), just downstream of the settlement, is a must. If water levels are high, you may have to paddle fairly hard to reach the shore on the island. Pulling up on the east side of the island (its right-most shore looking at the island from upstream), you can see the wooden "ways" that were constructed in 1913 by the British Yukon Navigation Company. These were used to pull the steamers onto the island for winter storage or repairs. Horses were used to turn the capstans, which in turn wound up the cables that were wrapped around the hull of a steamer. The ship was then levelled and blocked for winter storage, safe from ice damage. Resting atop the ways, set back from the river, is the *S.S. Evelyn,* a steamer built in 1908 in Seattle for American trade on the lower Yukon River. It was purchased by a Canadian company, Side Stream Navigation, in 1913, renamed the *S.S. Norcom* and put in service for one season between Whitehorse and the Bering Sea before being abandoned. The hull has deteriorated considerably in recent years, but is still

3

ROUTES & RAPIDS

Old buildings provide a unique backdrop for campers at Hootalinqua.

3

ROUTES & RAPIDS

The S.S. Evelyn slowly decays on cribs on Shipyard Island, near Hootalinqua.

relatively intact considering it has been retired from service for the better part of a century. Remains of shipyard equipment can be found on the site, including the huge capstans used to winch the boats up the ways.

About 14 kilometres below the shipyards, on the outside bend at km 320 (Map 25), lies the hull of the *S.S. Klondike #1*. In June of 1936, the steamer first hit bottom 10 kilometres upstream near Davis Point. From there to its final resting spot, the boat slowly sank, running out of control and hitting almost every sand bar on its way, causing more damage with every turn. Passengers were let off on dilapidated lifeboats, many just making it to shore before even the lifeboats sank! The crew, meanwhile, attempted to stop the boat each time it hit shore, jumping off and trying to tie it up. Crew and passengers ended up stranded on shore over several miles of river. Rescue efforts came quickly and everyone was rescued within a day. The only casualty, according to reports, was one cow. After coming to rest, the engines and much of the superstructure were salvaged and later installed on the *S.S. Klondike #2*. You can find the remains of the *S.S. Klondike* hull near the outside of the right bend, below the silty cutbanks on the left shore. It has become part of the sandbar over time, and you may think it *is* a sandbar until you get close enough. In high water, it may be completely submerged.

The stretch from here down to the Big Salmon River is a slower, meandering river. Once you are below Mazie Creek (km 332, Map 25), there are abundant low water campsites for your pleasure. You will pass a number of abandoned wood camps, including Bayer's Woodyard at km 327 and Big Eddy Woodyard at km 343.

The hull of the S.S. Klondike is slowly being claimed by the river.

Shortly downstream of Big Eddy camp, at which you can still see the remains of cabins and wood roads, Cassiar Bar hosted the best gold finds on the upper Yukon River. This was perhaps one of the reasons prospectors continued searching for the motherlode, hence finding the Bonanza. Perhaps you could get out your gold pan here and have a look for some "colours"!

Starting about three kilometres downstream of Lower Cassiar Bar, you will see the first signs of the huge fire of 1995. This fire burned an immense area over a number of months. You will see evidence of this fire on and off over the next 60 kilometres. This burn area, like many others, is covered in the magenta of fireweed, one of the first species to establish itself after a burn.

Big Salmon village (km 358, Map 26) is located just downstream of the **Big Salmon River** confluence, on river right. About half a kilometre upstream on river left lie the remains of an old telegraph building and NWMP site, burned in the fire of 1995. Luckily, Big Salmon village was spared the fury of the fire, and still hosts several intact buildings, as well as camping facilities. A small graveyard is located along a rough trail a short distance up the Big Salmon River. Please keep in mind that traditional burial grounds are sacred places to First Nation people, and visiting or photographing them is not encouraged. Please treat this whole site with respect.

The Big Salmon River was first prospected in the early 1880s. Gold in various quantities was found in the late 1890s, including the major find on Livingstone

A large forest fire in 1995 scarred the landscape between Big Salmon and Minto. Fireweed, gone to seed in this photo, quickly populated the burn area.

Several buildings remain at Big Salmon village.

BIG SALMON RIVER

The Big Salmon River is a long route into the Yukon River, and could be done as a trip in itself, taking out at Carmacks. The Big Salmon River is 235 kilometres long, with no opportunities for take-out along the way. Add that to another 119 kilometres from Big Salmon to Carmacks and your minimum journey is 354 kilometres, taking from eight to ten days. The Big Salmon River is also only for those with moving water skills. It is not as straightforward as many other tributaries of the Yukon River, and regularly features hazards such as rapids, sweepers, log jams and rocks.

Your journey starts at Quiet Lake, reached via the Quiet Lake campground, 77 kilometres north along the South Canol Road from Johnson's Crossing. After passing through a series of three lakes, Quiet, Sandy and Big Salmon, you enter the Big Salmon River, and should batten down the hatches and hang onto your hat! From here to the South Fork, about 155 kilometres, you must stay alert as the river is swift with many sweepers and log jams, some of which may cross the entire river.

After the South Fork, the river widens and slows somewhat. There are still rapids to be found, including one just below the entry of the North Fork. Sweepers and log jams are still evident, and apparently, the channels below Illusion Creek have changed due to flooding and log jams since the printing of government maps. For more information, Gus Karpes' guide, *The Big Salmon River from Quiet Lake to the Yukon River,* is an excellent resource.

Creek. As a result, Big Salmon Village was used for several decades as a steamboat landing, as well as a trading post, wood camp and native settlement.

At km 375, downstream of the 4th of July Bend, you will come across an abandoned gold dredge partially buried in the sand by the right shore, left there by a pair of prospectors in 1940. The dredge is a curiosity, assembled with machinery and materials from previous equipment, including a Caterpillar tractor, car motor, steam boiler and the ways from Shipyard Island. Although they did find about 72 ounces of fine gold using the dredge, it was not enough to recuperate the cost of the hand built dredge. Another abandoned gold dredge can be seen by looking up the slough on river right at km 382.

From **Erickson's Woodyard** (also known as Byer's Woodyard), just downstream of the second gold dredge, to Little Salmon Village, there are few opportunities for camping. The river meanders in a single channel among high forested slopes, with occasional cutbanks and high rocky bluffs. **Little Salmon village** (km 421, Map 29) is situated about one kilometre downstream of **Little Salmon River**. The graveyard is upstream of the village, located slightly upstream of the head of the island mid-river. It consists of many "spirit houses" and colourfully fenced-in graves. Again, please respect the First Nations' wishes against visiting or photographing these sites. Shortly downstream, the village hosts several buildings and a road that connects to the Robert Campbell Highway. The original

A unique old gold dredge didn't find enough gold to pay for itself, so it was abandoned.

Little Salmon village still sees some activity from time to time.

village was on the left shore of the Yukon River, across from the Little Salmon confluence. The village has seen only seasonal use since the influenza epidemic of 1917 to 1919 wiped out much of the village population.

Now that the river has neared the Robert Campbell Highway, you may start to see a few more signs of civilization, including road cuts, the odd cabin and fish camps. The road follows the valley to near Carmacks, where it meets the Klondike Highway. On river left, you could easily miss the abandoned village of **Lakeview**,

LITTLE SALMON RIVER

The Little Salmon River is not a common way to access the Yukon River, but some paddlers do it for a change of pace. It is a short run of about 50 kilometres from the put-in at the Robert Campbell Highway, completed easily in a weekend. You even have the option of taking out at Little Salmon, going down to Carmacks or continuing on to Dawson City.

The typical put-in is at the Little Salmon campground near the outlet of Little Salmon Lake, 85 kilometres east of Carmacks, along the Robert Campbell Highway.

The river starts off small and slow. One of its distractions is the highway that follows the valley and is visible at several points along the way. As you paddle down towards the Yukon River, the river speeds up and a few small rapids, up to Class 2, are encountered. You should keep your eyes peeled for sweepers. There are not a lot of camping spots along the river, so finding a place for the night could be a challenge.

Eagle's Nest Bluff stands like a sentry over the Yukon River.

nestled in the trees above the beach. Lakeview was once a woodcamp, then a small native settlement. Camping spots can be found both upstream and downstream of Mandanna Creek.

About 10 kilometres below the Little Salmon River, on river right at km 430, is **Eagle's Nest Bluff,** a prominent landmark. At one time, a hydroelectricity proposal was researched to dam and divert the river from this point, through an ancient channel along Frenchman and Tatchun lakes, to rejoin the Yukon below Carmacks at Tatchun Creek, 86 kilometres downstream. Although this issue has not been considered recently, it is hard to believe that a free flowing river as historically and recreationally significant as the Yukon could be considered for this kind of destruction.

About six kilometres further downstream at km 438 (Map 30) is **Columbia Slough**, the site of the wrecking of the steamer *S.S. Columbia*. In one of the most dramatic and disastrous steamboat accidents on the river, an innocent tripping of a deckboy carrying a gun set off three tons of gunpowder on board, near Eagle's Nest Bluff. The flaming steamer was sent out of control, and was subsequently rammed ashore here. The ship was then held to shore by metal hawsers or cables, evidence of which can still be seen. Six men were killed in the incident, including the boy who tripped.

After Columbia Slough, the river enters a sharply meandering stretch, with many islands and sand and gravel bars. The gravel bars make great spots for camping. The current has slackened in this stretch, making it necessary to stay in the main current to avoid ending up in an eddy. The many sloughs give the paddler choices along the way. One of these choices, at km 467 (Map 31), is **Raabe's Slough**. Taking this slough is like being on a completely different river, small and slow. Steamers were wintered here from the turn of the century to about 1920.

As you exit Raabe's Slough, you will see ahead on river right the bluffs of **Tantalus Butte**. This hill has several large coal seams through it, some as thick as six metres, which led to considerable mining in the 20th century. Two portals can be seen still up on the slopes, as well as remains of the docks used to haul the coal away. Another coal mine, the Tantalus Coal Mine, is situated on river left, just above the Klondike Highway bridge in Carmacks.

One thing that makes this trip unique over other extended canoe trips is the ability to stock up on fresh food at several points on the trip. **Carmacks**, at km 477 (Map 31), offers such an opportunity, the last major supply point along the route to Dawson. You may also check with local people, or the RCMP, about water conditions at Five Finger Rapids. If you wish to camp in Carmacks, you should pull out at the concrete launch ramp on river left immediately downstream of the highway bridge. The Tantalus campground is jointly managed by the Village of Carmacks and the Little Salmon-Carmacks First Nation and features a new visitor centre. The campground has 15 tenting/RV sites plus an area for tenting near the river. From here you can walk to the town's services. If you are not camping here, you can stop at the public dock about one kilometre downstream of the bridge to access the gas station and general store along the Klondike Highway, just a short walk from the river's edge.

Paddling near loons is a real thrill.

CARMACKS

Carmacks, originally called Tantalus, was a traditional First Nation fishing and trading site, where members of the Northern Tutchone met with coastal natives. Archaeological evidence points to inhabitants referred to as the "Microblade People" living here between 4,000 and 8,000 years ago. The tools they used consisted of small, disposable blades that fit into handles made of bone or antler. It is believed they were the ascendants of the Northern and Southern Tutchone that now live in the region.

George Carmack, co-discoverer of the Klondike gold, established a small trading post here in the 1880s after the discovery of coal in the area. Through the gold rush, Carmacks was the site of an NWMP post, located downstream of the Nordenskiold River. Later, a roadhouse was developed on the north side of the Nordenskiold, to be replaced by the one that still stands in the northern part of Carmacks. A telegraph office was also located here. Carmacks thrived over the following decades as a stopover for travellers on the river and the overland Whitehorse to Dawson stage road. It was conveniently situated almost midway between Whitehorse and Dawson.

Today, Carmacks is a small community of close to 500. It serves primarily as a service centre for highway traffic and the local mining industry. Past mining activities in the Carmacks area were centred around coal, gold and agate mining. The two large coal mines, the Tantalus Butte and Five Finger mines, saw large extractions of coal over the years. While in Carmacks, visit the Tage Cho Hudan Interpretive Centre run by the Little Salmon-Carmacks First Nation, which depicts the past and present lifestyle of the local Northern Tutchone people.

Carmacks Visitor Centre is a worthwhile stop.

3

ROUTES & RAPIDS

Lunch while floating is one way to make up time if you are behind schedule.

Distance: 404 kilometres
Time to complete: approximately 6 to 8 days
Challenges: Five Finger Rapids, Rink Rapids, finding clear drinking water, avoiding shallows
Rewards: changing scenery and enhanced wilderness below Fort Selkirk, increased wildlife sightings
Gradient: 1.7 metres per kilometre

This stretch can be divided into three distinct sections, each with its own characteristics. From Carmacks to Minto, the route is close to the Klondike Highway, with a more civilized feel to it. There are fish camps, cabins and the occasional sighting of the highway. You will likely see footprints of moose, bear and wolf. The section from Minto to the White River has more of a wilderness feeling to it. Wildlife is attracted to the life-giving water due to its relative clarity and the distance from civilization. The section from the White River down to Dawson has a very noticeable change — the White River adds silt to the Yukon, making it a less desirable drinking source for animals (and humans). In

Maps	page
31 • Carmacks	185
32 • Five Finger Rapids	186
33 • Yukon Crossing	187
34 • Hootchekoo Creek	188
35 • Minto	189
36 • Hell's Gate	190
37 • Fort Selkirk	191
38 • Threeway Channel	192
39 • Pilot Island	193
40 • Selwyn	194
41 • Isaac Creek	195
42 • Brittania	196
43 • Coffee Creek	197
44 • Kirkman	198
45 • White River	199
46 • Stewart Island	200
47 • Excelsior Creek	201
48 • Sixty Mile	202
49 • Reindeer Creek	203
50 • Indian River	204
51 • Swede Creek	205
52 • Dawson City	206

addition, many of the side valleys have mining camps at the base, so you will see cabins, camps and boat traffic.

Near the Pelly River, there is another marked change — the geology. Until this point, the pale silty cutbanks are characteristic of the Yukon River, seen at the outside of many bends. But near the Pelly confluence and for 20 kilometres downstream, the cutbanks are replaced by rock outcrops, showing the vertical columnar formations of quick-cooled basalt lava. The lava came from Volcano Mountain, lying about 15 kilometres north of the Yukon/Pelly confluence, which in its active days poured molten lava on the surrounding landscape and as far as the Yukon River. Between the Pelly River and the White River, the river also cuts through the Klondike Plateau and the Dawson Range, giving a little more variation to the topography. By the time you reach this area, it is a welcome change!

The Yukon River continues to flow quite quickly all the way to Dawson, making it possible to go long distances each day. Many parties also try a night drift to make up some distance if behind schedule. The long hours of daylight make such a thing possible. If you do this, it is wise to wait until downstream of Rink Rapids, and have at least one person awake to ensure you are not caught in an eddy or on a sandbar for the night. Floating lunches also help you maintain longer distances in a day.

AURORA BOREALIS — THE NORTHERN LIGHTS

For those who have experienced the northern lights, or aurora borealis, there is nothing else quite like it. Ranging from simple greenish-white arcs across the northern sky, to dancing curtains of green, red, blue and purple over much of the night sky, this phenomena has transfixed people through the millennia.

The aurora is a natural phenomenon caused by charged particles in the earth's magnetic field. These particles — protons and electrons — are released through sunspot activity on our sun, find their way to the earth in what is called the "solar wind," and are pulled towards the poles by our earth's magnetic field. When the particles penetrate the upper atmosphere near the poles, they react with oxygen and nitrogen and create the curtains of shimmering light. The colour of aurora, which can span the spectrum from white, green, pink and purple, is controlled by the particular mix of atmospheric gases through which the charged particles pass. Green or red light is derived from oxygen, while purple comes from nitrogen. The spectacle is most likely to be seen in the spring and fall, due to the relation of the planet's tilt to the sun's plane. However, they may be visible at any time of the year during hours of darkness.

The aurora is arrayed along a band known as the aurora oval. The shape, size and location of this band put the typical southern extent of the aurora over Carmacks and Faro. This is extended further south during periods of intense sunspot activity.

For those interested in increasing their chances of viewing the aurora borealis, the Geophysical Institute at the University of Alaska Fairbanks predicts aurora displays on their web site at www.gi.alaska.edu.

3

ROUTES & RAPIDS

The **Nordenskiold River** flows into the Yukon River from the south, rising near the headwaters of the Takhini River. One of the possible routes that the Yukon River may have taken before the last ice age is south through this valley, joining another branch where the headwaters of the Takhini River are now. From here, it is thought that the river went west, then south down the Dezadeash and Alsek valleys.

Downstream of Carmacks, for several kilometres, the river winds back and forth, almost meeting itself several times. It is about 36 kilometres to Five Finger Rapids, which should take between three and four hours. Camping spots are few and far between along here since many of the potentially suitable locations are taken up by fishing camps, especially in late July and August during the salmon run. However, some of the islands and gravel bars provide low water camping sites.

Once you have navigated the major twists and turns after Carmacks, you will find yourself facing Mount Monson, named after a constable with the NWMP who apparently later ended up prospecting with Robert Henderson, considered by some to be a co-discoverer of the Klondike gold.

Shortly after Murray Creek, also known as Myer's Creek after local woodcamp operators, you will encounter a sweeping left bend in the river. Once past the bend, you will be directly facing Mount Miller. This landform is named after a local character, Captain Charles Miller, who once developed the Tantalus Butte Coal Mine and built and skippered several river steamers.

The **Five Fingers Coal Company**, at km 503 (Map 32), is worth a stop. Coal was first discovered here by geologist George Dawson in 1887. The mine was operated first by C.J. Miller, followed by the Five Fingers Coal Company until 1908. The coal was used for heating homes and refuelling steamers. A tramway

3

ROUTES & RAPIDS

An old mine shaft and piles of coal are still visible at the Five Fingers Coal Company.

Five Finger Rapids is one of the few rapids on the Upper Yukon River.

was erected to carry the coal from the shafts to the river's edge. The tunnels, which once penetrated far below the river, have caved in and filled with water over the years. You can still see a few collapsed shaft openings, with piles of coal nearby.

About four kilometres downstream from the mine, you may see a few old buildings on river left. These are in the vicinity of **Kellyville**, a small community that once included a roadhouse, sawmill and woodyard. Then hold on to your hats, because Five Finger Rapids are a short five kilometres downstream! Be forewarned that you should keep close to the right shore when both approaching and entering the rapids.

Five Finger Rapids (km 513, Map 32) were a formidable barrier for the steamers earlier in the 20th century. With the swift waters

The islands of Five Finger Rapids are made of conglomerate rock.

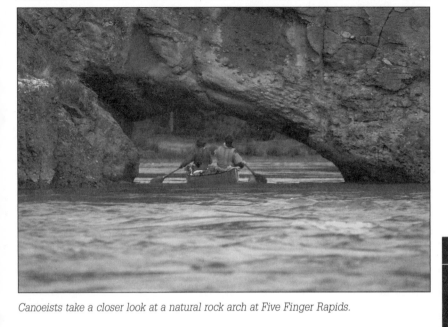

Canoeists take a closer look at a natural rock arch at Five Finger Rapids.

squeezed between rocky promontories, great precision and skill was required by riverboat pilots. Several boats were damaged in these rapids. Cables were used to guide all but the strongest boats upstream through the rightmost channel against the current. The rapids were improved in 1899 and 1900 by widening the right channel by about 20 feet and blasting out some of the rocks in the channel. Your best bet as you approach the rapids is to *keep to the right* and proceed down

These waves at Rink Rapids can be avoided by staying to the right.

the centre of the rightmost channel. The conditions here change considerably with various water levels. High water levels create large waves and turbulence. Do not make the mistake of underestimating the power of the water here. Beware of rough water as far downstream as **Tatchun Creek**, two kilometres hence.

Tatchun Creek would be the location of a hydro dam and power station, were the Eagle's Nest hydro project to go ahead. Five Finger Rapids itself has been proposed for several ventures, including a rail crossing and a hydro dam. Luckily for paddlers, these issues are no longer active.

The rocks of Five Finger Rapids are conglomerates of the Laberge Series. These were deposited in the Lower to Middle Jurassic age in near-shore coastal fans. The large boulders in the conglomerate, which eroded from a long chain of uplifted volcanic mountains to the west, indicate steep gradients. Shelly fossils are abundant, which confirms the ancient marine environment.

Now that you are beyond Five Finger Rapids, it's still not time to relax, because about six kilometres below Tatchun Creek, at km 522, is **Rink Rapids** (Map 33). Again, it is not a technical rapid, but you should be ready for some rough water, with your life jackets on, and kneeling positions in the boat. Rink Rapids consists of a series of haystacks caused by a shallow reef and rocks. The roughest water can be avoided by *keeping to the right shore*. In the early 1900s, this rapid was "improved" for river travel by blasting of several rocks midstream. Several steamers met their fate

Sam McGee's ashes are a particularly thick deposit of the White River Ash, and seem to be preferred by cliff swallows.

in Rink Rapids, and the wreck of one can just barely be discerned below the rapids. By crossing to the left below Rink Rapids and entering the first slough on the left, you can find the wreck of another *Casca* buried in the muck along the shore. It went down in 1936, only one month after the wreck of the *S.S. Klondike,* after hitting the wreck of the *S.S. Dawson* at Rink Rapids. There is not much left, and depending on the water levels, the remains may be hard to find.

Rink Rapids is the last bit of rough water on your way to Dawson. Now you can sit back and relax, although there are still some places of swift current over shallow bars. After the rapids, you enter a stretch of very braided river. Near the start of this, on river right at km 527, is what is referred to as **Sam McGee's ashes,** a particularly thick deposit of the White River Ash that has been exposed by the action of the river. The swallows don't seem to be put off by the ash, having made many nests in the white banks.

Where the river joins into one channel again, at km 530, lie the remains of **Yukon Crossing**. This community hosted McKay's Roadhouse, serving travellers on the old Dawson-Whitehorse stage road that was constructed in 1902. The stage road, which took 160 kilometres off the original winter route that followed the river ice, crossed over the Yukon at this point (hence the name), in winter by ice, and in summer by a primitive cable ferry. At one time there was a telegraph office, NWMP post, stables and roadhouse here. On river right, the remains of the cable tower can still be found. Primitive camping is available on the site. The best access is to paddle past the buildings on river left to a small slough, then paddle up this slough to behind the buildings. Beware of stinging nettle plants in the wood piles at Yukon Crossing!

Yukon Crossing once had a telegraph office, NWMP post, roadhouse and stables. Now it is a pleasant spot to camp among the ruins.

Minto now consists of a few dilapidated ruins, a small aircraft landing strip, a campground, a boat launch and Minto Resort.

After a few kilometres, islands start to appear in the river again, providing quite a few spots for camping. Given the proximity of the Klondike Highway, you will start to see a number of cabins and homes by the river, on both shores, so be mindful of private property when it comes to camping locations. On the left, near Merrice and Williams creeks, there are several cabins, now used for the considerable copper mining activity up both valleys. In 1907, a settlement called Boronite City was founded at the mouth of Williams Creek in response to copper deposits found on local creeks. The settlement reached a peak of 20 residents before it shut down two years later due to a lack of paying copper. You will also see more evidence of the big fire of 1995.

Further downstream on river right at km 560 is McCabe Creek. A settlement near the mouth of the creek had a small boom after 1952, when those few remaining at the now abandoned Fort Selkirk moved here. They established a post office here, and the settlement survived until 1970.

Minto lies at km 569 (Map 35), the last direct road access point before the Klondike Highway leaves the river. Originally called *Kitl-ah-gon,* meaning "the place between the high hills," Minto saw only seasonal use as a summer fish camp for the Selkirk First Nation. Although it once was a thriving community during and after the gold rush, including an NWMP post, roadhouse (to service the old stage road), general stores, a woodyard, steamboat landing and a number of farms, all that remains today are a few dilapidated buildings. There is a primitive campground here now, as well as an aircraft landing strip and boat launch. Minto Resort, shortly

| CHILKOOT TRAIL | HEADWATER LAKES | YUKON RIVER | **YUKON RIVER** |
| Dyea to Bennett | Bennett to Whitehorse | Whitehorse to Carmacks | **Carmacks to Dawson** |

3

ROUTES & RAPIDS

You may occasionally see work barges plying the waters of the Yukon River near Minto.

upstream of the campground, is one of the few places not burned by the fire of 1995. Boat tours to Fort Selkirk, about 40 kilometres downstream, begin here.

Now you will enter one of the most remote stretches of the Yukon River above Dawson City. Almost immediately after Minto, the Klondike Highway moves away from the river, and civilization drops off to a minimum. There are still some cabins and old homesteads along this stretch due to the old stage road and trails near the shores, but the river has a more remote feel to it. Although the highway leaves the river here, the river traffic steps up a notch. The only way miners have to reach the diggings on tributary creeks is by river transportation, so you may see the odd power boat or work barge.

Shortly after Minto, you may also see some wildlife, if you keep your eyes and ears open. The bluffs downstream from Minto are home to the largest breeding population of peregrine falcons in North America. Although this is a large colony, the peregrine falcon is considered endangered throughout the world. Please avoid disturbing these creatures; stay clear and avoid camping within two kilometres of nesting pairs. Two common calls are a repeated *we'chew* at rest, or a rapid *kek kek kek kek*.

From Minto to Hell's Gate, the river braids considerably, providing opportunities for low water camping on several of the many islands. **Big Creek**, at km 576, was once the location of a large homestead; hard to imagine today as you drift on by. The name Big Creek, according to Robert Coutts (*Yukon: Places and Names),* came about when a soldier with the Yukon Field Force took his leave and set up the homestead here. Upon asking locals the name of the creek, they indicated it was too big for a creek, hence Big Creek.

At km 586 (Map 36), you will reach **Ingersoll Islands**, where the river does a considerable amount of braiding. These islands caused the river to spread out so much that shallow bars impeded passage of the steamers. The main, left-most channel started off at the top of Ingersoll Islands with plenty of water, but lost some with each channel that branched off until it was too shallow at the downstream end, **Hell's Gate**, to allow passage. Many steamers got hung up on these bars over the years. The government's solution, implemented in the first decade or so of the 20th century, was to create pile and rock dams along the right side of the main channel to direct the water down this channel. The dams had to be lengthened several times as more gravel would be deposited at the lower end of the dams. It was constant work to keep the system working. The main route for canoeists today is the left-most channel. Very little can be seen of the works, except an iron mooring ring in the rock on the left shore, and some remains of the wing dam extending from the left shore below the ring. By travelling in the right-most channel, you may see the remains of Hell's Gate woodyard, but by this time, you may have seen enough of old woodyards (or not)!

Not far below Hell's Gate, you will begin to see high lava walls set back from the river. This marks a change in the geology of the valley that you will see for many kilometres downstream. Several volcano remnants are in this area to the east and north, the most prominent being Volcano Mountain, 15 kilometres to the north of the Yukon-Pelly confluence. This volcano is not visible from the river, but Ne Ch'e Ddhawa is, about five kilometres south of the Pelly confluence, on the east side of the river. Flows from these two breached cinder cones are visible along the right shore for about 30 kilometres. Paleomagnetic work on the flows indicates they

Flows from Volcano Mountain to the north resulted in these basalt cliffs visible along the river for about 30 kilometres near Fort Selkirk.

were laid down between 1.87 and 0.79 million years ago. Ash from this period is also visible downstream.

The **Pelly River** flows in from the right at km 604 (Map 37) through gates of basalt. The explorer Robert Campbell was the first European to set eyes upon this river in 1840. He named the stream after Sir John Henry Pelly, the governor of the Hudson's Bay Company at that time; previously it had been known as the Iyon River after the First Nation people who lived near its mouth.

Victoria Rock, near Fort Selkirk.

Robert Campbell and others considered the Pelly to be the real "Yukon" river, with the Yukon or "Lewes" River being a tributary of the Pelly. Shortly after the Pelly confluence, you will see a building on the left shore, the office of the Yukon Field Force. Then, one kilometre further downstream, is **Fort Selkirk**, now a beautiful restoration of a once-abandoned settlement. It is definitely worth a stop here for lunch, or for the night. It is incredibly picturesque, overshadowed by beautiful **Victoria Rock** just downstream. The site is now jointly managed by the Selkirk

3

ROUTES & RAPIDS

PELLY RIVER

The runnable stretch of the Pelly River is about 540 kilometres long, from the last point at which the Robert Campbell Highway allows access. I assume that those who are using the Pelly as a unique way to access the Yukon River in its wilder reaches wouldn't be interested in the upper part of the Pelly with some very difficult stretches of water. Putting in at Faro results in 356 kilometres (eight to ten days); the next good access is Pelly Crossing, 58 kilometres from the Yukon River (one to two days). Below Faro, moving water skills are required.

The river below Faro is framed by the Anvil Ranges to the north and the Glenlyon Ranges to the south. The mountains are soft and set back from the wide valley bottom. The large volume river meanders swiftly over gravel bars, but in about 70 kilometres, you will have to wake up for Little Fish Hook Rapids and Big Fish Hook Rapids, both Class 2 rapids.

With hundreds of kilometres to paddle, the river changes continually as you make your way downstream. There are areas with strong currents, rocks and riffles to watch for much of the way. Within 20 kilometres of passing the Macmillan River, you will encounter Granite Canyon. It is a large volume Class 2, with rocks and increased difficulty in high water.

Below Pelly Crossing, the river appears sluggish in comparison. Although the river is relatively gentle here, beware of strong currents near eddies and rocks. For more information, consult Mike Rourke's river guide, *Pelly River.*

FORT SELKIRK

Long before European habitation, the site of Fort Selkirk was used as a gathering place by the Selkirk First Nation. Members of the Tlingit, Northern Tutchone and Han First Nations would meet here to trade and celebrate. The prime focus of Fort Selkirk in terms of their seasonal round for fish and game was harvesting the salmon that spawn in the Yukon River in the summer and fall.

Fort Selkirk was first established as a post on river right, at the Pelly River confluence, by Hudson's Bay trader and explorer Robert Campbell in 1848. The post remained until flooding caused relocation to river left in April of 1852. However, by late 1852, the post was empty of people and supplies after it was looted in a confrontation with the Chilkats, angry at the competition to their trading business. White people were absent in the area for another 30 years before occasional prospectors started filtering in. A trading post was re-established on river right in 1889 by Arthur Harper, and interest slowly built from there. The post became an important stop along the route during the Klondike gold rush.

With the influx of Americans to Canadian soil during the Klondike gold rush, the Canadian government decided they needed a stronger law enforcement presence in the north. The Yukon Field Force was established and dispatched to build a post that still stands upstream of Fort Selkirk. From then on, the community thrived, with a school, two churches, a Taylor & Drury store, and by 1938, a Hudson's Bay post once again, after 86 years. With the construction of the Klondike Highway in the early 1950s, the steamer traffic ground to a halt and many river communities, Fort Selkirk included, were abandoned.

St. Andrews Church and other buildings have been preserved at Fort Selkirk.

Later in the season, morning fog becomes quite common on the Yukon River.

First Nation and the Yukon Heritage Branch and is being restored to its former glory. About 40 buildings stand in good repair, dating from 1892 to 1940, including two churches, a Taylor & Drury store, Hudson's Bay post, schoolhouse, NWMP post, Yukon Field Force site and several residences. You may get an interpretive tour from First Nation people here, or you can go hiking upstream to the Yukon Field Force building, or downstream to Victoria Rock. Camping facilities are available at the site, with outhouses, picnic benches, a well, fire rings, a kitchen shelter, bear-proof garbage containers and a warming cabin. Please note that, aside from the camping, there are no services here. There is access from Fort Selkirk by motorboat to the Pelly Farm on the northern shore at the outlet of the Pelly River. A gravel road provides access from the farm to Pelly Crossing on the Klondike Highway.

The river becomes increasingly braided as you head downriver from Fort Selkirk. Many of the suitable camping areas are located on the heads or tails of the many islands in the river. Often, at the transition of the cobble beaches and the overgrown portion of islands is a soft sandy area that is great for camping. These island spots tend to have fewer bugs and more firewood than shoreline sites. The river here is a little more silty due to the Pelly River. The topography becomes more dramatic as you head into the soft peaks of the Dawson Range.

It was common in the first half of the 20th century to take out homesteading claims in the Yukon valley. Old homestead sites are passed frequently in this stretch below the Pelly. Horsfall homestead, found at km 614 (Map 38), was occupied by a couple until the late 1920s, the female half of which was reported to be a daughter of Jack McQuesten. Adjacent to the Horsfall property was the Woodburn homestead. It was occupied by Harry Woodburn until about 1925, when he turned

PERMAFROST

Permafrost is considered to be soil or rock that remains below zero degrees Celcius for at least two years. More generally, permafrost terrain comprises a seasonally thawed active layer underlain by perennially frozen ground. Although the northern tip of the Yukon comprises continuous permafrost, much of the terrain you pass through on the Klondike Trail is widespread, scattered or alpine permafrost terrain. One of the main signs of permafrost is the "drunken forest," an area dominated by mosses, lichens, sedge tussocks and black spruce, many of which are leaning over in various directions due to the ice below. You may also see permafrost in the layers of cutbanks along the river with northern exposure. Permafrost is either "continuous," as it is in the far

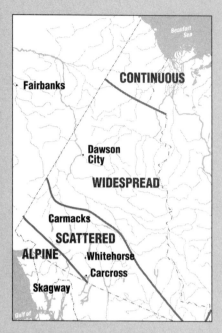

northern Yukon, or "discontinuous," or found sporadically, as in the southern Yukon.

Permafrost imposes huge challenges on development. Disturbance of any kind to permafrost can cause heaving and saturation of the ground. This can happen simply by covering the ground by a building, thereby changing the local surface climate. Most buildings in permafrost areas are built on stilts to allow air to circulate next to the ground. There are some examples in Dawson of the effects permafrost can have on buildings.

A drunken forest scene.

Bruce Bennett

3 ROUTES & RAPIDS

The Dawson Range provides topographical interest to the paddler, and mining opportunities to developers.

3

ROUTES & RAPIDS

it over to Horsfall. Further down at km 633 is Marshall's Ranch, occupied about the same time as the two homesteads upstream. **Pilot Island,** at about km 645, was owned by a woodcutter, who rafted much of the wood from the island down to Dawson.

The **Selwyn River** empties into the Yukon at km 659 (Map 40). The mouth of this river was once the location of a river crossing of caribou on their yearly migration. These magnificent creatures, likely part of the then-massive Forty Mile herd, have not been seen in this location for 60 years. At the mouth of the Selwyn was **Selwyn Station**. Activities here included an NWMP post, wood yard, First Nation settlement, and telegraph office. Remains of a couple of cabins can still be found in the underbrush upstream of the confluence.

Many valleys of the side creeks of this section of the Yukon River were prospected, and most of them had mining activity at one time or another. Mining camps were often located at the mouths of these creeks, with trails and rough roads up the valleys to the diggings. Many of them are still active and, therefore, are private property. Three examples are Isaac Creek, Brittania Creek and Ballarat Creek. **Isaac Creek**, at km 677 (Map 41), had several claims in the early 1900s before the valley was used to transport supplies to the Chisana gold rush in Alaska in 1913. The remains of some buildings are left today. **Brittania Creek,** at km 689 (Map 42), had several claims in the first half of the 20th century. Silver-lead (galena) mining operations are still carried out today. **Ballarat Creek**, at km 705, also has active placer gold mining operations about 25 kilometres up the valley.

Coffee Creek, at km 711 (Map 43), is named after an Indian trapper "Coffee Jack," and has seen many activities over the years. It was a meeting spot for First Nation groups for many years, and archaeological evidence indicates that it may have also been used by Russians. A homestead was established here in 1910. Beginning at the time of the Chisana gold rush, in 1916, a trading post was established by Taylor & Drury, and apparently, a trail led from here to Alaska.

Eventually, other homesteaders moved in and a telegraph office was opened. The site, about two kilometres below the creek confluence, continues to be occupied. In some years, pay camping has been available here, but you should check before you set up.

Kirkman Creek, at km 730 (Map 44), has seen a considerable amount of prospecting in the last century, which actually resulted in a fair amount of gold being extracted over the years. This resulted in homesteading activity at the mouth of the creek, and a post office that was operated for a decade. The building is still standing, and used as a private residence. The owners have been known to welcome canoers and sell pies, cookies, home-made root beer and candy bars. Below Kirkman Creek are shallow bars that posed a hazard and a challenge to the steamers. Over the years, the bars were dredged and scraped several times, with minimal success. Rumour has it that the steamboat pilots were leery of the woodcutter there. It is said that if anyone argued about the wood quantity or price, he would order the wood put back on shore and put a curse on the boat. The boat would then proceed to run aground in the shallows, and in the process of getting off the sandbar, would then end up needing the wood from Kirkman Creek (sold at an even higher price!)

Many of the side creeks are still providing gold to modern prospectors. **Thistle Creek**, at km 744, is one such valley that saw considerable mining in its time, and still provides gold to a fourth generation miner living in Dawson. In the late summer of 1997, a $15,000 nugget was removed from Thistle Creek, weighing approximately 27 ounces. When in Dawson, drop by the Gold Claim to see the latest results of the Thistle Creek operations. This creek was apparently named by the Scots who first staked claims on the creek, after their country's national emblem.

One member of the Burian family still runs a store on Stewart Island.

At km 757 (Map 45) you have reached the **White River**. It was named by Robert Campbell in 1851 after the unusual colour of the water. The river rises in the Wrangell and St. Elias mountains, where the volcanic blast that caused the White River Ash occurred. The thick deposits in the headwaters, up to 30 metres thick, are constantly being eroded and absorbed into the river, causing the water to look like thin chocolate milk. Along most of its length, the fast flowing river braids along a wide, flat bottomed gravel valley. It enters the Yukon at breakneck speed, dumping its load into the relatively clear river. Downstream of the White River, the Yukon is full of fine silt and ash. You can hear the gritty sound of it scraping on your paddle and the hull of your boat. The views up the White River valley are stunning.

The northern-most channel of the White River, called **Bellinger's Slough**, creates Sullivan Island. A sawmill once operated here, and downstream of Bellinger's Slough, a community of sorts existed through the years, especially around the time of the Chisana gold rush. Slightly downstream is **Becker's Island**, also the site of a homestead and woodcamp.

Between the White River and Stewart Island and below, there are plentiful islands and bars, laid down as a result of the heavy sediment load in the river. Due to the very fine grained nature of the sediments in the river now, the soil is very unstable when saturated. You will often find when you pull your boat up or step out onto the sand beaches, it will suck at your feet. Watch your step and choose your campsites carefully in this regard.

Stewart Island (Map 46) is situated a few kilometres downstream of the mouth of the **Stewart River**, which is in turn about 14 kilometres below the White River. A number of long sloughs create several large and small islands downstream of the Stewart River confluence, including Split-up and Stewart islands. Stewart Island, from some accounts, has been occupied on and off for several centuries, possibly by Russian traders long before Robert Campbell's company arrived on the scene in 1849. The area saw its first boom in 1885, when paying quantities of gold were discovered on the Stewart River, originally called *Na-Chon-De* by local First

3
ROUTES & RAPIDS

Below the Stewart River, mid-river camping opportunities are plentiful.

3

ROUTES & RAPIDS

STEWART RIVER

The Stewart River between Stewart Crossing and the Yukon River is 190 kilometres of easy paddling, taking between four and six days to reach the Yukon. The river valley is wide, with soft hills set far back from the river. The river is large, with a steady current of silt-filled water.

Between Stewart Crossing and the McQuesten River, the road parallels the river. While driving the Klondike Highway, you get many views of the large river, which for paddlers always piques their curiosity. The flip side is that when you are on the river, you can see the road cuts and hear the occasional traffic. However, this is short-lived. Soon after the McQuesten River, the road veers away from the river, leaving you with that wilderness feeling all the way to the Yukon River at Stewart Island and beyond. Few hazards should be encountered in this stretch, although you should always be on the lookout for sweepers on these northern rivers, and there are some faster stretches.

Rivers of the Yukon, by Graham Wilson and Ken Madsen, gives more detail on paddling the Stewart River.

Nations. Local miners started referring to it as the "Grubstake River," since one could find just enough gold to pay for another year of prospecting. Shortly thereafter, a post was established at the mouth of the river. The community reached its peak during the Klondike gold rush, with a population of about 1,000 and many services. They came and went quickly, and by the summer of 1898, the air was quiet once again. However, various activities kept the site occupied over the years, seeing both a Hudson's Bay post and a Taylor & Drury store. An ore transfer site was located in a slough behind Stewart Island, where silver ore from the mines at Elsa was put onto larger steamers for the run up to Whitehorse. The sole resident of the island now is Robin Burian, son of one of the prominent families of Stewart Island over the years. He watches over things and runs the Burian Store that can be seen from the river. The growing conditions here are good, with nutrient-rich soils built of the White River silt. Unfortunately, the action of the river has always been a problem on Stewart Island, eating away several feet of shoreline each spring, especially in years with ice jams. Several buildings have been lost to the river (in the summer of 1997, the family house could still be seen in a slough about two kilometres downstream from Stewart Island), and several others moved. You may also see buildings on the island directly across the river from Stewart Island, including an old telegraph office.

Building a sauna is a rewarding layover day activity.

Even 100 years later, dipping a gold pan into the cold waters of the Yukon River still fills one with anticipation.

Split-Up Island, located just upstream of Stewart Island, was named after numerous stampeders who, upon reaching this point after many months of travel in close quarters, dissolved their partnerships and parted company. It was also in this vicinity, up Henderson Creek behind these islands, that the famous author Jack London's cabin was ultimately discovered by author Dick North. You can see the cabin in Dawson at the Jack London Interpretive Centre.

Hopefully, you have seen your fair share of wildlife on your voyage so far. In summer, in the vicinity of Dead Man Island, around km 795 to 800, you may see Dall sheep, either down by the river or up on the bluffs above the river.

The **Sixty Mile River** comes in from the left at km 812 (Map 48), so named for its distance along the Yukon River from Fort Reliance. This post, situated on the Yukon River 10 kilometres downstream of the Klondike River, was set up by the three early pioneers of the Yukon, Arthur Harper, Al Mayo and LeRoy (Jack) McQuesten. It was the focus of early life in the Yukon, and the basis for naming several features along the river. The Sixty Mile River and its tributaries supplied considerable gold over the years, and continue to produce paying quantities today. Ogilvie Island, across from the Sixty Mile mouth, has seen resulting occupation for as long as 125 years. Arthur Harper and Joseph Ladue, an early prospector, set up a trading post here shortly before the Klondike strike, running it for several years. This location has also seen a sawmill, post office, NWMP post, telegraph office and homesteading. Today, cabin remains and farm equipment can still be found on the island.

By now, most if not all of the side creeks that could otherwise be considered as camping locations are taken up by cabins dedicated to mining. It is best if these

3

ROUTES & RAPIDS

sites are considered to be private property. Given the braiding of the river around the many islands, there is lots of opportunity for camping mid-river. Many of the smaller side creeks are clear but coloured with organics. With the Yukon River being so grey-white with silt and ash, the creeks look distasteful where they enter the bigger river, like iced tea flowing into chocolate milk. However, it may be better to take your water from these creeks, since harmful organisms may attach themselves to suspended sediments in the Yukon's waters, and the sediments tend to clog filters quickly.

The mouth of the **Indian River**, at km 841 (Map 50) was once used by First Nations (for which it was named). This site has also been home to an NWMP post and homestead. Considerable prospecting was done on the Indian River prior to the Klondike strike. Several of its tributaries flow from King Solomon's Dome, the mountain that is believed to supply the gold to Bonanza and Eldorado creeks. Now that you are approaching the outskirts of Dawson, most of the creeks like this have seen use throughout the last century, many of them for homesteading or prospecting. Across the river, at the mouth of Galena Creek, there was once a trading post for miners and other travellers in the area.

After passing Swede Creek at km 872, you will have reached the **Sunnydale** farming area (Map 52) on the outskirts of Dawson. On river left, Sunnydale was established as an agricultural area very early in the 20th century. Although some fields are still used, much of it has gone fallow. A nine-hole golf course now occupies a large chunk of this area. Golfing here at midnight on the longest day of the year is a popular activity. Just below Sunnydale is **Steamboat Slough**, a channel of the Yukon River that rarely has current except during high water levels. It was a place where steamboats were laid up for the winter and allowed to freeze into the slough. Since the current was minimal, ice damage was infrequent.

Hatch's Island is the large island which separates Steamboat Slough from the main stem of the Yukon. This island was purchased in 1901 by George Hatch, who

Dawson City is easily identified by Moosehide Slide on the slope behind it.

The George Black Ferry runs 24 hours a day during the ice-free days of the year.

3

ROUTES & RAPIDS

turned it into one of the most profitable farming operations near Dawson. He grew potatoes, grains and vegetables, and raised hogs and chickens.

As you near the outlet of Steamboat slough on the left, you reach **Lousetown** or **Klondike City** on the right. Across the Klondike River from Dawson, this "less desirable" part of Dawson housed the seedier aspects of humanity after they were driven out by the high society of Dawson City. A ferry and footbridge once crossed the Klondike River between Dawson City and Lousetown. Used by First Nations in years gone by, this remains an important place for the Han people, and is an important archaeological site.

The **Klondike River** comes into the Yukon River with the sweet promise of gold. Its waters are clear but dark, pushing the muddy waters of the Yukon River aside for a short distance downstream. The river was originally known to the local First Nation people as *Thron-diuck*, meaning "hammer-water," which referred to stakes that were pounded in the river bed to anchor the salmon nets. Robert Campbell, when he travelled by in 1851, named it the Deer River, a name used by local traders for a time before its return to First Nation beginnings. Klondike was eventually derived through mispronunciation of its First Nation name.

By this time, you will see the cheerful waterfront buildings of **Dawson City,** partially hidden behind the dike that protects the city from spring flooding of the Yukon River. The city's backdrop is Midnight Dome, with its distinctive scar, the **Moosehide Slide**. This was the landmark that told the weary stampeders that they had, as you have now, reached the end of a most remarkable journey.

Shortly downstream of the steamer *S.S. Keno,* there is a public dock on the Yukon River which is the most convenient place to dock and take out. Undoubtedly it will be a moment of mixed feelings for you! The sadness of leaving this great

DAWSON CITY

Before the Klondike gold rush, the site of Dawson City was a swampy lowland at the confluence of the Yukon and "Thron-diuck" rivers, undesirable for human habitation. The site across the Klondike River had seen some First Nation use for fishing on the Klondike River, and prospectors sometimes camped in the area.

After Carmack and his friends made the discovery claim in August of 1896, word spread and prospectors from all over made their way to the Klondike. Sourdough Joe Ladue saw riches on the mud flats at the confluence, staked out a town which he called Dawson City and floated a sawmill down from Sixty Mile. It was a more profitable venture than many found on gold-laden Bonanza Creek. Land value quickly went from $10 an acre to $1,000 for a lot, and later to $40,000 for the prime lots.

Today, many century-old buildings can be found in Dawson. Due to several fires just before the turn of the century, few buildings still standing pre-date 1900. An early government landmark was the post office, built in 1900 by the Canadian government to link Dawson and the Klondike goldfields with the rest of Canada. It became a symbol of civic pride and a reminder of the government's commitment to the region. Dawson was also the logical choice as the original capital of the Yukon when it was established in 1898. It was stripped of that title in 1953, and as compensation, was linked to southern Yukon by the Klondike Highway.

Today, Dawson City is a quaint, frontier town. Its 2,000 residents still cash in on the gold rush, even 100 years later. Tourism in the summer bolsters the economy, which otherwise still subsists primarily on mining. The townsite is a National Historic Site, with 35 buildings having been restored, reconstructed or stabilized for viewing tourists. In the summer, mounted "Red Serge" patrols by the RCMP can be seen around town. The Tr'ondëk Hwëch'in Cultural Centre has displays and information on traditional native life.

Dawson City from the air, with a view up the Klondike valley.

river that has tugged you along for the last several weeks is softened by the thought of flush toilets, showers, night life, cushy mattresses and fresh food (cooked by someone else). Prior reservations for hotels or campgrounds are advised because, at times, Dawson is very busy, with few rooms available spontaneously.

If you wish to have one last night of camping, the Yukon River campground is located on river left in West Dawson, just downstream of the ferry landing. This campground has 98 sites, including several tenting sites near the water. A fee is payable; check for current rates at the vehicle entrance. A paddlewheeler graveyard is located on the left shore of the Yukon River a short hike downstream of the campground. From the campground, you can pack up your gear and haul it across the river by ferry when you are ready to arrange your final departure from Dawson.

Now that you have arrived, congratulate yourself! You have just made a journey through history, touching upon the lives of many who passed this way before. You have gained an appreciation for life 100 years ago, before the age of modern conveniences. Although it is hard to understand the circumstances which would drive ordinary people like you and me to complete an epic journey so unbelievable, we can get a small taste of it by dipping our plastic gold pans in the sandy shores of the Yukon River, hoping for just a single speck of "colour." In an age where everything is known and no earthly discoveries seem to remain, you have made a discovery of the heart and soul of humanity.

3

ROUTES & RAPIDS

The effects of permafrost are especially evident in Dawson.

3

ROUTES & RAPIDS

Dredges left a legacy of tailings throughout the lower Klondike valley.

KLONDIKE GOLDFIELDS

A visit to Dawson City, whether by road or by river, is not complete without a tour of the Klondike goldfields. After all, the region would be quite devoid of people were it not for the famous strike on what was once known as Rabbit Creek, on August 16, 1896.

A trip up the Bonanza valley will take you past many worthwhile stops. Several Government of the Yukon signs tell of some of the more lucrative areas of the Bonanza valley, such as the White Channel and Cheechako Hill. One of the first tourist places you will encounter is Claim 33, where you can pay a few dollars to try panning some

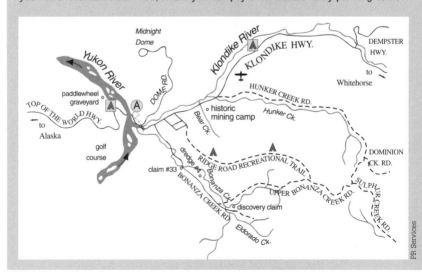

gravel. Next is the restored Dredge #4, which created many of the huge piles of gravel tailings seen in the Klondike valley. The Discovery Claim, at the confluence of Bonanza and Eldorado creeks, is now a Parks Canada heritage site. You can return the same way or take a loop out via Hunker Creek Road.

GOLD MINING METHODS

Upon reaching the Klondike, staking a claim for many was the easy part. Next came the task of getting the gold that lay hidden in the soils. Materials and mining equipment were scarce in the early Klondike days. Although some miners worked on open cuts, most dug underground through the permafrost to the pay gravels. This, of course, involved thawing the permafrost, a tedious task usually undertaken through the use of wood fires. Much of this work was done in the winter, so the pay gravels had to be stockpiled on site. Finally, in the spring, melting snows brought the water required to operate rudimentary sluices.

As more people and equipment reached the Klondike, the mining methods began to change. Shortly after the turn of the century, permafrost was being melted by steam. This involved large surface boilers that delivered steam to the working face. With the railway to Whitehorse from Skagway, heavier equipment entered the picture, giving the large conglomerates an edge over the independent miners. In 1905, the first of the very large bucket-line dredges began operation. These huge dinosaurs worked the valley bottoms in the Klondike until the 1960s. The bench deposits were worked through a system called hydraulics, which used high pressure water to move the soils.

Hydraulic mining is still used in the goldfields today.

LOWER YUKON RIVER

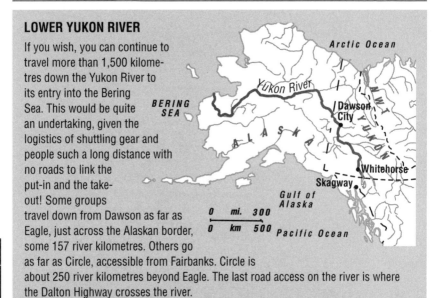

If you wish, you can continue to travel more than 1,500 kilometres down the Yukon River to its entry into the Bering Sea. This would be quite an undertaking, given the logistics of shuttling gear and people such a long distance with no roads to link the put-in and the take-out! Some groups travel down from Dawson as far as Eagle, just across the Alaskan border, some 157 river kilometres. Others go as far as Circle, accessible from Fairbanks. Circle is about 250 river kilometres beyond Eagle. The last road access on the river is where the Dalton Highway crosses the river.

Certainly, the section below Dawson is the wildest stretch of the Yukon River, with only three isolated vehicle access points. The river is large and braided for much of its length. The major tributaries which contribute to the flow include the Porcupine River, Tanana River and the Koyukuk River. The river passes through several mountain ranges including the Ogilvie Mountains, White Mountains, Ray Mountains, Kuskokwim Mountains, Kokrines Hills, and Haiyuh Mountains. This is truly a wilderness experience; help is not close at hand if anything goes wrong. However, like the upper river, this long stretch is relatively gentle but with a strong current.

Below Dawson City, the lower Yukon River beckons.

3

ROUTES & RAPIDS

CHAPTER 4...MAPS

*T*he following chapter contains a key map with a legend, and 52 strip maps of the Klondike gold rush route from Dyea to Dawson City. The strip maps are oriented such that travel is from the bottom to the top of the page. The scale of 1:50,000 for the trail section, and 1:100,000 for the lake and river sections, provides for considerable detail, while still covering areas alongside the route. There is approximately one kilometre of route overlap between each map, and match lines to line up adjoining maps are shown on each page. North arrows indicate the approximate position of the magnetic north pole in 2000. Contour lines, separating 200 metres of elevation, give the traveller some perspective on the surrounding topography, including valleys, peaks and bluffs. Significant historical and natural features are indicated on the maps, as well as a selection of camping locations. Most of these are mentioned and described in the previous chapter. You may find campsites that are not marked here, or not find campsites that are marked. Things can change from year to year, especially on islands and gravel bars. Plus, when it comes to primitive camping, everyone has a different definition of a campsite! Information on these maps and in the descriptions is accurate to the summer of 2000. Some changes may occur over time, and the sizes of gravel bars can vary greatly from year to year, and during a season, with changes in water levels.

Please note that the lines on the maps are approximate, and should not be considered fully accurate for backcountry navigation.

A welcome sheltered bay on Lake Laberge.

■ LIST OF STRIP MAPS

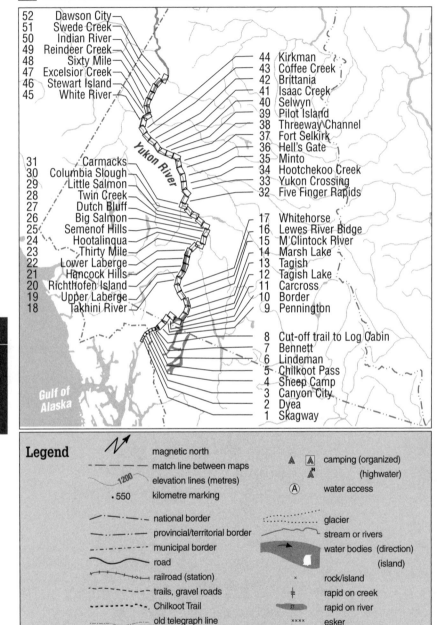

52 Dawson City
51 Swede Creek
50 Indian River
49 Reindeer Creek
48 Sixty Mile
47 Excelsior Creek
46 Stewart Island
45 White River

44 Kirkman
43 Coffee Creek
42 Brittania
41 Isaac Creek
40 Selwyn
39 Pilot Island
38 Threeway Channel
37 Fort Selkirk
36 Hell's Gate
35 Minto
34 Hootchekoo Creek
33 Yukon Crossing
32 Five Finger Rapids

31 Carmacks
30 Columbia Slough
29 Little Salmon
28 Twin Creek
27 Dutch Bluff
26 Big Salmon
25 Semenof Hills
24 Hootalinqua
23 Thirty Mile
22 Lower Laberge
21 Hancock Hills
20 Richthofen Island
19 Upper Laberge
18 Takhini River

17 Whitehorse
16 Lewes River Bidge
15 M'Clintock River
14 Marsh Lake
13 Tagish
12 Tagish Lake
11 Carcross
10 Border
9 Pennington

8 Cut-off trail to Log Cabin
7 Bennett
6 Lindeman
5 Chilkoot Pass
4 Sheep Camp
3 Canyon City
2 Dyea
1 Skagway

Yukon River

Gulf of Alaska

Legend

magnetic north
match line between maps
1200 elevation lines (metres)
•550 kilometre marking

national border
provincial/territorial border
municipal border
road
railroad (station)
trails, gravel roads
Chilkoot Trail
old telegraph line
bridge
airstrip
feature
settlement (large)
cabins/buildings

camping (organized)
(highwater)
water access

glacier
stream or rivers
water bodies (direction)
(island)
rock/island
rapid on creek
rapid on river
esker
marsh/swamp
mountain summit
lava cliffs

4

MAPS

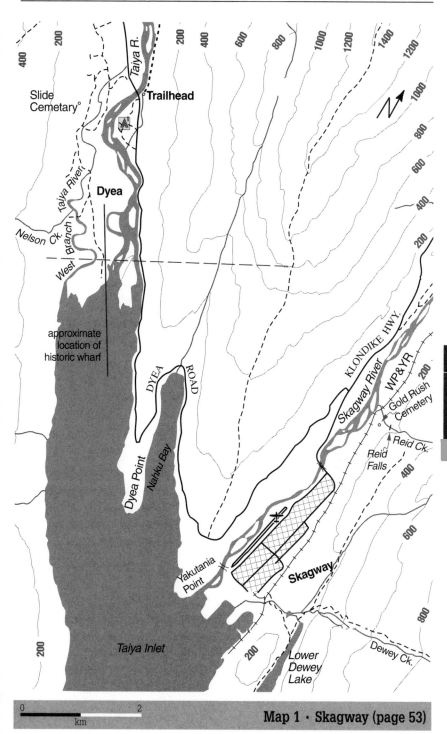

Map 1 · Skagway (page 53)

CHILKOOT TRAIL
Dyea to Bennett

HEADWATER LAKES
Bennett to Whitehorse

YUKON RIVER
Whitehorse to Carmacks

YUKON RIVER
Carmacks to Dawson

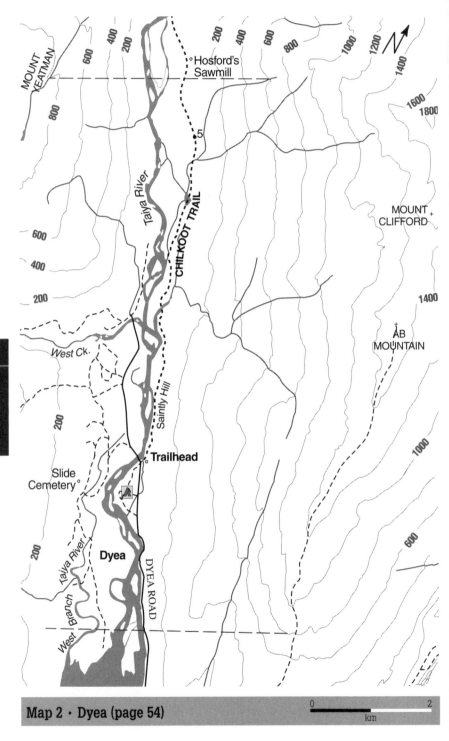

MOUNT YEATMAN

Hosford's Sawmill

5

Taiya River

CHILKOOT TRAIL

MOUNT CLIFFORD

1400

AB MOUNTAIN

West Ck.

Saintly Hill

Trailhead

Slide Cemetery

Taiya River

Dyea

DYEA ROAD

West Branch

Map 2 · Dyea (page 54)

0   km   2

4

MAPS

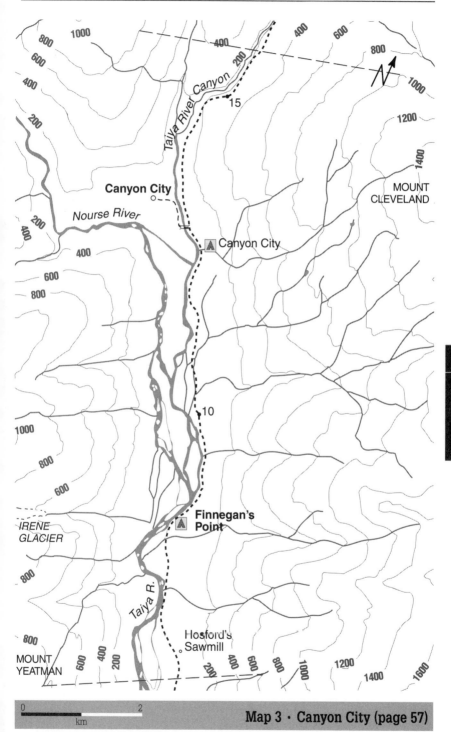

CHILKOOT TRAIL
Dyea to Bennett

HEADWATER LAKES
Bennett to Whitehorse

YUKON RIVER
Whitehorse to Carmacks

YUKON RIVER
Carmacks to Dawson

1000
800
600
400
200

400

400

600

800

1000

1200

1400

Taiya River Canyon

15

MOUNT
CLEVELAND

Canyon City

Nourse River

200
400

400

600

800

Canyon City

10

1000

800

600

*IRENE
GLACIER*

**Finnegan's
Point**

800

Taiya R.

800

600 400 200

Hosford's
Sawmill

200 400 600 800 1000 1200

1400 1600

**MOUNT
YEATMAN**

0   2
km

Map 3 · Canyon City (page 57)

4

MAPS

CHILKOOT TRAIL
Dyea to Bennett

HEADWATER LAKES
Bennett to Whitehorse

YUKON RIVER
Whitehorse to Carmacks

YUKON RIVER
Carmacks to Dawson

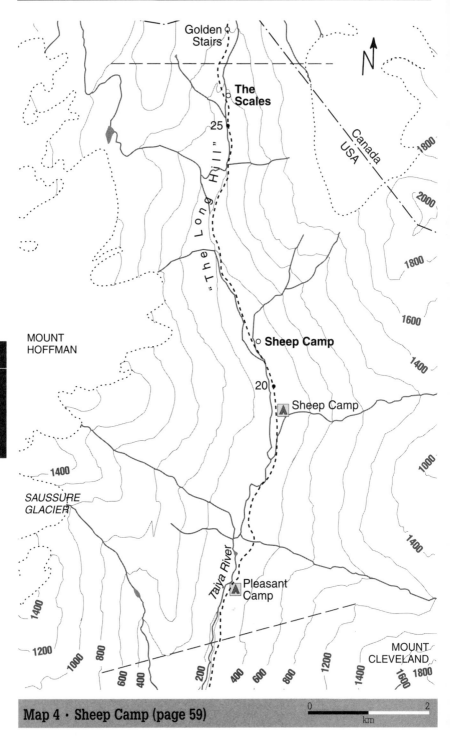

4

MAPS

Map 4 · Sheep Camp (page 59)

CHILKOOT TRAIL
Dyea to Bennett

HEADWATER LAKES
Bennett to Whitehorse

YUKON RIVER
Whitehorse to Carmacks

YUKON RIVER
Carmacks to Dawson

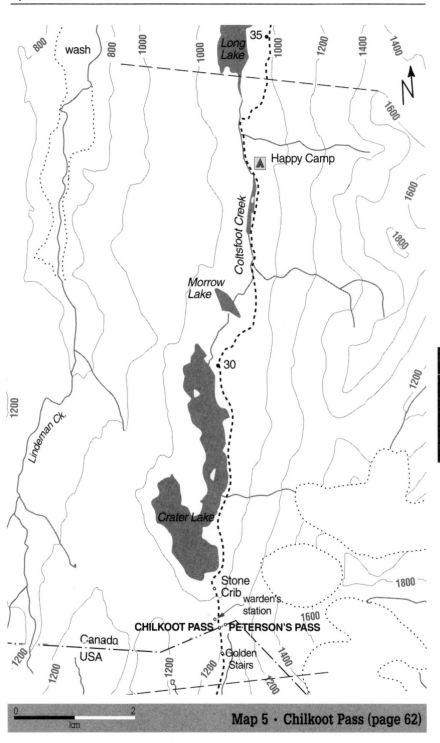

Map 5 · Chilkoot Pass (page 62)

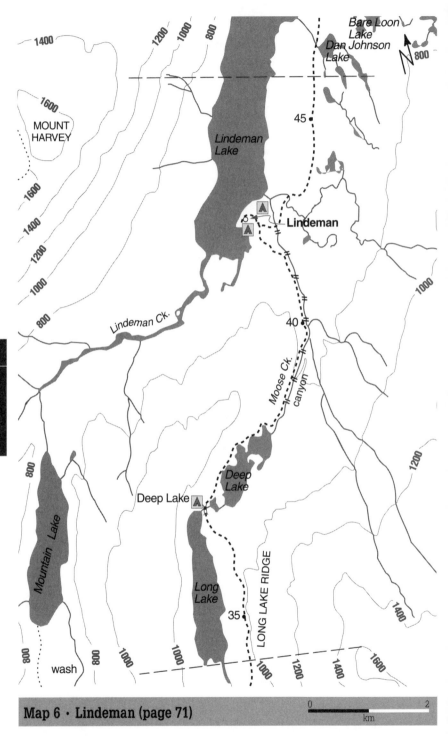

Map 6 · Lindeman (page 71)

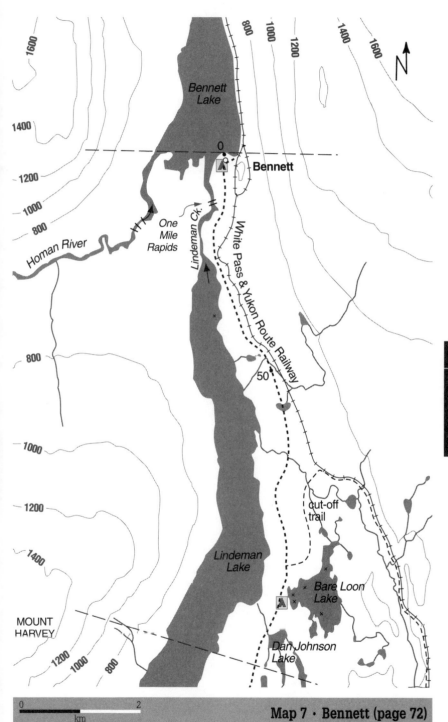

1600

1400

1200

1000

800

Bennett Lake

800 1000 1200 1400 1600

N

0

Bennett

Homan River

One Mile Rapids

Lindeman Ck.

White Pass & Yukon Route Railway

800

50

1000

1200

cut-off trail

1400

Lindeman Lake

Bare Loon Lake

MOUNT HARVEY

1200 1000 800

Dan Johnson Lake

0   2
km

Map 7 · Bennett (page 72)

4

MAPS

CHILKOOT TRAIL
Dyea to Bennett

HEADWATER LAKES
Bennett to Whitehorse

YUKON RIVER
Whitehorse to Carmacks

YUKON RIVER
Carmacks to Dawson

Map 8 · Cut-off trail to Log Cabin (page 74)

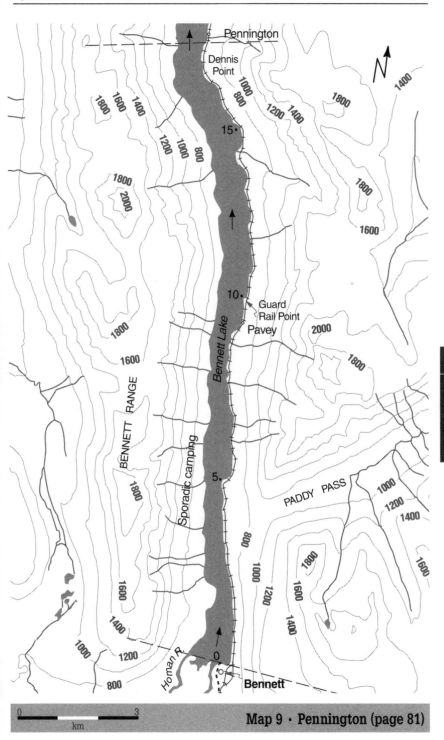

Map 9 · Pennington (page 81)

CHILKOOT TRAIL
Dyea to Bennett

HEADWATER LAKES
Bennett to Whitehorse

YUKON RIVER
Whitehorse to Carmacks

YUKON RIVER
Carmacks to Dawson

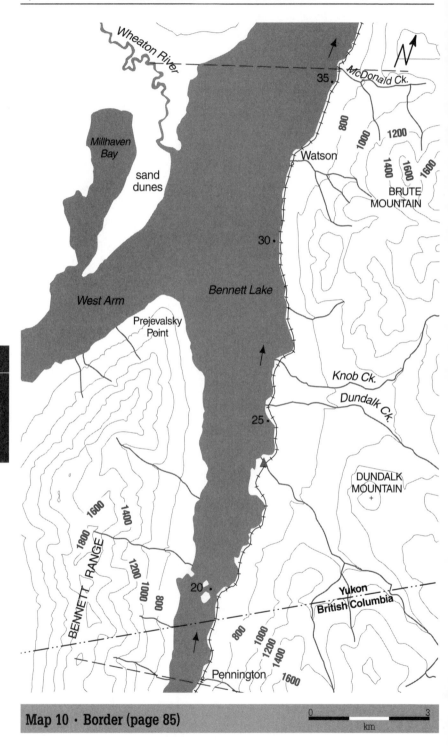

Map 10 · Border (page 85)

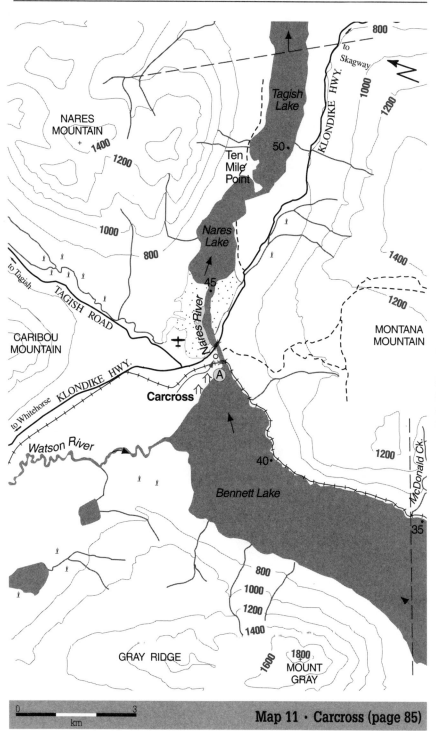

Map 11 · Carcross (page 85)

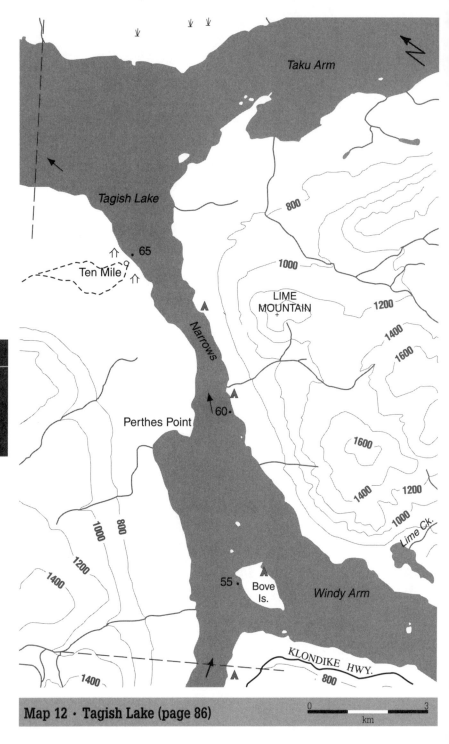

4

MAPS

Map 12 · Tagish Lake (page 86)

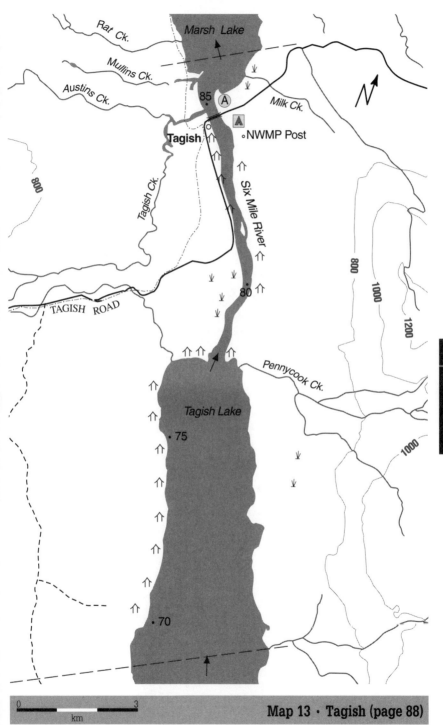

Map 13 · Tagish (page 88)

CHILKOOT TRAIL
Dyea to Bennett

HEADWATER LAKES
Bennett to Whitehorse

YUKON RIVER
Whitehorse to Carmacks

YUKON RIVER
Carmacks to Dawson

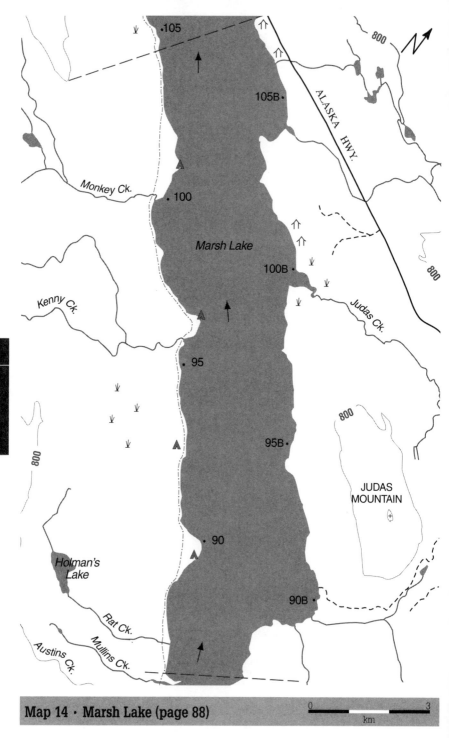

Map 14 · Marsh Lake (page 88)

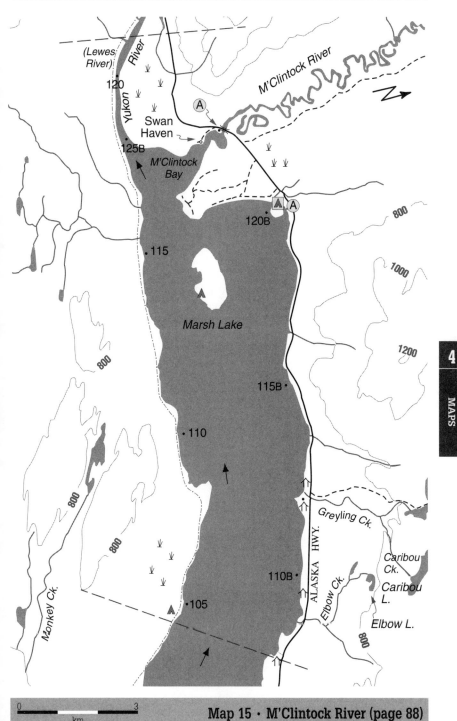

Map 15 · M'Clintock River (page 88)

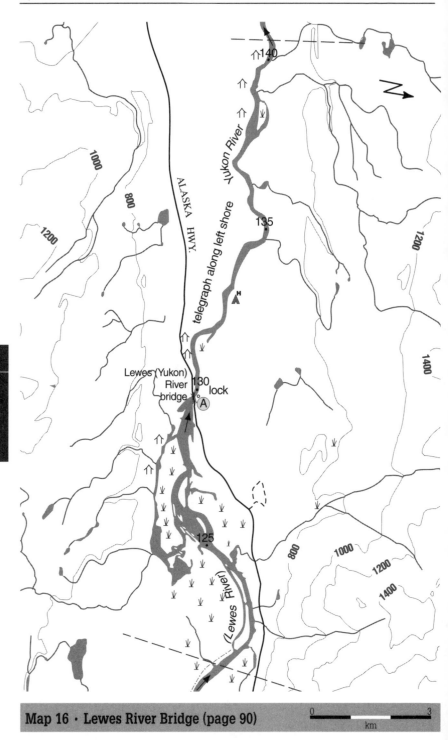

Map 16 · Lewes River Bridge (page 90)

CHILKOOT TRAIL
Dyea to Bennett

HEADWATER LAKES
Bennett to Whitehorse

YUKON RIVER
Whitehorse to Carmacks

YUKON RIVER
Carmacks to Dawson

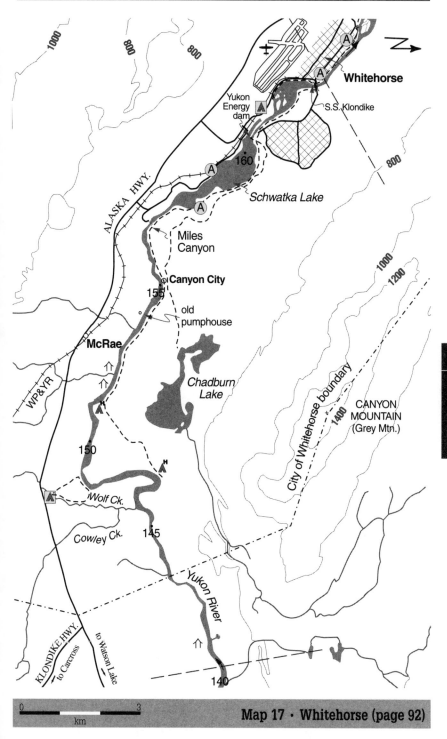

4

MAPS

Map 17 · Whitehorse (page 92)

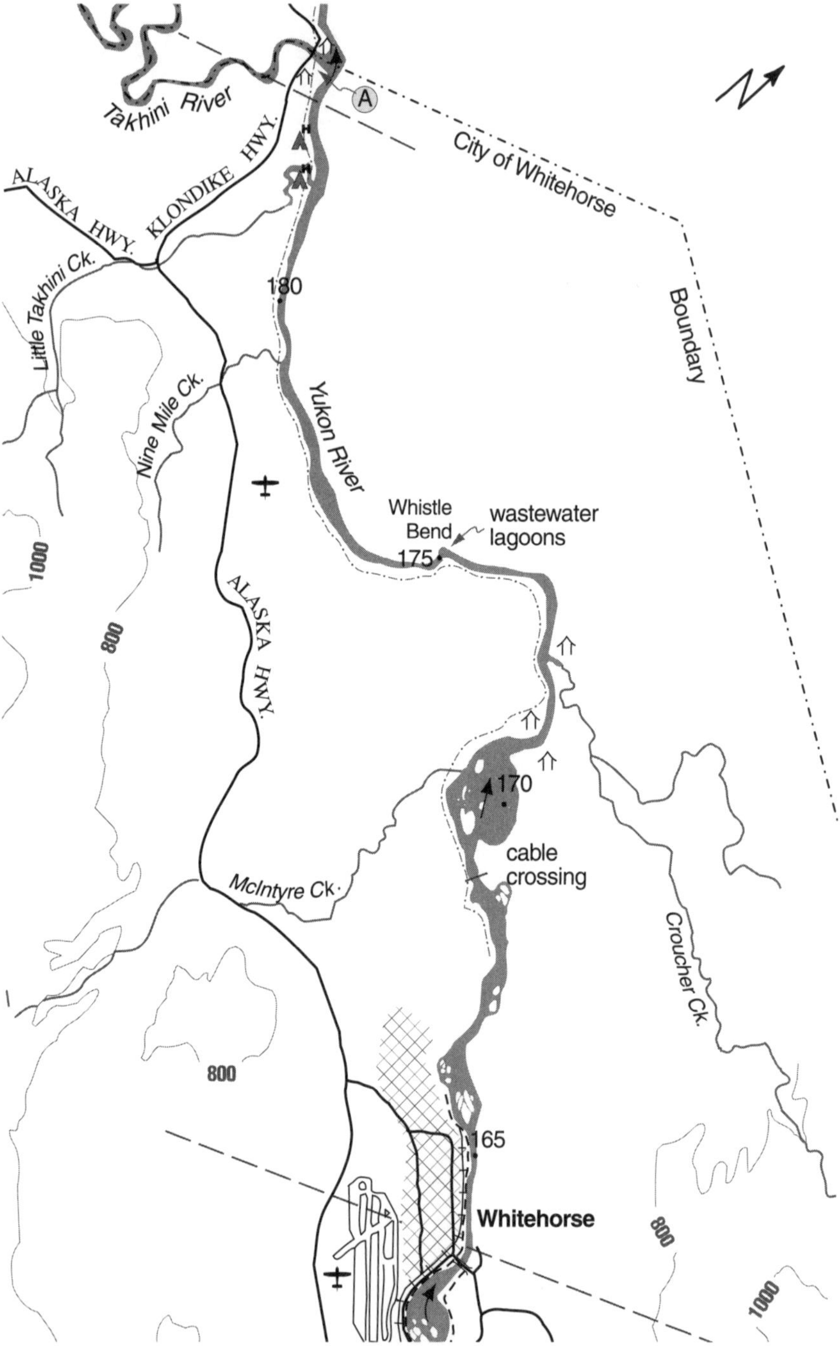

CHILKOOT TRAIL
Dyea to Bennett

HEADWATER LAKES
Bennett to Whitehorse

YUKON RIVER
Whitehorse to Carmacks

YUKON RIVER
Carmacks to Dawson

Takhini River

City of Whitehorse

Ⓐ

Boundary

ALASKA HWY.

KLONDIKE HWY.

Little Takhini Ck.

Nine Mile Ck.

180

Yukon River

1000

800

ALASKA HWY.

Whistle Bend
175

wastewater lagoons

170

cable crossing

McIntyre Ck.

Croucher Ck.

800

165

Whitehorse

800

1000

4

MAPS

Map 18 · Takhini River (page 102)

0
km
3

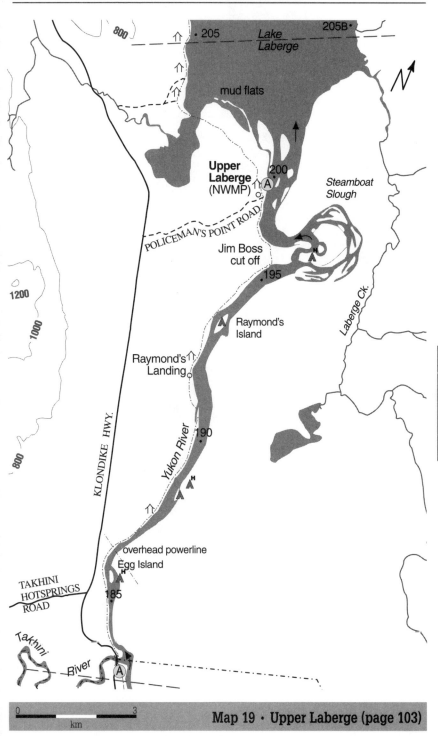

Map 19 · Upper Laberge (page 103)

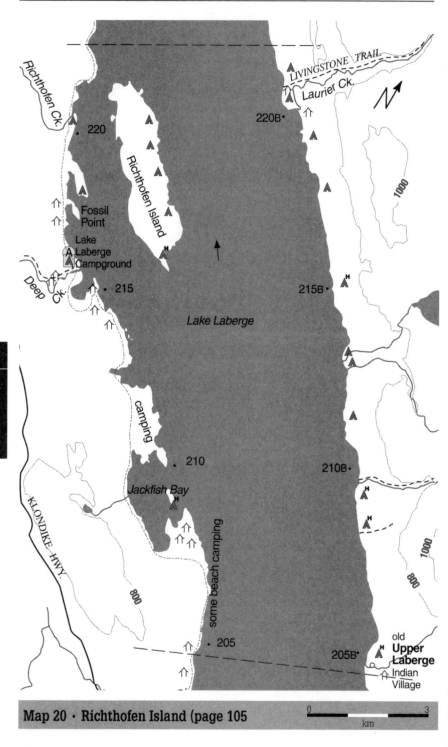

Map 20 · Richthofen Island (page 105

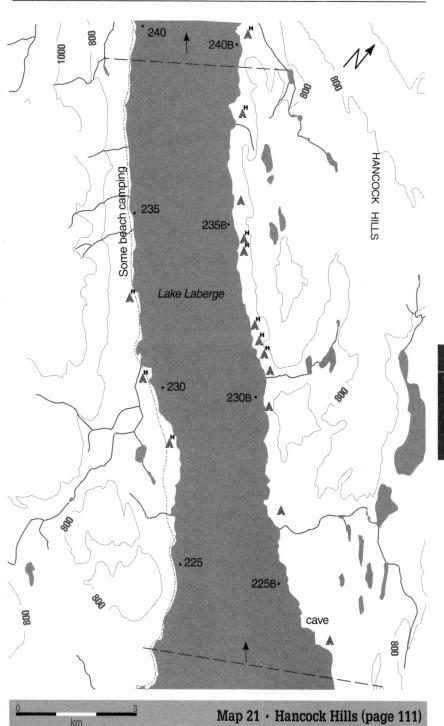

Map 21 · Hancock Hills (page 111)

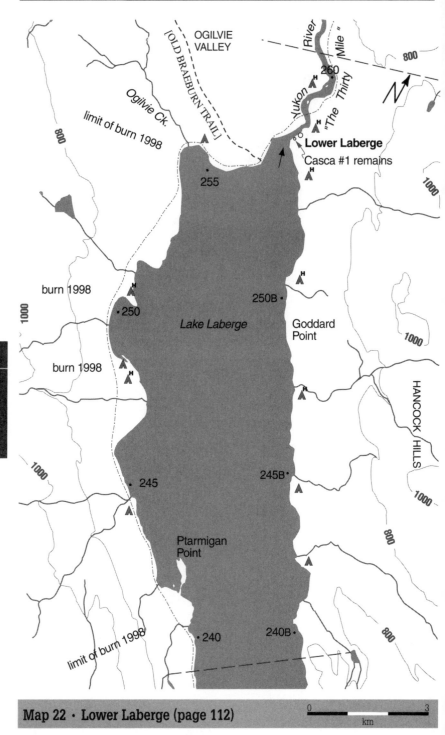

Map 22 · Lower Laberge (page 112)

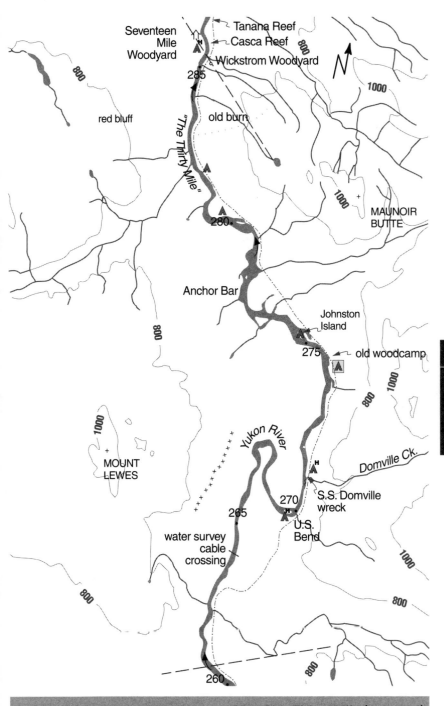

Map 23 · Thirty Mile (page 114)

CHILKOOT TRAIL
Dyea to Bennett

HEADWATER LAKES
Bennett to Whitehorse

YUKON RIVER
Whitehorse to Carmacks

YUKON RIVER
Carmacks to Dawson

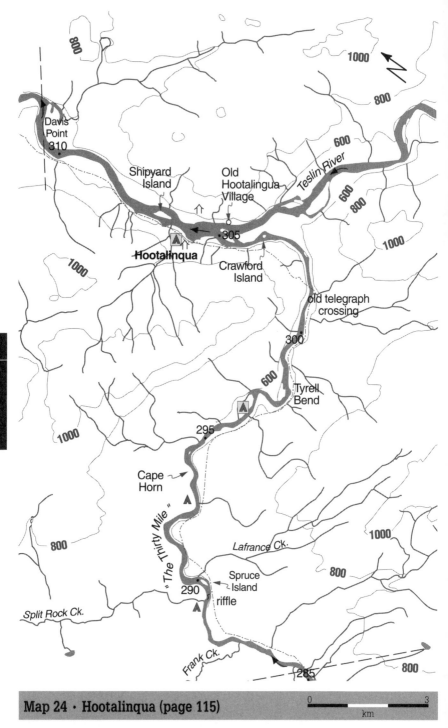

Map 24 · Hootalinqua (page 115)

0 ——— 3
km

CHILKOOT TRAIL
Dyea to Bennett

HEADWATER LAKES
Bennett to Whitehorse

YUKON RIVER
Whitehorse to Carmacks

YUKON RIVER
Carmacks to Dawson

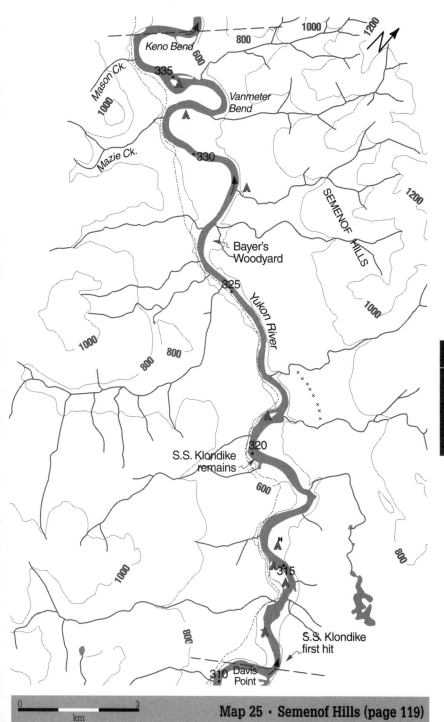

Map 25 · Semenof Hills (page 119)

CHILKOOT TRAIL
Dyea to Bennett

HEADWATER LAKES
Bennett to Whitehorse

YUKON RIVER
Whitehorse to Carmacks

YUKON RIVER
Carmacks to Dawson

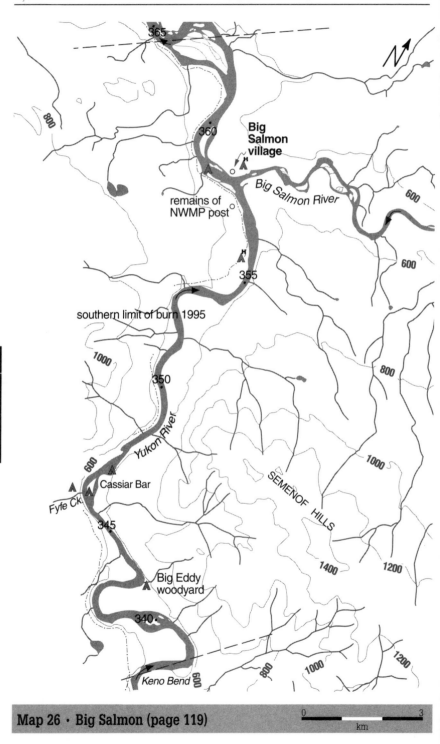

Map 26 · Big Salmon (page 119)

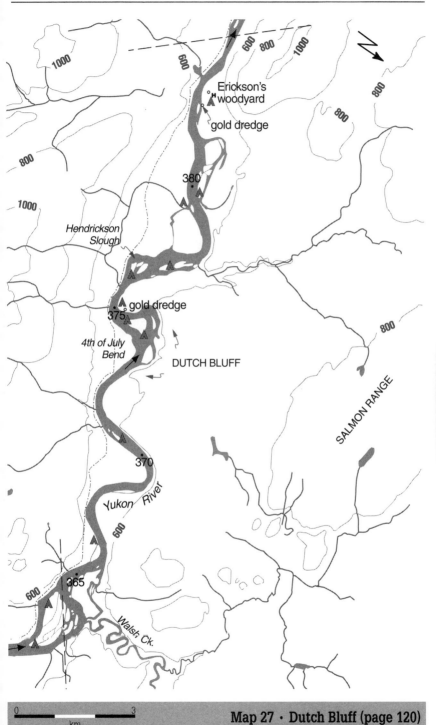

Map 27 · Dutch Bluff (page 120)

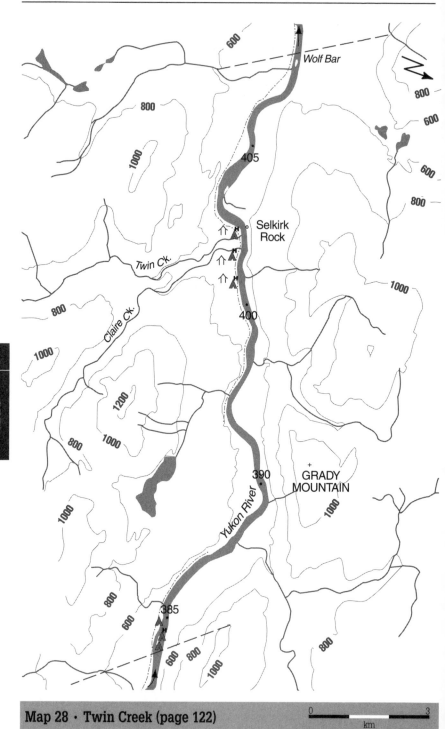

Map 28 · Twin Creek (page 122)

0   km   3

CHILKOOT TRAIL
Dyea to Bennett

HEADWATER LAKES
Bennett to Whitehorse

YUKON RIVER
Whitehorse to Carmacks

YUKON RIVER
Carmacks to Dawson

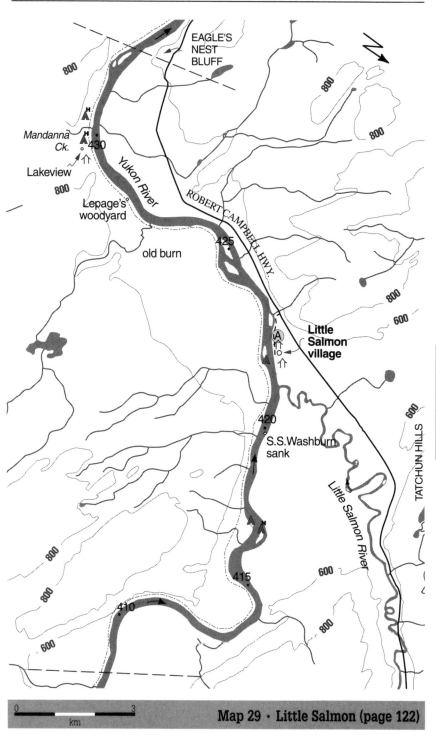

Map 29 · Little Salmon (page 122)

CHILKOOT TRAIL
Dyea to Bennett

HEADWATER LAKES
Bennett to Whitehorse

YUKON RIVER
Whitehorse to Carmacks

YUKON RIVER
Carmacks to Dawson

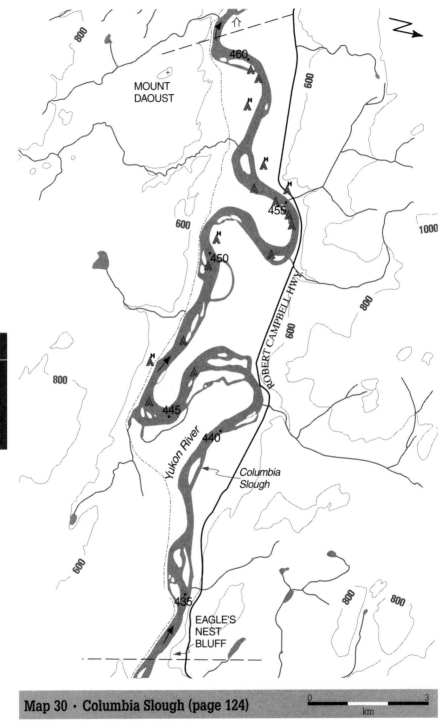

4

MAPS

Map 30 · Columbia Slough (page 124)

0 _____ 3
km

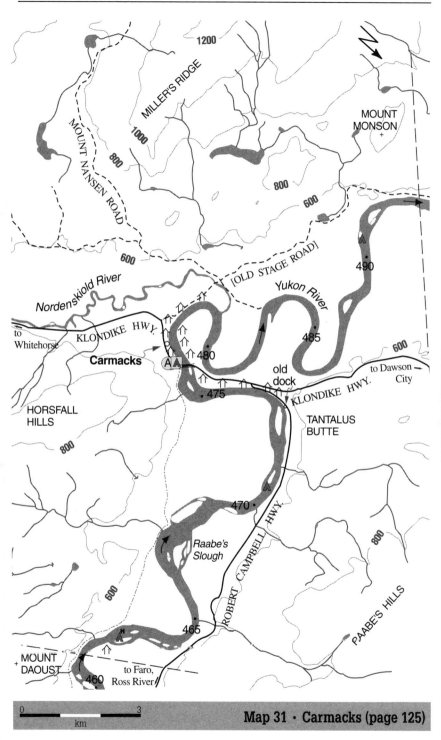

Map 31 · Carmacks (page 125)

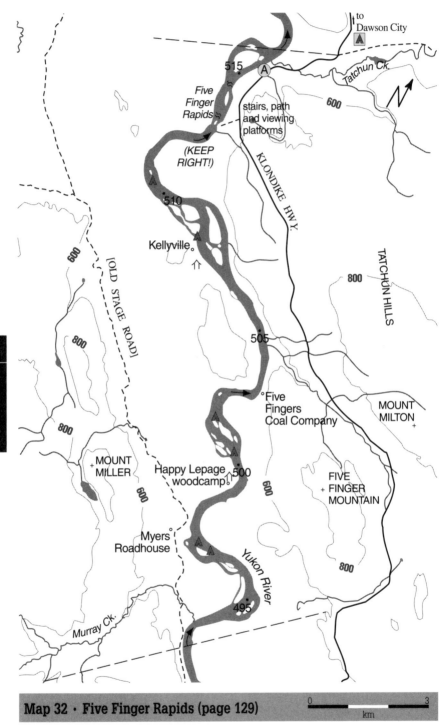

Map 32 · Five Finger Rapids (page 129)

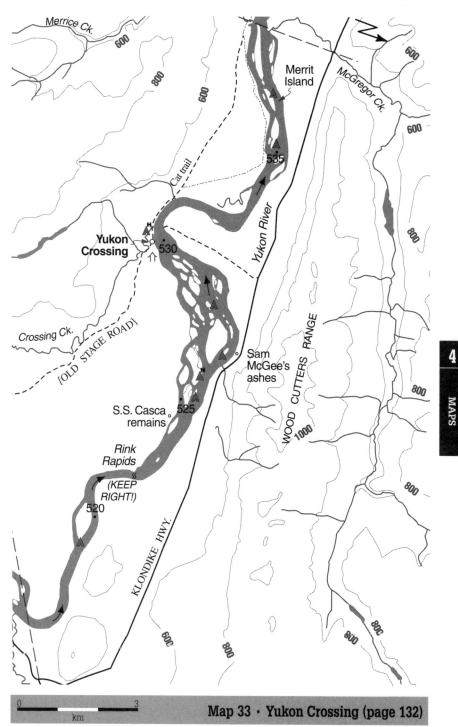

CHILKOOT TRAIL
Dyea to Bennett

HEADWATER LAKES
Bennett to Whitehorse

YUKON RIVER
Whitehorse to Carmacks

YUKON RIVER
Carmacks to Dawson

Merrice Ck.

600

800

600

Merrit
Island

McGregor Ck.

600

535

Cat trail

**Yukon
Crossing**

530

Yukon River

800

4

MAPS

Crossing Ck.

[OLD STAGE ROAD]

Sam
McGee's
ashes

WOOD CUTTERS RANGE

1000

800

S.S. Casca
remains

525

*Rink
Rapids*
(KEEP
RIGHT!)

520

KLONDIKE HWY.

800

800

800

800

0   3
      km

Map 33 · Yukon Crossing (page 132)

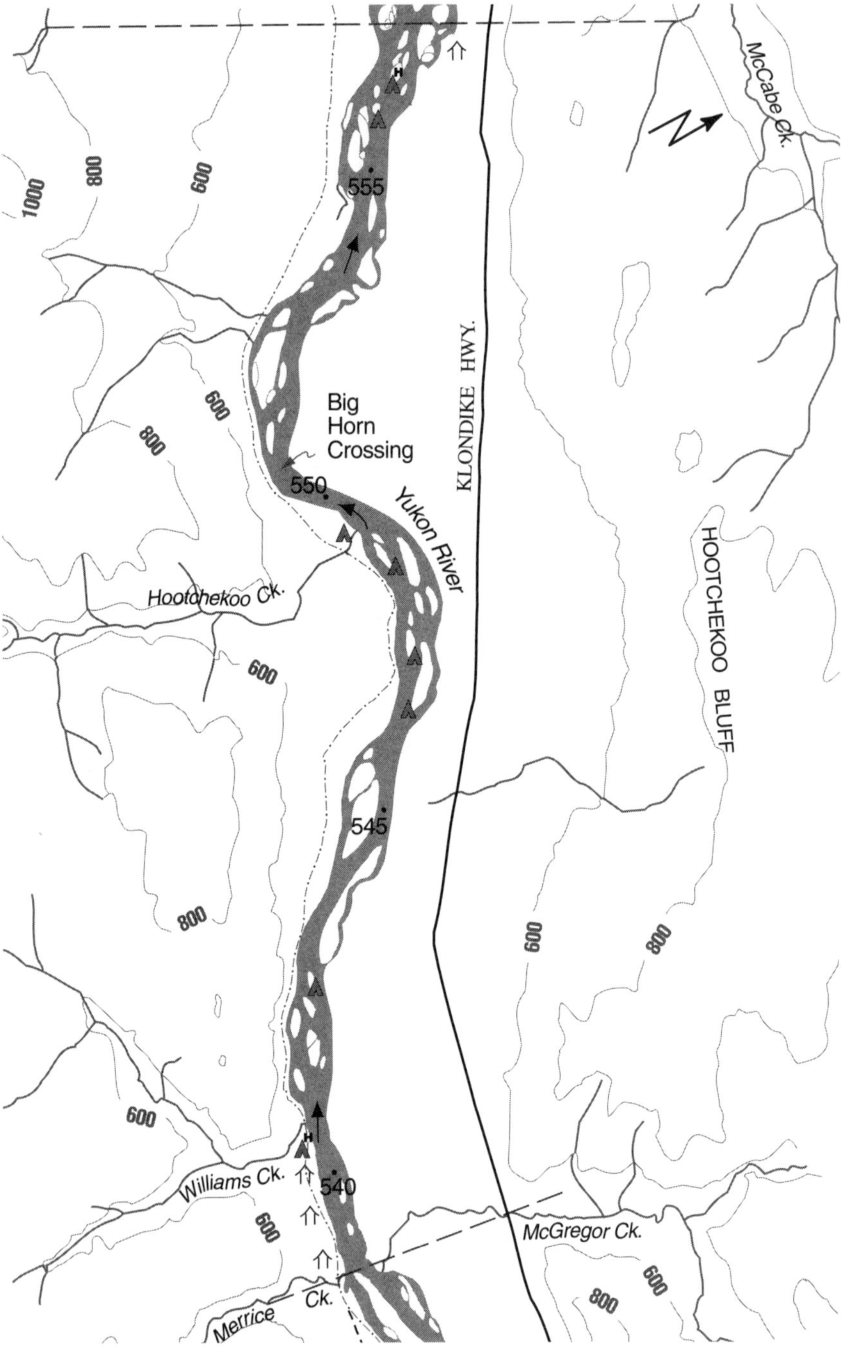

CHILKOOT TRAIL
Dyea to Bennett

HEADWATER LAKES
Bennett to Whitehorse

YUKON RIVER
Whitehorse to Carmacks

**YUKON RIVER
Carmacks to Dawson**

McCabe Ck.

1000

800

600

555

Big
Horn
Crossing

KLONDIKE HWY.

550

Yukon River

Hootchekoo Ck.

600

HOOTCHEKOO BLUFF

545

800

600

800

600

600

Williams Ck.

540

McGregor Ck.

600

Merrice Ck.

800

600

Map 34 · Hootchekoo Creek (page 132)

0 _____ 3
km

CHILKOOT TRAIL
Dyea to Bennett

HEADWATER LAKES
Bennett to Whitehorse

YUKON RIVER
Whitehorse to Carmacks

YUKON RIVER
Carmacks to Dawson

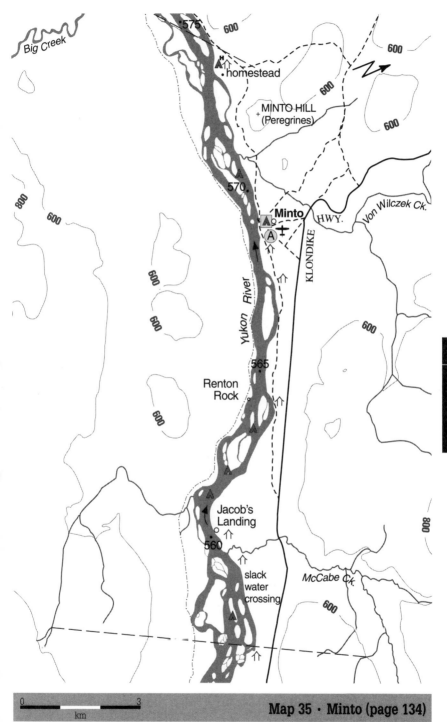

4

MAPS

Map 35 · Minto (page 134)

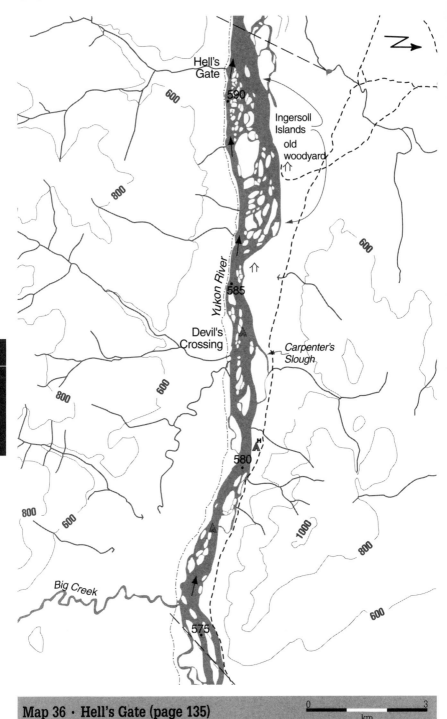

Map 36 · Hell's Gate (page 135)

0   3
km

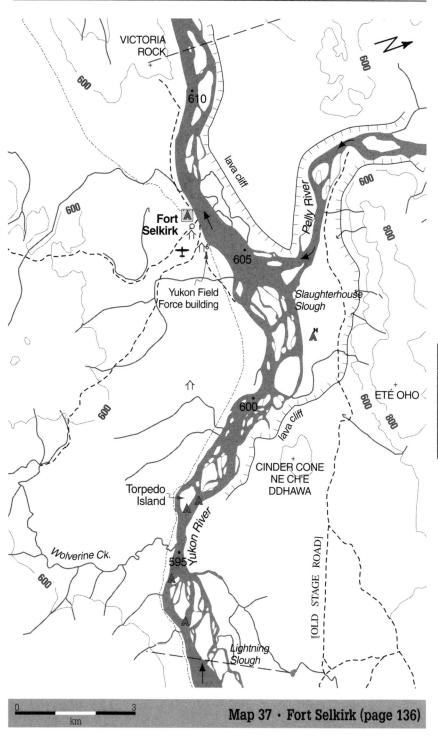

4

MAPS

Map 37 · Fort Selkirk (page 136)

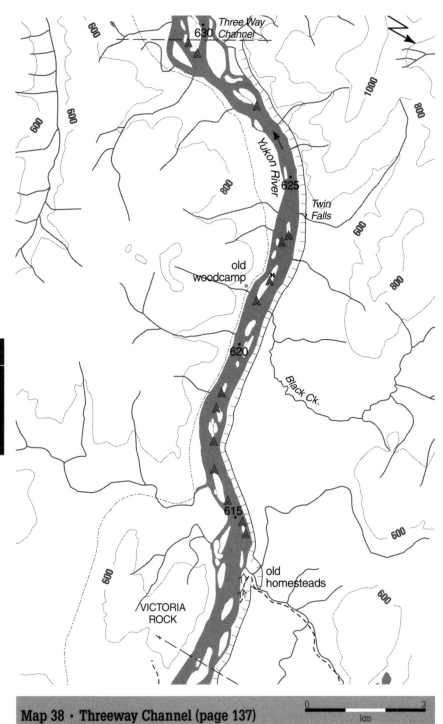

Map 38 · Threeway Channel (page 137)

0   3
km

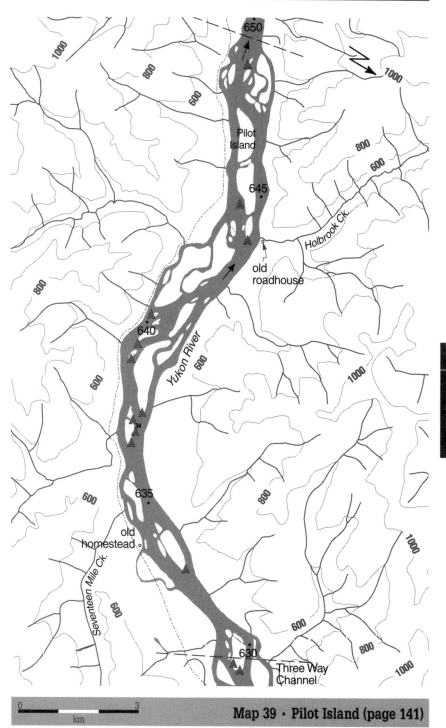

Map 39 · Pilot Island (page 141)

0 _____ 3
km

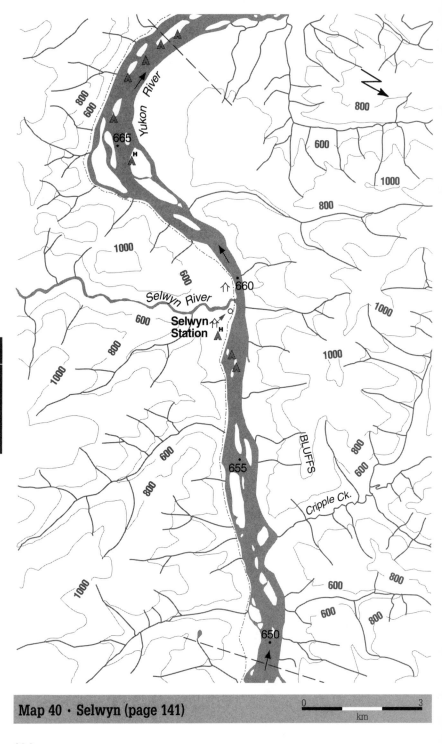

Map 40 · Selwyn (page 141)

0 _____ 3
km

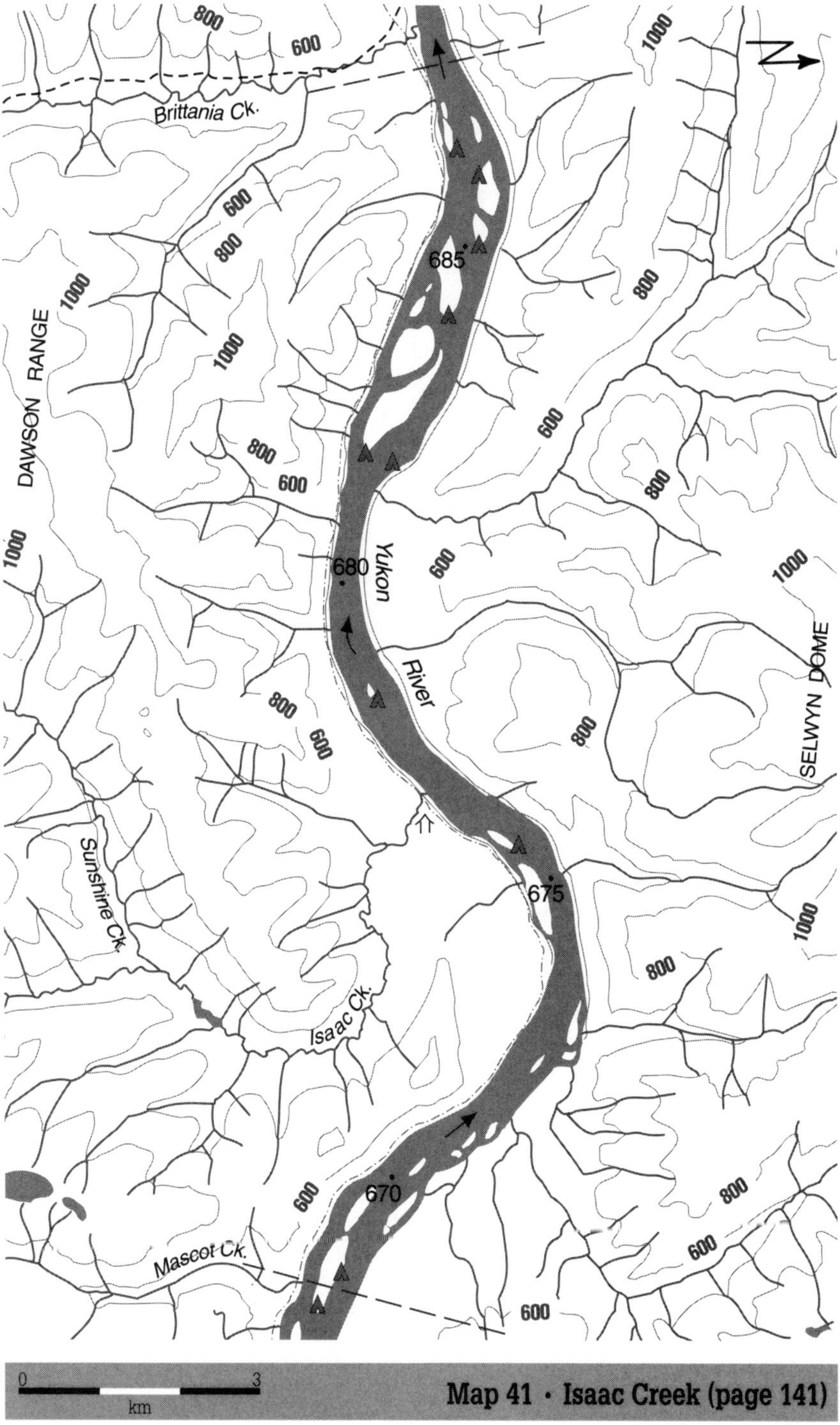

CHILKOOT TRAIL
Dyea to Bennett

HEADWATER LAKES
Bennett to Whitehorse

YUKON RIVER
Whitehorse to Carmacks

YUKON RIVER
Carmacks to Dawson

Brittania Ck.

DAWSON RANGE

800
600
1000

685

680

Yukon

River

675

Sunshine Ck.

Isaac Ck.

670

Mascot Ck.

600

SELWYN DOME

4

MAPS

0   3
km

Map 41 · Isaac Creek (page 141)

CHILKOOT TRAIL
Dyea to Bennett

HEADWATER LAKES
Bennett to Whitehorse

YUKON RIVER
Whitehorse to Carmacks

YUKON RIVER
Carmacks to Dawson

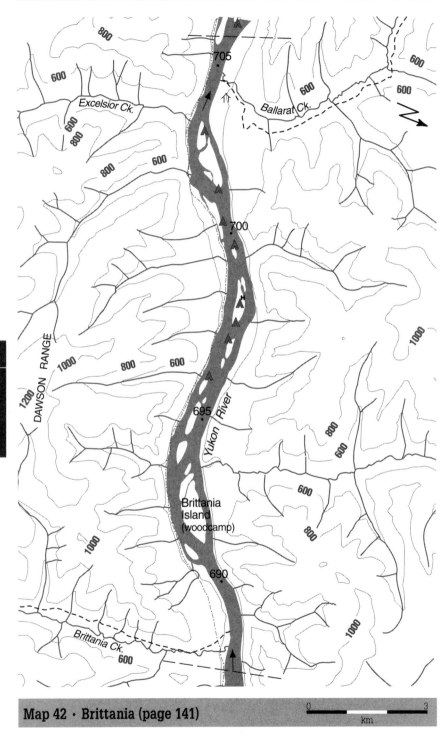

Map 42 · Brittania (page 141)

CHILKOOT TRAIL
Dyea to Bennett

HEADWATER LAKES
Bennett to Whitehorse

YUKON RIVER
Whitehorse to Carmacks

YUKON RIVER
Carmacks to Dawson

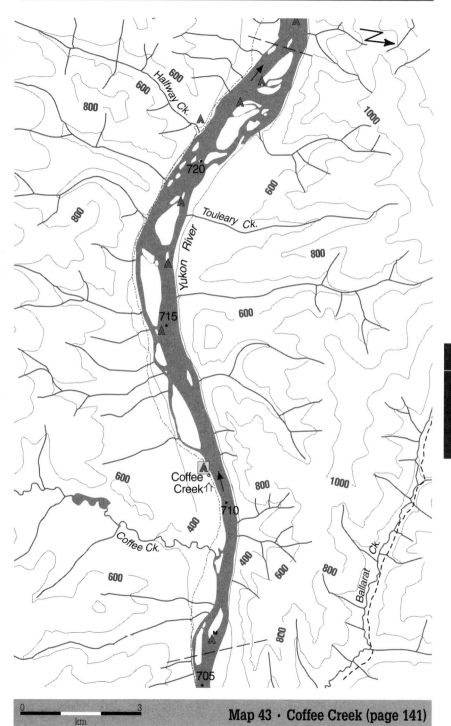

Map 43 · Coffee Creek (page 141)

CHILKOOT TRAIL
Dyea to Bennett

HEADWATER LAKES
Bennett to Whitehorse

YUKON RIVER
Whitehorse to Carmacks

**YUKON RIVER
Carmacks to Dawson**

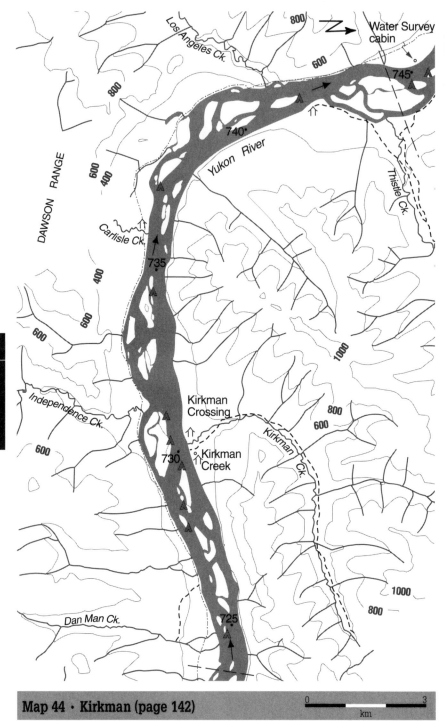

Map 44 · Kirkman (page 142)

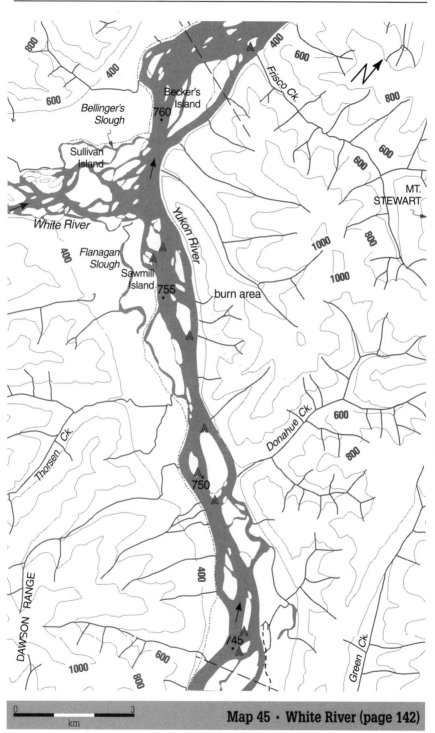

Map 45 · White River (page 142)

4

MAPS

CHILKOOT TRAIL
Dyea to Bennett

HEADWATER LAKES
Bennett to Whitehorse

YUKON RIVER
Whitehorse to Carmacks

**YUKON RIVER
Carmacks to Dawson**

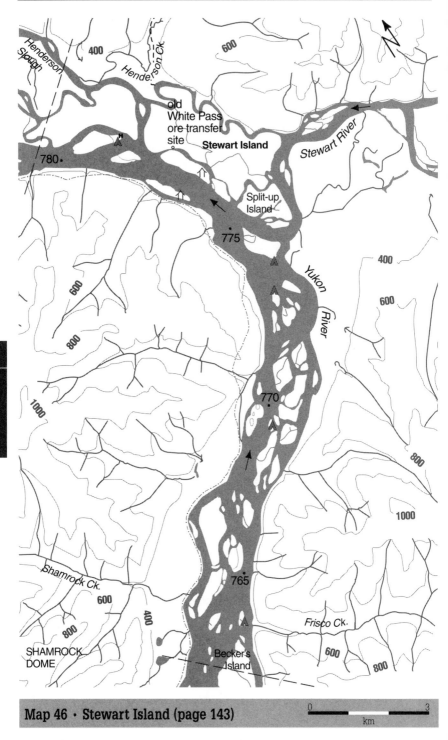

Map 46 · Stewart Island (page 143)

0
km
3

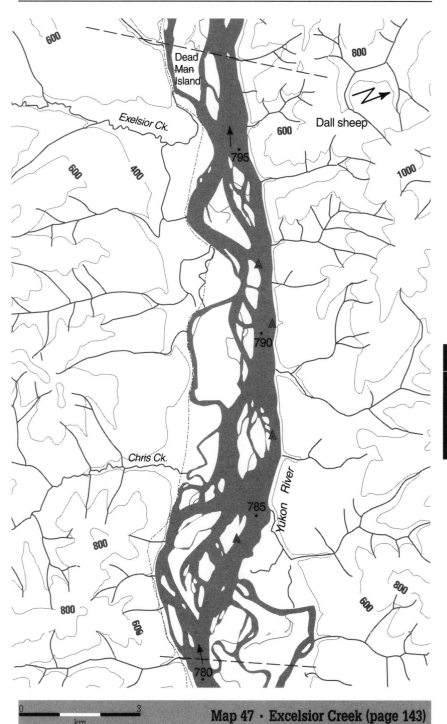

Map 47 · Excelsior Creek (page 143)

CHILKOOT TRAIL
Dyea to Bennett

HEADWATER LAKES
Bennett to Whitehorse

YUKON RIVER
Whitehorse to Carmacks

YUKON RIVER
Carmacks to Dawson

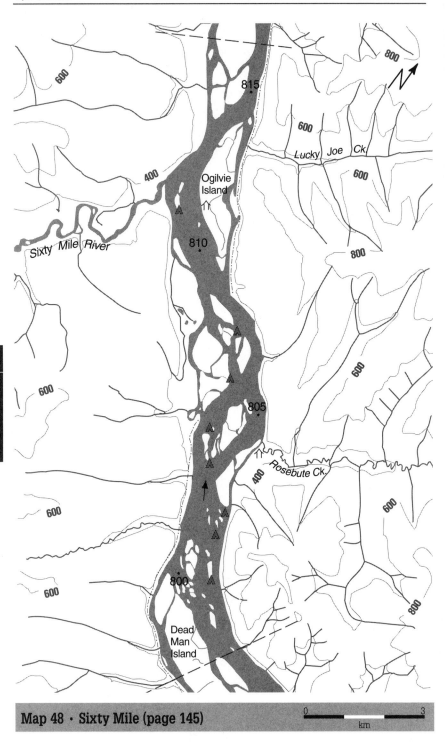

Map 48 · Sixty Mile (page 145)

CHILKOOT TRAIL
Dyea to Bennett

HEADWATER LAKES
Bennett to Whitehorse

YUKON RIVER
Whitehorse to Carmacks

**YUKON RIVER
Carmacks to Dawson**

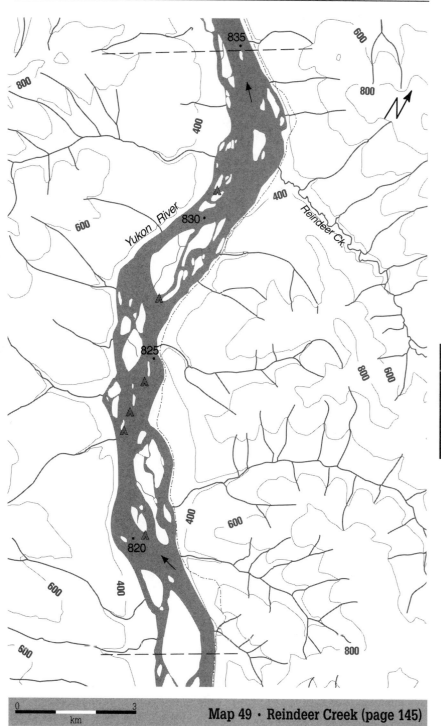

835

400

800

800

600

Reindeer Ck.

400

Yukon River

830

600

400

825

800

600

4

MAPS

400

600

820

600

400

600

800

0 ———— 3
km

Map 49 · Reindeer Creek (page 145)

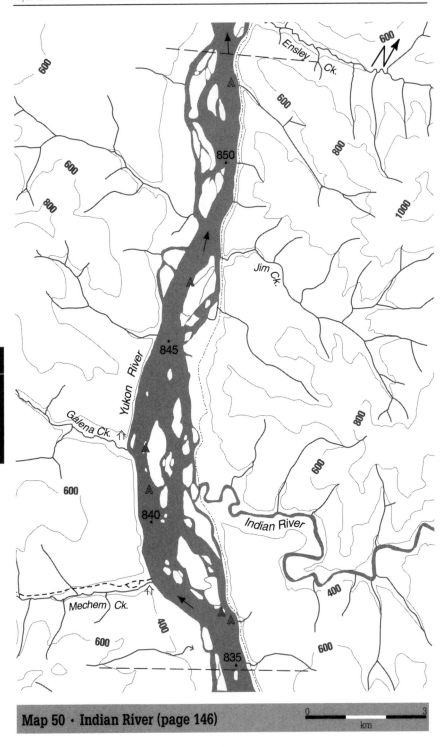

Map 50 · Indian River (page 146)

0   3
km

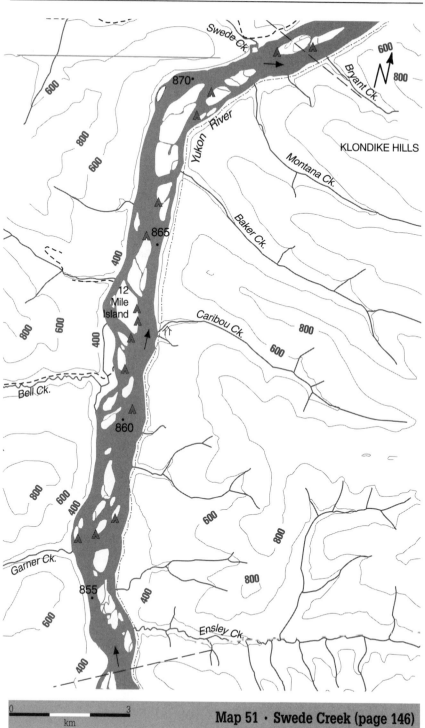

4

MAPS

Map 51 · Swede Creek (page 146)

CHILKOOT TRAIL
Dyea to Bennett

HEADWATER LAKES
Bennett to Whitehorse

YUKON RIVER
Whitehorse to Carmacks

YUKON RIVER
Carmacks to Dawson

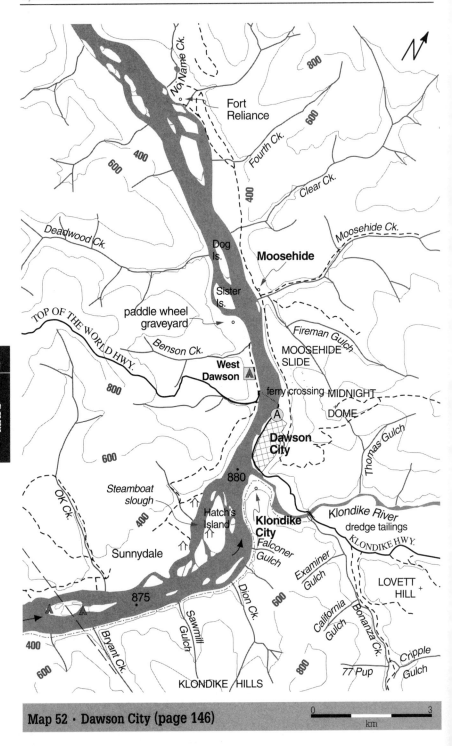

No Name Ck.

800

600

Fort
Reliance

Fourth Ck.

400

600

400

400

Clear Ck.

Deadwood Ck.

Moosehide Ck.

Dog
Is.

Moosehide

Sister
Is.

paddle wheel
graveyard

Fireman Gulch

TOP OF THE WORLD HWY.

Benson Ck.

MOOSEHIDE
SLIDE

**West
Dawson**

800

ferry crossing MIDNIGHT

DOME

Thomas Gulch

600

**Dawson
City**

880

Klondike River

OK Ck.

Steamboat
slough

400

Hatch's
Island

**Klondike
City**

dredge tailings

KLONDIKE HWY.

Falconer
Gulch

Examiner
Gulch

LOVETT
HILL

Sunnydale

600

875

Dion Ck.

Bonanza Ck.

California
Gulch

Sawmill
Gulch

400

800

Cripple
Gulch

600

Bryant Ck.

77 Pup

KLONDIKE HILLS

Map 52 · Dawson City (page 146)

0   3
km

4

MAPS

*T*he Chilkoot Trail and the Yukon River watershed have long been in use by First Nations people, from a time long preceding the arrival of the first newcomers to the north. Of the many First Nations in Alaska, British Columbia and the Yukon, there are five distinct language groups that have historically occupied the area that you will be travelling through:

- Tlingit;
- Tagish;
- Southern Tutchone;
- Northern Tutchone; and
- Han.

First Nations people lived in a certain equilibrium until the mid-1800s, when explorers started to travel to the central Yukon. But it was the Klondike gold rush that instigated the greatest change, bringing a sudden influx of 30,000 to 40,000 people over a few short years. Once the gold rush subsided, the remaining people had to pick up the pieces and adapt to a new reality in their homeland.

F. Schwatka, A summer in Alaska, J.W. Henry, 1894, p. 221

First Nation people and their birch bark canoes at Fort Selkirk with Victoria Rock in the background, 1883.

■ FIRST NATIONS

The region surrounding the Chilkoot Trail and the Yukon River has a long and rich history, made even more amazing by the adverse conditions of the north. As far as can be established through legends and archaeology, Alaska and the Yukon have been inhabited for at least the 10,000 years since the last great ice age, and possibly up to 25,000 or 30,000 years, particularly the northern Yukon area called "Beringia," which was ice-free. Flaked stone tools, referred to as microblades, have been found near Carcross and date back 4,500 years. Copper tools have been found that are up to 1,200 years old. Archaeological finds indicating the possibility of earlier human habitation have been found in Bluefish Caves, near Old Crow in northern Yukon. This latest "evidence" has not been fully accepted in the scientific community, but it sparks the imagination.

Today, First Nations people of the region are from five linguistic groups: Tlingit, Tagish, Southern Tutchone, Northern Tutchone and Han. The Tlingit have traditionally been a coastal people, with a culture similar to others living along the west coast of Alaska and British Columbia. However, some Tlingit, such as the Teslin Tlingit, have extended their territory inland. The other four groups are of the larger Athapaskan language family, each speaking different dialects of the Athapaskan language.

The Tlingit language has two dialects within our area of interest — one spoken by the coastal Chilkats and the other, interior or Inland Tlingit. Of the Athapaskan families, six "First Nation" groups are evident. First Nation people have organized themselves this way in part to settle their land claim and self-government agreements with Canada and the Yukon:

- Carcross/Tagish — a blending of traditional Tagish Athapaskan and coastal Tlingit due to their position in the middle of the extensive trade between the coastal Tlingit and Tutchone;
- Kwanlin Dun — a blending of primarily Southern and Northern Tutchone, centred around Whitehorse;
- Ta'an Kwach'an — Southern Tutchone people traditionally located between the Takhini area and Hootalinqua;
- Little Salmon/Carmacks — Northern Tutchone people, centred around Carmacks;
- Selkirk First Nation — Northern Tutchone people, centred in the lower Pelly valley surrounding Pelly Crossing, Minto and Fort Selkirk; and
- Tr'ondëk Hwëch'in — speakers of the Han dialect, centred in Dawson City, spanning from the Stewart River to the Yukon boundary with Alaska along the Yukon River.

Before the arrival of Europeans along the coast of Alaska and, later, into the Yukon interior, the First Nations had established a sophisticated system of trading. Generally, trading occurred between coastal communities, which had an abundance of fish oils, dried seaweed, shells and other marine products, and the interior communities with their furs, meats, clothing and copper. The Tlingit had a strong and powerful position in this trade, and jealously guarded the passes that were the only routes from their lands to those of the interior. Tlingit people would make trading trips to the interior several times each year, moving as far inland as the Fort Selkirk area to gather, mingle, trade and fish. All First Nations communities lived, for the most part until quite recently, nomadic or semi-nomadic lives. As a result,

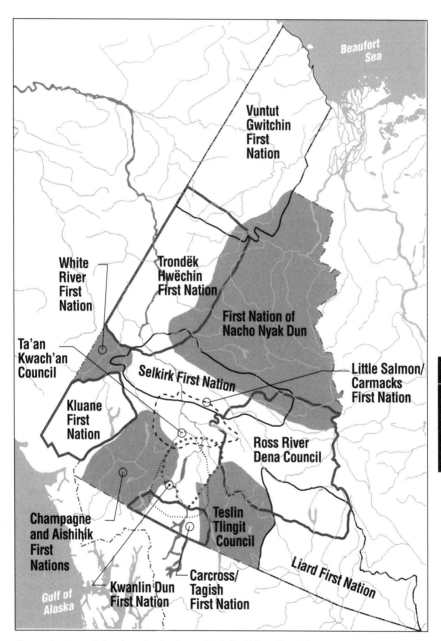

Approximate traditional territories for each of the Yukon First Nations.

the Yukon and Alaska are criss-crossed with well-established trail systems linking seasonal sites for fishing, hunting, trapping and berry picking, and allowing trade to occur between distant groups.

After several millennia of established relations between the various First Nations communities of the north, the balance was first disturbed, primarily along the Alaska coastline. In the 1700s, the Russians came down from the Bering Strait, reaching the Aleutian Islands by the 1740s. Their approach was to aggressively exploit both the First Nations people and the wildlife. This was compounded later in the century with the arrival of the Spanish, British and American explorers from the south. Initially, disease and conflict caused population declines in the First Nation populations. Ultimately, around the turn of that century, a new balance was reached. The Tlingit, through their control of trade to the interior, supplied the Russians' voracious demand for furs, while receiving in exchange new tools, materials, guns and ammunition. This contact initiated the rapid and permanent change to the Tlingit culture, with impacts reaching far inland to the Athapaskan people of the Yukon.

The rush to the Klondike late in the 19th century changed the lives of this region's First Nations people forever. The Tlingit benefited for a time by their monopoly on packing gear over the Chilkoot and White passes. Interior peoples were simply overrun by the masses, which overtook trading routes, and put a strain on all limited northern resources. After the gold rush, First Nation people faced new challenges from white society, including church, police and government. Life would never be the same. Efforts to provide widespread education resulted in disruptive and damaging residential schools that generations to this day are struggling to recover from. The changed economic environment had put a further strain on resources and relationships.

Further, and in many ways more drastic, change came to the First Nations in the 1940s and 1950s when the federal government took increased interest in the territory. Highway and industrial development, mining claims, oil and gas leases, outfitting licenses and private property deeds all served to take traditional land away from native populations. Despite the Royal Proclamation of 1763 that required treaties with aboriginal peoples, no land treaties had been struck in the Yukon, and the federal government claimed absolute dominion over the land. Organized efforts on the part of First Nations to initiate meaningful treaty negotiations began in the mid-1960s. In 1973, in an effort to protect their cultures, the First Nations presented the first comprehensive land claim, entitled "Together Today for our Children Tomorrow" to the Government of Canada. Thus began a long, drawn out process of negotiation. Land claim agreements have resulted from this effort, which provide several First Nations with land, financial compensation and self-government. Once more, First Nation peoples are self-governing.

Tlingit

The Tlingit First Nation covers a vast area of the Alaskan coastline and points further inland, from Wrangell in the south to Yukatat in the north. Some theorize that the Tlingit came to North America about 10,000 years ago from Asia over the Bering land bridge, then found their way to the coast over the glaciers via the Chilkat River. From here they spread south as far as the Stikine River. The two tribes that were most impacted by the gold rush are the coastal Chilkat Tlingit, and, to a lesser extent, the Inland Tlingit. Related to the Chilkats, the Inland Tlingit, apparently moved from the Alaskan coast to facilitate trade to the interior tribes, settling in the areas of Teslin, Carcross and Atlin.

Traditional Tlingit activities and settlement revolved around availability of food. The Chilkats' traditional food was salmon, but they also enjoyed eulachon (a small fish high in oils), herring, shellfish, seaweeds, harbour seal, fur seal, sea otter, black-tail deer, bear, Dall sheep, and mountain goat. Summers were spent on the land and sea, fishing, hunting and gathering. In the winter, they stayed in larger communities along the coast, enjoying the fruits of the summer gathering. Occasionally, they would move inland over established trails to trade with the interior tribes.

The Teslin Tlingit were led by different rhythms, since local resources were quite different than on the coast. Due to their location and environment, their seasonal round followed the availability of caribou, moose, sheep, fish and berries.

Theirs was a totemic culture, like most of the coastal peoples. Their log homes featured intricately carved corner posts or totem poles. The Tlingit society is divided into two divisions or moieties, the Ravens, and the Eagles. In the cultural tradition, marriages must occur between the two. A spiritual people, they produced

First Nations packers hauling stampeders' loads up the Chilkoot Trail near Sheep Camp, 1898.

legends to explain natural processes, and used storytelling to pass on information from generation to generation. Dancing is very important to the Tlingit, often as a means of enhancing their storytelling. In modern times, the Chilkat dancers, based out of Haines, Alaska, have attained world renown for their energetic and colourful dances. The Chilkats are also well known for their intricate woven blankets.

Tagish

The Tagish, although primarily Athapaskan, have close ties to the Tlingit through marriage and the extensive trading that took place between the two cultures. The Tagish people were nomadic, following the movements of moose, woodland caribou, sheep, fish and berries. The land provided food, clothing and shelter. Although the Tagish people are now concentrated primarily in the Tagish and Carcross area, until the 20th century they lived in temporary structures due to their nomadic existence. They had camps in areas such as Carcross, Log Cabin, Annie Lake and Bennett.

Generally, the summer was spent fishing at camps on the various lakes. Fall was spent picking berries, hunting moose and caribou, and preparing and storing food for the winter. Winter was a social time, with some trapping of small game to provide fresh meat and furs. Spring was heralded with the annual beaver hunt.

The Tagish were well positioned to acquire goods through well-established trade links with both the coastal Tlingit and the inland Kaska and Tutchone. In addition to acquiring goods from the coast, such as shells, eulachon oil, dried clams, wooden boxes and seaweed, in exchange for excess furs, tanned hides,

Anchorage Museum of History and Art, B87.7.103

First Nation woman and children of the Carcross-Tagish First Nation, at Carcross, about 1905.

Low-flying eagle.

clothing, and lichens and mosses for dyeing, the Tagish people acted as middle people in trade between the coast and the inland people. This became a more powerful position with the arrival of Europeans and the fur trade.

As with many other First Nations people, the Tagish have a culture rich in storytelling, art and dance. Their social structure includes the Crow and Wolf clans. Storytelling is used for teaching, to explore favourite themes such as how the world began, and to pass on information on hunting, trapping, family life, place names and survival.

Southern Tutchone

The Southern Tutchone dialect covers an area along the Yukon River from approximately Marsh Lake to Hootalinqua. Two main groups along the Klondike Trail are the Ta'an Kwach'an, based around Lake Laberge and the Kwanlin Dun, centred around Whitehorse. The Lake Laberge basin, or "Tage shaw jadali," was their storehouse of resources. In the spring, they fished for spawning salmon and grayling with the use of willow traps. Sheep and moose were hunted in the mountains and valleys surrounding the lake.

As part of the extensive system of trade in the Yukon, the Southern Tutchone traded most frequently with the Chilkat Tlingit. In exchange for their winter furs, the Southern Tutchone received fish oils, seaweed, shells, guns and ammunition,

Group of Pelly First Nations people at Fort Selkirk, 1894.

clothing, blankets, glass beads and metals. Close ties to the Northern Tutchone were also maintained by the Kwanlin Dun.

The gold rush brought many changes to the Southern Tutchone culture. The plentiful resources around The Thirty Mile and Lake Laberge were severely depleted by the sheer quantity of people. Many natives took seasonal jobs as woodcutters, pilots and deckhands for the riverboat industry, while pursuing traditional activities like hunting and trapping during winter. These changes brought new impacts to their culture.

Northern Tutchone

The Northern Tutchone dialect covers a large area of the upper Yukon basin, from Hootalinqua to north of the Stewart River. Although made up of several groups, the main people in this region are the Little Salmon/Carmacks people, now based out of Carmacks, and the Selkirk people, now based out of Pelly Crossing and Mayo. They belong to either the Crow or Wolf clans, similar to other Athapaskan cultures.

The realities of the north resulted in a nomadic existence for the Northern Tutchone. Summers saw them fishing on the Yukon and its tributaries in camps, such as those at the sites of modern day Fort Selkirk and Pelly Crossing. The fall led them to higher ground, hunting big game, such as caribou, moose, and sheep, in the local mountains. Late fall marked the salmon runs, which led to winters spent either fishing in large groups at the main fish lakes, or hunting and trapping in small family groups. Spring involved beaver and moose hunting, and fishing. The land provided all they needed: game, fish and plants for food; stone and copper for tools; and hides for clothing and shelter.

Han

The Han dialect spans the Yukon River drainage from the Stewart River to downstream of the Yukon/Alaska border. The main people inhabiting this region were the Tr'ondëk Hwëch'in, now centred in Dawson City. The Han were fortunate to live in an area rich with wildlife and fish. The focus of their diet was fish, provided by the river of life, the Yukon River. The word "Han" is a First Nation word meaning "people of the river." Spring was spent on the banks of the Yukon River preparing canoes, fish nets and fish weirs for the upcoming summer fishing season. Summers were an active time, with the primary activities being fishing, drying, tanning hides, hunting and picking berries. In the fall, they moved up into the higher tributaries to prepare for the winter caribou hunt by constructing and repairing corrals into which to drive the caribou. After a brief fall hunt, groups returned to the Yukon River to prepare for winter, stocking up caches and sewing clothes. Then, winter was spent on the winter caribou hunt.

Because of their heavy reliance on the river, the Han were somewhat less nomadic than other northern groups. There is evidence they developed semi-permanent villages, consisting mostly of moss houses, semi-subterranean dwellings made of wood and dirt. When they moved, they stayed in portable caribou or moose skin houses.

For further reading on Yukon First Nations culture and history, see *Part of the Land, Part of the Water* by Catharine McClellan, Douglas and McIntyre, 1987.

First Nations camp at the Klondike River, around 1895.

Yukon Archives, Coutts Coll. #82/358.

5

THEN & NOW

■ THE NEWCOMERS

Although there was significant European activity on the coast in the 18th and 19th centuries, the influx of European influence directly to the interior came later and slower. Robert Campbell of the Hudson's Bay Company was the first non-native, in recorded history, to see the Yukon interior. His arrival in the 1840s began with his exploration along the Pelly River and resulting establishment of Fort Selkirk in 1848. After Fort Selkirk was pillaged by Chilkats in 1852, there was little non-First Nation activity until the 1870s. Then, in the last few decades of the 19th century, there was a slow influx of prospectors followed by traders, then missionaries. A deal made between Captain Beardslee of the U.S. Navy and the Chilkats allowed miners to travel the Chilkoot Trail on the condition that they would not interfere with the fur trade. By 1890, there were between 300 and 500 prospectors in the Yukon, many of whom had come over the Chilkoot.

Mineral strikes were spotty during the first few decades of prospecting in the upper Yukon River drainage. The first payable quantity of gold discovered in the territory was on the Big Salmon River in 1881. Gold was also found on the Stewart River, Forty Mile River and at Cassiar Bar on the Yukon River in 1880s. Each small strike only served to further convince prospectors that they would find the motherlode that they were sure existed.

Klondike gold rush

The big strike did occur, sparking one of the largest movements of people in recorded history. It was August 16th, 1896, when George Carmack, Skookum Jim and Tagish Charlie, passing through the Rabbit Creek valley, stumbled upon heart-

Museum of History and Industry, Seattle, #12757

Stampeders boarding a steamship in Seattle, bound for the Klondike,1897-1898.

stopping quantities of gold. The next day, George Carmack registered their claims with the mining recorder at Forty Mile, over 100 kilometres downstream, taking for himself the discovery claim.

The strike on what soon became known as Bonanza Creek quickly caused a stir among the prospectors in the Klondike region. Most left their camps, many from the Forty Mile area, and rushed to the creek to stake a claim. Many who did not act, however, regretted not taking "Lying George" seriously — Carmack had a reputation of embellishing the truth.

By the end of August of 1896, all of Bonanza Creek was staked. Gold on Eldorado Creek was discovered shortly after, and that creek too was quickly fully staked. Word was slow to spread to the outside world. It wasn't until two ships bearing gold, the *S.S. Excelsior* and the *S.S. Portland*, arrived at the wharves of San Francisco and Seattle in July of 1897, that the rest of the world was introduced to the words "Klondike" and "ton of gold!" Mostly due to a recession at the time, the pandemonium that followed was completely out of proportion to the amount of gold that lay in the Klondike valley.

By the time these two ships landed, it was too late in the season for all but the first few (about 2,500 people) to get to the Yukon before freeze-up. That didn't stop tens of thousands of people from dropping everything and rushing north. People came from all over the world, including many Canadians, Americans and Europeans. They came by boat, by foot, by horse, by rail. It is estimated that, over the months of the Klondike gold rush, 100,000 people set out from their homes, aiming for the goldfields. Only 30 to 40 percent of these made it to the Klondike and only a tiny percentage of them fulfilled their Klondike dreams.

There were many routes taken to reach the Yukon, some more amazing than others. Some goldseekers went north from Edmonton, Alberta along various routes, travelling such rivers as the Athabasca, Peace, Mackenzie, Peel, Bell, Porcupine, Liard, Pelly and Stewart. Others travelled overland from Ashcroft, British Columbia or up the Stikine River from the coast to Glenora, then overland to the Teslin River system. Dalton's Trail involved a trek over the Chilkat Trail from Pyramid Harbour, Alaska, overland to Fort Selkirk, then down the remainder of the Yukon River to Dawson City. Those with money came on a long ocean steamer ride up the British Columbia and Alaska coastline to St. Michael near the mouth of the Yukon River, then up the river by flat-bottomed river steamer. However, the most popular routes by far were over the White and Chilkoot passes to Bennett and down the lakes and Yukon River by raft or boat.

When stampeders reached the end of Lynn Canal on the Alaskan coast, they had to choose either the White Pass or Chilkoot Pass. Many who chose the White Pass did so because the elevation was lower than on the Chilkoot, and the ascent less steep, making it seem more desirable. Unfortunately, they did not recognize or heed warnings about the lack of a proper trail, the difficulty of traversing the high terrain past the pass, and the high avalanche hazard along the route. In reality, the Chilkoot Trail, despite its higher elevation and steep climb up the Golden Stairs, was the safer of the two options.

To reach the Chilkoot Pass, stampeders were let off boats at either Dyea or Skagway. Skagway was the more popular option because of its superior docking facilities. Those dropped at Dyea often had to be transferred in smaller vessels, with their livestock swimming to shore. There was chaos on the beach at Dyea, with stampeders trying to find their gear from among tons of supplies scattered along the shore.

Skagway was an American-style frontier town, with the degree of lawlessness that goes along with that, if not more. This was in stark contrast to the Canadian portion of the route. The North West Mounted Police, despite being understaffed, underequipped and undergunned, for the most part kept things quite orderly and controlled on Canadian soil.

NWMP Superintendent Samuel B. Steele saved many lives by making the trip to the north safer. He was also a main factor in the good behaviour of Americans on Canadian soil.

By early winter, 1897, the North West Mounted Police had imposed an order that each stampeder must carry a year's worth of provisions over the pass, equal to a ton of goods. This was to ensure stampeders' survival in a country with no network of supply depots. A ton of gear meant as many as 30 trips up the trail, usually ferrying gear from camp to camp. Only those with money could take advantage of packers and aerial trams from Canyon City over the pass.

Most stampeders were unprepared for the arduous trail and the miserable conditions. The 27 kilometres up to the pass were in a lush rain forest, making for sloppy, wet and cool conditions in spring, winter and fall. Overloaded horses collapsed in the mud under monstrous loads.

The more entrepreneurial at the time figured out ways to exploit the other stampeders; they would "mine the miners" as the saying goes. Some of the more committed ventures were the aerial trams constructed between Canyon City and the Chilkoot Pass. Three companies went at it over the winter of 1897–1898: the Dyea-Klondike Transportation Company, the Chilkoot Railroad and Transport Company and the Alaska Railroad and Transportation Company. Two tram systems were working by late spring of 1898, but by 1900, with the White Pass & Yukon Route railway opening over the White Pass, there were no stampeders on the Chilkoot to keep the trams in business. The WP&YR bought out the tram companies and had the tramways moved or demolished to eliminate any potential future competition.

The Golden Stairs, the steepest section leading up to the Chilkoot Pass, was the biggest bottleneck of the trail. Many people today are familiar with the photo images of a thick line of men and women with heavy packs on their backs, trudging their way up the steep, snow-covered Golden Stairs. An individual on the Stairs dared not step aside for a break for fear of not being let back in. The word "rush" seemed out of place here — the line moved so slowly that it could take up to six hours to make a single trip up the Stairs that would otherwise take only one hour. Another option was to hire Tlingit packers, who would pack up to 150 pounds per trip over the pass.

Once on top, stampeders still had a long way to go to get to either Lindeman or Bennett Lake. Those with money could hire packing services. Horses and mules were used to take gear overland to the south end of Long Lake, where it was loaded onto boats. From the quays at the north end of the lake, remains of which can still be seen, the gear was transferred to wagons for the trip down to Lindeman. Those without money had to handle the loads on their own, but at least it was now mostly downhill.

Stampeders had another decision to make at the end of the trail — Lindeman or Bennett. Many chose to end their overland journey at Lindeman, tired of the rigours of the trail. Others continued on the trail, past One Mile Rapids, to Bennett. Both centres became large tent cities by the end of the winter of 1898, with hundreds of boat-building operations actively working away. The folks at Lindeman may have underestimated the hazards of the One Mile Rapids that separated them

National Archives of Canada, C4688

Boat building kept the stampeders busy over the long winter and spring.

Dawson City was a bustling metropolis in 1898, the largest city west of Winnipeg and north of San Francisco.

from the relatively calm waters of Bennett Lake. In the spring, these rapids were to claim boats, gear and at least one life.

The challenge didn't end here. Boats were required to navigate the waters of the Yukon River, and the only means to secure one, aside from dragging it over the pass, was to build it. The main tool for cutting the lumber was the whipsaw, a long flexible saw that needed a large contraption consisting of stands on which the log was placed, and room for the saw to move. Two men were required to work it: one at the top and one at the bottom. The extensive boat building, as well as the need for fuel and shelter, also had a major impact on the forests surrounding the two settlements.

After a long, difficult winter, the end came on May 29th, 1898, when the ice finally broke on Bennett Lake. Within 24 hours, an estimated 7,000 boats left to sail and float down the Yukon River system. On their way, they had to navigate the rough, windy waters of the headwater lakes, the difficult rapids of Miles Canyon and Whitehorse Rapids, the unpredictable seas of Lake Laberge, and the strong currents of the Yukon River. The rapids above Whitehorse were probably the most life-threatening of all they would encounter, claiming both boats and lives before the NWMP enforced a requirement in June of 1898 that all boats passing through the rapids must be navigated by a proven pilot. Most stampeders unloaded their gear at Canyon City and, for a fee of $25, had it transported to below the rapids by tramway, while their boat was skilfully navigated through the raging waters. Although sections below, such as The Thirty Mile and Five Finger Rapids, also took lives, they were calm in comparison to the maelstrom at Miles Canyon.

When they finally arrived at Dawson City, the stampeders were no doubt devastated to learn that the region had been completely staked for the better part of a year. Many dropped everything and returned home, penniless but somehow enhanced by the experience. Others stayed on, however, attracted by the freedom and vastness of the land, finding various jobs or ways to exploit those who had struck gold. Dawson continued to boom for several years, becoming the largest town north of San Francisco and west of Winnipeg. Dubbed the "San Francisco of the North," Dawson City had a lively culture born of gold dust.

The rush continued through 1898 and into 1899. The face of it changed in 1899 when the White Pass & Yukon Route railway was completed between Skagway and Bennett. At this point, the White Pass suddenly became a much more desirable route into the Yukon than the Chilkoot Pass. The Chilkoot Trail was virtually abandoned overnight, including all the settlements along its route — Dyea, Canyon City, Sheep Camp and Lindeman.

The Klondike gold rush had far reaching impacts, not only on the region but on the world. People all over the globe were able to dream of untold riches, and many were able to act on those dreams. The First Nation population of the Yukon would be changed forever, as would the 30,000 to 40,000 stampeders who travelled over the various trails to the Klondike. The gold rush marked the beginning of the settlement of the Yukon, forever changing its social, economic and environmental future.

Old cabins are often seen along the Klondike trail.

The riverboat era

Although a few small riverboats had plied the waters of the Yukon River before, the Klondike gold rush really was the start of extensive river travel through the Yukon. Not only did the rush of goldseekers provide an initial clientele for the boats, but increased traffic in the territory led to further mining discoveries and increased settlement. The steamboats were sustained for decades by the movement of people, mining products, mail and other freight at a time when there were virtually no roads. It wasn't until after the opening of the Klondike Highway

MSCUA, University of Washington Library, Special Coll. Division, 2476A

At the height of the gold rush, close to 69 paddlewheelers plied the Yukon River.

Remains of the ways used to haul boats up for the winter are still evident at Shipyard Island, near Hootalinqua.

between Whitehorse and Dawson City in 1952 that the last of the Yukon riverboats stopped running. During the time of the riverboats, men worked hard for their money, under harsh conditions, and they were proud to do it. Many came from outside the Yukon, but the experience stayed with them for a lifetime, endearing them to the north. Many stayed on in the Yukon after their steamboat days were over, unable to turn their backs on the Yukon River or the people who lived there.

Names such as the *S.S. Klondike, S.S. Whitehorse, S.S. Tanana* and *S.S. Keno* will live on in the minds and hearts of Yukoners for years to come. Some of these names, such as *S.S. Columbia, S.S. Casca*, and *S.S. Domville*, will live on on maps, marking the spots where the great boats met their demise. It seems from our modern perspective that few runs on these ships were uneventful, whether it was a sinking, running aground on a sandbar, watching caribou cross the river by the thousands or running with ice flows in the late season. The large boats drew approximately three to six feet of water when loaded, and required great alertness and skill to avoid the many sandbars in the river, especially below the White River, where the water became thick with silt and ash.

The riverboats required an amazing amount of resources to complete a single round trip between Whitehorse and Dawson City. Typically, these boats needed between 15 and 25 crew. This generally consisted of a captain, pilot, first and second mate, purser, three engineers, three firemen to load the boilers full of wood, a chef and second cook, four stewards, and five to eight deckhands. An average steamboat required a cord of wood per hour to run. A typical run was about one and a half days downstream to Dawson, and five days upstream to Whitehorse.

In winter, most of the boats were taken out of the water at communities like Whitehorse, Carcross, Carmacks, Hootalinqua and Dawson to avoid hull damage by the ice. The boats were pulled up on ways, consisting of large timbers laid up the shoreline, coated with tallow and fish oil. The ship was winched up carefully, lifted and levelled, then set in a cradle constructed to hold it for the winter. In the spring, the ships were carefully lowered onto the ways, then released back into the river. Another method of winter storage was in shallow sloughs with little flow. Examples include Raabe's Slough upstream of Carmacks, and Steamboat Slough near Dawson City. These sloughs were shallow and still enough that ice damage was rare.

This truck at Lower Laberge was once used to haul wood for use by the riverboats.

A challenge for steamboat companies was to extend the season as long as possible. One constraint early in the season was the ice on Lake Laberge, which generally stayed frozen weeks after the river was clear. White Pass tried several methods to help the ice go out earlier. These included spraying "lamp black" and old crank-case oil on the ice to attract the sun's warmth, and the use of the Marsh Lake control structure to flush out the ice. The "lamp black" was the most successful, and with the help of the first boat of the season breaking up the resulting slush, the route was opened two weeks before the usual time. White Pass also jumped the season by about a month by wintering a smaller steamer at Lower Laberge. In the spring, the company would send a tractor with a sleigh full of supplies over the Lake Laberge ice. The load was then taken down the ice-free river to Dawson, where residents were anxious for fresh supplies after a long winter.

The Whitehorse to Dawson Stage Road, built in 1902, runs parallel to the Yukon River and was used primarily for winter travel with horse-drawn sleighs. Its main purpose was to handle the winter mail contract to Dawson; it also carried passengers and some freight. Roadhouses spotted the trail along its length, providing accommodations, food and supplies to those on the trail. The stage road was used until the late 1930s, when air mail service began. The existing Klondike Highway follows portions of the route. The construction of the Klondike Highway spelled the end of many communities along both the river and the stage road.

It must have been a nostalgic time for many when the opening of the Klondike Highway caused the end of the riverboats, and as a result, the demise of many Yukon River communities, such as Fort Selkirk and Minto. The river went from being a community 450 miles long, to a quiet and lonesome waterway, returned for the most part to the bears, wolves and moose. To get a feeling for the size and power of these riverboats, you can tour the *S.S. Klondike* in Whitehorse. The *S.S. Keno* is currently being restored in Dawson City and will be open for tours in the future.

■ MODERN TIMES

After the gold rush, many communities settled into a quiet existence in comparison to the turn-of-the-century heyday. The gold rush had opened up the territory to other mining, which brought more development to the region. Strikes and smaller rushes continued on rivers and creeks throughout Alaska and the Yukon. Gold was discovered in the Mayo region in 1902, and the rich silver and galena deposits near Keno in 1919. Regular silver operations were carried out in the region from the 1930s to 1980s, with the community of Mayo serving as a major transportation centre. As mining technology improved, the Klondike region continued to produce significant quantities of gold for several decades. Dredges operated on the creeks in the Klondike until the 1960s.

The outbreak of World War Two brought more development and access to the Yukon with the construction of the Alaska Highway. After the bombing of Pearl Harbour in December 1941, the U.S. felt vulnerable to an attack on Alaska by Japan. Constructed between March 9 and October 25, 1942, the Alaska Highway was built to allow overland access to the north for defence. The route, selected in a hurried fashion, followed an existing line of airfields from Edmonton to Fairbanks, called the Northwest Staging Route, also using existing winter roads, First Nation trails, rivers and "sight" engineering. The highway was built through a cooperative agreement between the two countries. Canada furnished the highway right-of-way, waived import duties, sales taxes, income taxes and immigration regulations, and provided construction materials. The United States paid for the construction and agreed to turn over the Canadian portion after the war. The highway went

Dredge No. 4 National Historic Site can be viewed on Bonanza Creek, near Dawson.

from Dawson Creek, British Columbia to Delta Junction, Alaska, a total of 1,390 miles, or 2,237 kilometres.

The Alaska Highway was originally only accessible to the military. The opening of the highway to the public in 1947 did probably as much for shaping the future of the Yukon as did the Klondike gold rush, setting the stage for the next 50 years of development. Transportation corridors changed from rivers to roads, allowing better access to some mineral-rich areas that had no access before.

Mining had a boom with the development of the Faro mine. Silver and zinc deposits found in the area prompted development of the mine and resulting townsite in 1969. This provided a temporary boom to the Yukon economy. However, the transportation and infrastructure required,

Modern day gold mining is more sophisticated than 100 years ago.

as well as taxes paid to the territory, helped the struggling northern economy. After the mine's closure in 1982, the WP&YR railway was forced to close, and a depression hit the territory that lasted for several years. After opening again in 1986, the Yukon economy began to rebound. The mine has continued its boom and bust routine since that time, most recently closing in 1997.

Today, the northern economy is primarily based on government, tourism, mining and lumber. Tourists come in great numbers to travel the Alaska Highway and other highways such as the Top of the World and the Klondike Loop. The WP&YR railway has re-established itself as far north as Bennett, due to a growing demand from tourism. Mining of gold, silver, copper and other resources continues in the north. Unfortunately, the dependence on world prices for metals and minerals causes the mining industry to be quite cyclical. Lumber industry is restricted to the southern areas of the region due to poor access, low timber productivity and minimal species values in the north.

■ PROTECTION

Despite its significance as a natural, historical and recreational corridor, not much of the Klondike gold rush route is actually protected by park or other status. Of the entire 934 kilometres, only 103 kilometres of the route has been given any form of protection. Although there have been proposals to protect the complete Klondike Trail, no movement has yet come through to make it a reality. The logistics of such an undertaking would be quite complex.

As it stands, three sections of the route have some form of protection. The Chilkoot Trail is protected on the American side by the Klondike Gold Rush National Historic Park, and on the Canadian side by the Chilkoot Trail National Historic Park. The third section that has been given a degree of protected status is The Thirty Mile, which has been designated a Canadian Heritage River. Although this does not in itself provide protection for the waterway, it provides a framework for management, and formally recognizes its importance, hopefully resulting in more comprehensive and conservation-based management of the river.

The National Park Service (NPS) has a full-time presence in Skagway at the Klondike Gold Rush National Historic Park Visitor Centre at Broadway and 2nd Avenue. NPS staff also have a part-time presence at the Parks Canada Trail Centre across the street. Park rangers and interpretive staff are located above Sheep Camp along the trail. Parks Canada, in addition to running the trail centre in Skagway, has a presence at the Chilkoot summit and at the Lindeman campground. Also designated as historical sites are the *S.S. Klondike* in Whitehorse and the *S.S. Keno*, Dredge No. 4 and 37 buildings in Dawson City.

Bruce Bennett

5

THEN & NOW

Wolf track and human track come close.

Peter Long

Swans over the Yukon River.

5

THEN & NOW

CHAPTER 6...ROCKS, RABBITS & RAINFOREST

*A*laska and the Yukon comprise a vast, astounding wilderness that is rich in natural wonders. Many travellers have outdoor pursuits that they enjoy, that enhance their experience of a place. These include rock hounding, birding, wildflower identification, wildlife photography or fishing. An understanding of the natural world can deepen your appreciation of the region through which you are travelling, and give you perspective on your place within it. This chapter provides a general overview of the geology, flora and fauna surrounding you as you travel through this great northern land.

Fireweed, the official territorial flower, is widespread in the Yukon.

In following this great route through the northwestern corner of North America, you will travel through an immense land shaped by amazing events. Over the 934 kilometres, you will pass through several very distinct environments, each with its own characteristics. Variations in geological and climate history have left each zone with different topography, geology and vegetative environment. These factors then create different habitats, influencing the diversity and type of life in each place.

For the purposes of categorizing the natural world in the region, I have divided the route into four environmental zones. The first, from the coast to about 900 metres elevation (between Sheep Camp and the Scales), is the coastal rainforest. The second and smallest, which reaches from the rainforest to between Happy Camp and Deep Lake Camp, is the alpine. From there to Bennett Lake is the subalpine boreal forest. Then the largest zone, from Bennett Lake through to Dawson City is the northern boreal forest.

This chapter describes the natural world in a way that is easy for travellers to reference as you journey along the trail and down the river.

The flats by Dyea have risen out of the sea by 1.3 metres since the gold rush.

Climate

The coastal rainforest, along the trail from tidewater to north of Sheep Camp, is typified by a wet, maritime environment. Generally, summers are cool and winters mild, but temperatures and rainfall are greatly influenced by elevation and distance inland. Along the coast, summers tend to be long and cool, although some days can be quite warm and pleasant; the locals count on it! Winters are very wet and short, with most of the precipitation falling as snow between November and March. At higher elevations, the winters are longer, with snow falling to great depths over the season. Although hikers may not feel it due to the thick forest cover, the winds blow heavily up the valley for much of the summer.

Vegetation

Due to the high amounts of rainfall, the coastal rainforest is lush and productive. Before the gold rush, the valley bottom would have been rich with old growth western hemlock, western red cedar and mixed spruce. Since the valley was denuded during the gold rush, this area is primarily second growth alder, cottonwood, aspen, western hemlock and Sitka spruce. The higher regions of this zone comprise mostly mountain hemlock, subalpine fir and amabilis fir. Understory plants that you will see along the trail include devils club, salmonberry, ferns, lichen, mosses and a huge variety of interesting mushrooms and fungi. Watch out for sharp spines on the stems and undersides of the large leaves of devil's club.

Evidence of why the stampeders had such a rough time of it in the coastal rainforest zone.

6

ROCKS, RABBITS & RAINFOREST

Devil's club in bloom. Watch yourself around this plant! It's the bane of hikers.

Mammals

Mammals are quite common in this bountiful forest, but your chances of seeing wildlife are reduced by the popularity of the trail for humans, the thickness of the forest and the shy nature of the wildlife. The best times to see most wildlife are generally dawn and dusk, which can last quite some time this far north.

Black bear is probably the most common large animal, with mountain goats, coyote and lynx being seen less often. Mountain goats are quite rare, but may be seen in the higher regions of this zone. Black bears are especially abundant near the creeks in the fall during fish spawning. The lynx is rarely seen, but keep your eyes peeled for its tracks. The lynx is primarily nocturnal, saving its energy by sleeping during the day for its pursuit of the snowshoe hare at night. The hare usually spends its days hiding under a log or in a burrow. Small mammals that you may see in or near the rushing water include river otter, mink, marten and weasel. The red squirrel and deer mouse are common in the campgrounds, looking for wayward crumbs. Porcupines tend to spend quite a bit of their time up in trees. And bats are most likely seen flying around after insects for a short period at dusk.

Birds

The diversity of bird life in the Taiya Valley is quite incredible. Due to its proximity to the coast, there are both coastal and interior species, plus a huge variety of migrating birds during the shoulder seasons. Near the shore you can see goldeneyes, terns and great blue herons. Along the rushing rivers, you might spy bald eagles roosting, harlequins swimming the rapids, and the little brown dipper bobbing in the shallows. In the forest, the Rufous hummingbird is sometimes seen, and you may hear the deep hooting of the blue grouse, or the drumming of the male ruffed grouse.

Fish

The four primary fish species found in the Taiya River and its tributaries are the pink and chum salmon, the Dolly Varden and eulachon. Salmon are an important commercial fish, although not on this river since it is within a park. The pink salmon typically spawn in July and August. The chum spawn from July to October. The eulachon, a small oily fish, has long been an important resource for the Tlingits. The Dolly Varden is a popular game fish.

If you want to fish within Alaska, you require a fishing license from the state. This can be obtained at several retailers in Skagway.

Amphibians

There are three species of amphibians found in this zone. These include the wood frog, the Columbia spotted frog and the boreal toad. All three of these are fairly well distributed along the coast, but considerably less common in the interior. Amphibians are an indicator species, since they are very sensitive to pollution and other environmental changes. Many amphibians worldwide have been mysteriously on the decline in recent years; a worrisome trend.

Insects

Biting insects are generally not too much of a problem in this environmental zone, although midges and no-see-ums can be irksome in some years. Although they can be bothersome in the depths of the rainforest, they are nothing compared to what is found in the boreal forest.

Bruce Bennett

Spotted frog at Log Cabin.

6
ROCKS, RABBITS & RAINFOREST

Geology

This zone is contained within the Boundary Ranges of the Coast Mountains. This extremely rugged belt of mountains rises from the Pacific Ocean between Washington State and the northern end of the Alaskan Panhandle. The Boundary Ranges are among the most rugged and ice-covered sections of the Coast Mountains. Amazing forces have shaped this land, primarily tectonic and glacial.

This ridge of high mountains was formed as a result of the interaction of the oceanic and continental crusts. As pressure mounted between the two opposing crustal plates, the oceanic crust "subducted" or thrust under the continental crust. This action caused melting of the subducted crust, and the resulting magma rose as granodiorite batholiths or plutons. Much of this activity occurred in the mid-Cretaceous period, or between 125 and 90 million years ago.

Glacial action has added to the rugged appearance. Due to the weight of the massive ice sheets that once covered this area, the land is still experiencing glacial rebound. As a result, the land near the south end of the Chilkoot Trail at Dyea is rising by approximately 13 millimetres per year. Since the Klondike gold rush, the Dyea estuary is estimated to have risen 1.3 metres.

The rugged Coast Mountains fringe the Taiya River valley.

Climate

A very small part of the Klondike Trail is alpine, from The Long Hill to Deep Lake, but it is so unique that it warrants separate classification. Given the high elevation, the alpine is subject to severe weather, very short summers and long cold winters. Since this zone is adjacent to the coast, it also tends to be very wet, with 75 percent of its considerable precipitation falling as snow. Accumulations of five to 10 metres of snow at the pass are not uncommon. The ground is usually snow covered between mid-September and early July. Because the summers are cool and short, snow may lie near the pass throughout this period, only to be covered by fresh snow the following winter. Therefore, avalanche hazard can be high, even in the summer. Generally in summer, cloud and rain are the norm, making the chance of seeing sunshine on the pass quite slim. Winds tend to be very strong over the pass. In summer, low pressure systems coming in from the coast are in contrast to generally high pressures deeper in the interior. This imbalance draws air rapidly from the coast to the interior, funnelling it through the passes such as the Chilkoot.

Vegetation

The main thing you will notice when you enter this zone is that there are no trees. At least there are no obvious trees as most people are used to. But aside from stunted subalpine fir you will see on the borders of the zone, such as near the Long Hill and Happy Camp, there actually are shrub birch and dwarf willow, which grow very close to the ground to take advantage of the warmer microclimate there. And despite the desolate look of the alpine, there is an abundance of

Snow patches can lie near Chilkoot Pass throughout the year.

Cotton grass.

plant life. Many varieties of heaths, lichens, mosses, herbs, sedges and grasses abound. Over 100 species of wildflower bloom during the summer months, including paintbrush, lupine, wintergreen, anemone, fireweed, grass of Parnassus, Labrador tea and mountain avens. Despite the short growing season, those plants that can survive here have done so by being very productive in that short period of growing time. However, since the climate is so harsh, and it takes a long time for these plants to establish themselves, this is a very sensitive habitat. Please stay on trails while in the alpine zone.

GEOLOGICAL TIME SCALE

It is amazing to think of the span of time over which this landscape has developed. To classify various stages of evolution of the earth and its creatures, geologists have developed the Geological Time Scale.

The time since the earth was created (it is commonly believed that the earth is four to five billion years old) is divided into eras, and within each era, periods. This time scale, though useful to geologists, does not help us to visualize the length of time during which there has been life in comparison to the length of the earth's history. One simple way to imagine this is to stand with your arms outstretched to the sides. Imagine that the distance between your left and right fingertips represents the 4.5 billion years of the earth's history. Consider your left fingertips to be the beginning of earth. The Precambrian era, from your left hand all the way to your right wrist, denotes the vast time period before 600 million years ago, before life began on earth.

The next era is the Paleozoic era, meaning "old life," from 600 million to 230 million years ago. This era spans from your right wrist to the base of the fingers on the right hand. Beginning with the appearance of abundant and complex life, fish, land vertebrates and reptiles were formed during this time.

Next is the Mesozoic era, meaning "middle life," from 230 million to 65 million years ago (between the base of your fingers to the last knuckle on your right hand). Reptiles were dominant on land, and dinosaurs evolved and became extinct.

Finally, we have the Cenozoic era, meaning "new life," spanning 65 million years ago to the present, the last inch of your right fingers. During this era, life was very much as we know it now. Human life takes up only the last three million years, which could be wiped away with the swipe of a nail file. Feel small?! I do!

Arctic ground squirrel.

Mammals

At one time, several large mammal species thrived in the mountains near the Chilkoot Pass. These included caribou, mountain goat and Dall sheep. Today, you can count yourself lucky if you see any large animals here. Some mountain goats winter here. Few caribou, moose and coyote have been spotted. Dall sheep are very rare. However, small mammals are abundant, including the arctic ground squirrel, hoary marmot and pikas. Look and listen for marmots and pikas in rocky talus slopes. Marmots use a loud, high-pitched whistle to warn of potential danger, leading to their nickname of whistlers. Pikas make short high peeps.

Birds

The two bird species you are most likely to see are the white-tailed and rock ptarmigans. Watch your footing so you don't step on a well disguised hen and her chicks. These birds are found in rocky alpine areas. Other birds you are likely to spot include water pipit (otherwise known as American pipit), Wilson's warbler, gyrfalcon, snow bunting, and golden-crowned sparrow.

Fish

No fish are known to inhabit the lakes above Moose Creek Canyon.

Amphibians

No amphibians are found in this harsh environment.

Insects

Due to the frequent winds and the open nature of the alpine, the nuisance of biting insects is minimal.

Geology

You have reached the high point of your journey here, the Chilkoot Pass. This area has been subject to the greatest concentration of tectonic forces, and as a result, is the highest and most rugged area of the Boundary Ranges.

This area has been subject to considerable glaciation, both continental and alpine. Of the two types of glaciation, alpine glaciers have, by far, had the most effect on the landscape you see here. Icefields and alpine glaciers, such as Irene Glacier high above the Taiya valley, build when the supply of ice and snow in the winter exceeds the rate at which it melts in the summer. After the melt, the remnants of the previous winter's snow becomes "firn." Firn is like dense, granular snow, weakly cemented together by ice. As subsequent layers form over the years, the pressure on the lower layers turns the firn to ice, thus building icefields. Once icefields are big enough, glaciers flow from the edges under the force of gravity, down mountain slopes and valleys. The movement of the glaciers breaks off the underlying rock and grinds it to fine glacial flour. This gives glacier rivers a silty look, and slower moving water and lakes their characteristic blue-green colour.

Alpine glaciers leave behind their visual legacy. Grooves and striations on the underlying rocks can be seen. Characteristic U-shaped valleys, such as the Taiya River valley, are sure signs of a previous valley glacier. As alpine glaciers recede, they often leave behind mounds of ground-up soil called moraine. The glaciers carve out such shapes as cirques (large bowl-shaped depressions formed at the head of the glaciers), arêtes (sharp ridges caused by glaciation on both sides) and nunataks (high rugged peaks). You will see examples of these as you pass through the alpine area.

The alpine zone, although it does not always appear so, supports an amazing variety of life.

Climate

The subalpine boreal forest zone, along the trail from Deep Lake to Bennett Lake, is typified by short warm summers and long cold winters. Compared to the zones you have come through, the weather here is quite dry, with approximately 380 to 760 millimetres of rain annually. Of this, about 25 to 50 percent falls as snow. Even so, snow accumulations of 2.5 metres are not uncommon in the higher and more southerly regions of the zone.

Vegetation

Vegetation varies considerably through this zone, which is a transition area between the harsh alpine and the more productive northern boreal forest. In the higher regions, growing conditions are quite marginal, while near the larger lakes, they are considerably more productive. Primary tree species include lodgepole pine, subalpine fir, and white and black spruce. Subalpine fir is found mostly in the upper regions of this zone. Lodgepole pine is quite abundant between Deep Lake and Bennett Lake. Because of the dry conditions, the forest is more open than that of the coast. Low areas have plentiful wetlands, where black cottonwood, trembling aspen and balsam poplar grow. Understory plants include a variety of berry bushes, such as bearberry, buffalo berry, blueberry, cranberry, saskatoon berry, strawberry and raspberry. Caribou lichen abounds on the forest floor.

6

ROCKS, RABBITS & RAINFOREST

A dry region of the subalpine boreal forest zone.

Mountain hemlock at Log Cabin.

Bruce Bennett

Mammals

The wetlands in this zone make good habitat for moose. Black bear, caribou and wolf also make this zone their home, although it is rare to see either caribou or wolf. Caribou are limited to a few remnant animals from the original massive herds, and wolf tend to be quite shy, knowing you are about long before you would ever know they were there. They are more likely to be heard than seen. Smaller animals in this zone include wolverine, porcupine, beaver, snowshoe hare, weasels, and the squirrels and mice that you may encounter in camp.

Birds

You may hear the ruffed grouse drumming as you hike down the trail through this subalpine zone. It is a haunting and magical sound that is almost felt more than heard. Other birds you are likely to see include golden eagles, common loons, ravens, magpies, robins, juncos, redpolls, crossbills, chickadees and the

A moose in the river.

Bruce Bennett

white-throated sparrow. Rufous hummingbirds are often seen at Lindeman.

Fish

The only fish found alongside the trail in this region reside in Lindeman Lake. Due to the high sediment load in the lake during the spring and summer months, productivity is low. Known species include round whitefish, lake whitefish, grayling, lake trout, burbot, northern pike and long-nose sucker. Please remember that no angling is allowed within Chilkoot Trail National Historic Park.

Amphibians

Three species of amphibian are known to inhabit the subalpine boreal forest. These are the same as those found in the coastal rainforest: the wood frog, the Columbia spotted frog

Grouse, master of camouflage.

and the boreal toad. Although the wood frog is found as far north as Old Crow, Yukon, the Columbia spotted frog and the boreal toad here are on the very northern edge of their range. These hardy creatures survive the winter by hibernating underground, under ponds or under leaf litter beneath a thick blanket of snow. You may hear the chorus of either the spotted frog or the wood frog in the spring.

Fresh Arctic grayling for supper; what a treat!

Skipper on arnica.

Insects

Well, say hello to your constant companion from here–on in. Likely, you have heard of the reputation of the northern biting insects long before your feet hit the soil here. The stampeders, having dealt with many adversities along the length of the trail, were introduced to a new one at Lindeman Lake. Mosquitoes!

The abundance and ferocity of the mosquitoes will depend on the time of your visit. If you picked late August or September to come, you will likely encounter only a few of these menaces. However, if you decided your top priority was long hours of daylight, then make sure you have good bug spray and bug shirts. The abundance of mosquitoes varies from year to year depending on water levels and other conditions; a drier year means fewer bugs.

Mushrooms for lunch, anyone? A rodent made a good meal of these mushrooms, but don't try it yourself!

A mushroom grows right out of a tree.

Geology

This zone is still entirely within the Boundary Ranges of the Coast Mountains. The mountains you see along Lindeman and Bennett lakes, although still craggy and spectacular, have a softer and more rounded look to them than those you see on the coast side of the pass. These peaks are cauldron-style volcanoes from the early Cretaceous period, between about 145 to 125 million years ago. The rocks of these volcanoes have been hardened by subsequent granitic intrusions. Glaciation has also played a big part in shaping these mountains.

The Boundary Ranges tower over Lindeman Lake.

CONTINENTAL GLACIATION

During the Pleistocene age (between 1.8 million and 11,000 years ago), the average temperatures were three to 10 degrees Celsius colder than they are now, leading to the advance of the great ice sheets that covered much of North America. In response to intervals of cooling and warming, the Cordilleran (covering the western continent) and the Laurentide (covering the main part of the continent) ice sheets in North America advanced and retreated at least six times, with huge effects on the underlying land. Much of what you see south of the Pelly River has been hugely impacted by these glaciers.

The effects of the great ice sheets on the landscape are varied and significant. The most obvious effect is the scoring, erosion and polishing of the underlying land by the movement of the ice sheets. Another common effect is the deposition of the soil, called till, that the glaciers created in their advances and retreats. Rivers flow-

ing away from glaciers leave thick expanses of gravel and silt. At times, ice sheets would dam rivers, creating large lakes. One such lake in southern Yukon was Glacial Lake Champagne. The pale silty cliffs and cutbanks near Whitehorse were laid down in Glacial Lake Champagne. But one of the most remarkable effects of the glaciation was the altered flow of many of the rivers of the Yukon.

Effects of glaciation are evident in much of the alpine zone.

BERINGIA

Beringia is a name given to a vast area in the northern Yukon, Alaska and northeastern Asia that was free of ice during the last great ice age, approximately 10,000 years ago, when most of North America and Europe were covered by massive ice sheets. The name is derived from the Bering land bridge that is believed to have existed during this time. The land bridge was created between Asia and North America when the vast amount of water locked up in the ice sheets lowered the sea level by up to 100 metres. The Klondike goldfields, nestled within the "U" made by the Klondike, Yukon and Indian rivers, were within the refuge of Beringia.

The land bridge allowed the migration of people and animals between the two continents. Many of the animals were different than those that roam the earth now. The habitat was also considerably different. Although the climate was still severe, the earth was covered in grasslands on which large herds of ancient animals grazed. It is believed the deposition of loess — fine silt blown from the outwashes of ancient glaciers — provided an abundance of nutrients to the soil, making the vegetation more lush than would otherwise be expected in such a harsh climate.

With the passing of the last ice age, conditions in Beringia changed dramatically. The climate warmed, causing the ice to melt, and the oceans to rise and cover the Bering land bridge. Precipitation increased, and what was once a lush grassland began to change into forested regions. The various species of animals at the time reacted differently to these changes depending on their habitat requirements and adaptability. Approximately 40 species became extinct, including animals such as the Jefferson's ground sloth, woolly mammoth, American mastodon, giant horse, dire wolf, North American short-faced bear, American lion, giant beaver, American Scimitar cat, Steppe bison and Alaskan camel. Others stayed and evolved into smaller cousins of the original giants; some moved to similar habitats elsewhere, while still others remained as they were.

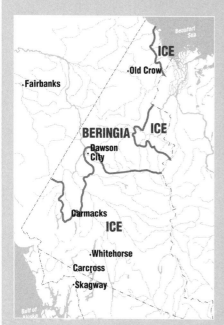

Maximum extent of ice during the latest ice age.

Amazingly enough, it was the Klondike gold rush that has brought us much of our knowledge of Beringia. The methods used during the gold rush to find gold — deep diggings into the permafrost — brought Beringia to light and uncovered many pieces to the Beringia puzzle. Miners today still recover ancient bones as they dig to reach gold-bearing gravel.

FOREST CYCLES

You will pass through several burn areas of different ages, including the Fox Lake fire of 1998 that burned to the shoreline at the north end of Lake Laberge. Although to the average person the thought of a forest fire or insect infestation causes an unpleasant feeling, these are natural and usually beneficial processes that keep forest and vegetation communities healthy. Other "healthy" disturbances include wind, drought and fungal attack. All these disturbances help regenerate forests and restore soil fertility. They just don't do much for short-term forest economics or scenic values.

The evolution of a forest involves many factors, relating to the type of disturbance, exposure, climate and so on. However, the typical cycle of a forest involves three stages. The first, which would occur after a full-scale disturbance, is a dominance of grasses and shrubs that thrive under sunny or full light conditions. As they die off annually, they provide valuable nutrient input to the soil. In the second phase, deciduous trees such as aspen, poplar and willow, need more nutrients than grasses and shrubs and begin to thrive. These grow taller and eventually shade the forest floor, changing the composition of the

understory. In the third and final phase, conifers such as the dominant spruce gradually take over. Under the canopy of the deciduous trees, these shade-tolerant species thrive until they dominate and shade the deciduous trees, causing them to die off. Since conifers like spruce slowly rob the soil of nutrients and deny the forest floor light and heat, mosses, fungi and lichens thrive. It could take several centuries to complete the cycle.

In the Yukon, fires burn most forests on average every 150 to 250 years. After each burn, the forest begins its cycle anew. However, where fires are more or less frequent, regeneration may take on a slightly different character. For instance, where forest fires hit with greater frequency, certain species may not have developed to an extent that allows them to regenerate easily. Certain species may be depleted under this circumstance.

As you will see on your travels, especially along certain stretches of the Yukon River, forest fires are a reality in the Yukon. Other disturbances, such as insect infestations and wind, tend to eliminate not entire stands of forest, but select the less healthy specimens within a forest. Regeneration occurs then on a smaller scale, creating a multi-age forest. This is just as important as regeneration by fire, which creates a single-age forest.

An old burn area ultimately creates a healthy forest.

NORTHERN BOREAL FOREST

By far, the northern boreal forest zone covers the largest part of the Klondike Trail, as it does much of northern Canada and Alaska. Basically the entire paddling portion of the route is within this northern zone. Although subtle changes occur as you head downriver and northward, much of the route you travel will be relatively similar.

Climate

The climate in the northern boreal forest varies between the north and south extremes of the region. However, generally the summers are very short but productive, due to long hours of daylight. You can expect to enjoy long hot sunny days as you paddle on the headwater lakes and down the river to Dawson. Winters are long and c-c-cold, with temperatures reaching down to among the lowest on the planet. Due to the mountainous terrain, the weather is quite unpredictable. The southern areas are moderated to some degree by low pressure systems or storms sneaking over the Coast Mountain barrier, which also makes the weather quite changeable. The northern areas, due to the longer hours of daylight and their distance from the coast, tend to have more extreme annual weather patterns. The weather here is a little more predictable than farther south, and travellers can count on clearer skies and warmer days in summer. In winter, temperatures can stay extremely low for long periods of time.

A typical forest of the northern boreal forest zone.

Vegetation

The northern boreal forest is primarily comprised of white and black spruce on rolling hills and plateaus, with aspen and sagewort grasslands on south-facing slopes. Paper birch grows in places where conditions are cool and wet. Burned areas, which are commonly seen along the river, encourage certain plant species, such as fireweed and lodgepole pine, to grow. The cones of the lodgepole pine activate with the high heat of a burn, and open to release seeds. Muskeg is also common, especially in areas of permafrost. Muskeg is recognizable by sparse, scrubby black spruce, sphagnum moss, sedge tussocks and lichens. Where permafrost underlies the muskeg, you will see what is referred to as a "drunken forest," where the spruce are leaning over in various directions (not in the same direction, as found in a blowdown).

Mammals

Given the harshness of the environment in the northern boreal forest, the biodiversity is quite amazing. The terrain offers a number of different types of habitats, such as mountain, bottomlands, fast-moving water and still water. Keep your eyes raised to higher regions for caribou, mountain goat, and Dall sheep; going on a mountain hike or using

(top) Strawberry blite can be found on sandy beaches. (middle) Fox tail is a common plant in the Yukon. (bottom) Wild crocus come early in the season.

binoculars will increase your chances of spotting one of these species. In the forested bottomlands along the river, you can expect to see moose and black bear. These are most common in the more remote stretch of the Yukon River between Minto and the White River. You will almost definitely see their tracks on sand bars in the river, along with the tracks of wolf and probably beaver. Other boreal forest dwellers, especially in or along the fringes of the river, include river otter, marten, snowshoe hare, lynx, mink and muskrat. Red squirrels will likely be seen at several of your campsites, looking for handouts. Evidence of beavers is abundant much of the way down the river — beaver lodges, beaver-chewed stumps and beaver mounds, small mounds of mud scented with castorium secreted by this creature. At dusk, in June through August, you may see the little brown bat flying around after insects.

A northern saying goes: "when fireweed goes to cotton, summer is forgotten."

Birds

Although there are literally hundreds of bird species that call this region home at some point in the year, there are some that you are more likely to see or hear as you travel along the Klondike Trail. For the most part, these are birds that prefer a habitat around moving water.

Several birds of prey can be spotted if you keep your eyes peeled overhead. You will likely see and hear bald eagles throughout your journey. Ospreys can sometimes be seen overhead looking for fish in the waters of the Yukon River. Peregrine falcons, although once very rare due to pesticide poisoning,

Beavers mark their territory with a "beaver mound," a pile of mud mixed with castorium, secreted by the anal gland.

Bald eagle surveys a campsite.

have been reestablishing themselves in the Yukon. A breeding colony is located on the bluffs shortly downstream of Minto. These birds are still endangered. Please give them a wide berth.

Other birds you may see on the river include the kingfisher, nighthawks, harlequins and mergansers. In camp, you will likely be visited by gray jays (also called camp robbers), known for their marauding skills. Starting in mid-August, multi-species flocks begin to gather, including warblers, sparrows and flycatchers.

It is unlikely you will catch any early northward migration activity, however, in late August and September, you will likely hear and see huge Vs of geese in the sky. If you happen to be at Marsh Lake in mid- to late April, you can witness migrating trumpeter and tundra swans stopped over for a rest and food at Swan Haven. If you happen to be near Dawson City in late September, you may see the lesser sandhill crane migration, with as many as 250,000 passing from Alaska on their way south down the Tintina Trench.

CYCLES OF NATURE — THE SNOWSHOE HARE

The snowshoe hare seems to be a trigger species to a natural cycle of population in the wilds of the north. The snowshoe hare has several predators, including the wolf, wolverine, coyote, goshawk and owl. But the most significant predator is the lynx, which has a diet that includes up to 75 percent hare. Generally, the prey and predator species populations build to a high point, at which time the snowshoe hare experiences a population crash. The trigger of this likely has to do with several factors, the most important being a limited food supply. This is followed by a crash of the predator species, especially the lynx. Other prey species are also affected as predators try to round out their food supply once hares become scarce. After a few starvation years, the populations begin to build and the cycle begins again. This cycle tends to be about 10 years long.

Fish

Fish are plentiful in the Yukon River system, especially in the clear headwater lakes and Lake Laberge. Twenty-eight species can be found within the watershed, many of them prime species for angling.

Three species of salmon spawn in the Yukon waters. Coho can only be found in the Porcupine River and downstream on the Yukon River, so you will not see any on this route. Chum is the most widely found salmon in the Yukon watershed, preferring to spawn from mid-August through October in major tributaries such as the Porcupine, White, Stewart, Pelly and Teslin rivers. Chinook, or King, prefer the freshwater lakes and quiet backwaters of the Yukon. To conserve salmon, sport fishing of salmon in the Yukon has been quite limited in recent years. Check for current rules and guidelines.

Freshwater species include Arctic grayling, lake trout, northern pike (or jackfish), whitefish, rainbow trout and burbot. These fish spend much of their time in frigid, unproductive lakes, resulting in slow growth and reproduction. This makes them highly susceptible to overfishing.

If you are interested in identifying species, check the fishing regulations or obtain a guide such as the *Peterson Field Guide to Freshwater Fishes*, by L.M. Page and B.M. Burr.

Amphibians

Aside from the Columbia spotted frog and the boreal toad, which are found only in the very south by Bennett Lake, the only amphibian found throughout the region is the wood frog. Found as far north as Old Crow, the wood frog uses glucose in its cells to lower its tolerance to freezing by about five degrees Celsius. This trait helps it survive while hibernating under forest litter and snow. It also has the fastest rate of development of any North American frog. If you are north of Carcross and hear a chorus of duck-like quacks, it is probably wood frogs.

Insects

If someone mentions the Yukon and bugs, what do you think of? Mosquitoes, the territorial bird, right? In reality, you have a lot more to worry about than mosquitoes: black flies, deer flies, horse flies and biting midges, to name a few. But much of the insect life in the north is perfectly harmless, and, as a matter of fact, can enhance your journey. Think of butterflies, caterpillars, dragonflies and iridescent beetles. Most of the species that have learned to thrive in this habitat do so very well and are extraordinarily abundant.

Geology

The northern boreal forest zone comprises most of the Yukon. Many geological events have shaped this land over the millennia, although the prevalent forces are plate tectonics and glaciation.

The Tintina Trench is a long, northwest-trending trough that is the northern continuation of the Rocky Mountain Trench in British Columbia. As shown in the map on the page 254, this trench passes just north of Dawson City, and is followed by the Pelly River for a portion of its length. This line approximates the boundary

INSECT LIFE IN THE NORTH

To survive in such a hostile climate, the insects living in this region have adapted in various ways to protect themselves. One form of winter survival involves selection of a winter habitat that suits the insect's needs. This may involve finding sheltered areas, such as under leaf litter and under snow, that buffer cold temperatures and sudden changes.

In contrast, some species choose exposed sites for overwintering, which allows them a jump start when warmer spring temperatures hit. Most of these species are either freezing-tolerant, or lay eggs that are. Some aquatic insects, such as mayflies, can survive in water deep enough that it does not freeze to the bottom.

A second category of winter survival is labelled microhabitat modification. This involves the formation of structures such as earthen cells, winter cocoons and galls. Galls are used by many insects living in temperate zones, and involve injecting hormones into trees, prompting the tree to grow in a way that provides a winter refuge for the insect.

A third category of cold-hardiness involves freezing and super-cooling. Some insects simply freeze. Other freezing-intolerant species lower their freezing or super-cooling temperatures to incredibly low temperatures. This is usually done through the synthesis of anti-freeze or cryoprotectant compounds, together with a process that removes agents from the cells that will freeze. Cryoprotectants include alcohols, carbohydrates and amino acids, of which glycerol is the most common.

The arctic environment has differences from more southern regions of the temperate zone. The most obvious is that the temperatures in summer and winter are much lower than areas to the south. Less obvious is the static nature of the arctic winter. In winter, low temperatures are sustained over long periods, and the temperature variations within each day are small due to the lack of solar energy. This may actually lead to a lower winter mortality rate than more southern climes that experience considerable freeze-thaw throughout the winter.

between two geological regions: Ancient North America, which lies northeast of the Tintina Trench and was formed in place, and the Accreted Terranes, which lie southwest of the Tintina Trench and were formed elsewhere and joined Ancient North America through tectonic forces. As a result, the land that underlies the Yukon River is based on rocks which were formed in an entirely different part of the world, then moved to their present location, after which further forces continued to shape the land. Ancient North America was built between one billion and 300 million years ago. The terranes joined the continent between 190 and 120 million years ago.

Since the formation of the continent, plate tectonic processes have continued. Uplifting of the crust and intrusions of granitic plutons (molten rock that subsequently cooled) near the "subduction" zone where the oceanic and continental plates meet have created the high ridge of the Coast and St. Elias mountains. Volcanic events have deposited formations such as the Miles Canyon and Fort Selkirk lavas and the White River Ash. A few sedimentary formations, such as the

The Tintina Trench east of Dawson City.

Tantalus Formation which hosts the coal deposits near Whitehorse and Carmacks, have been laid down. Faulting, such as along the Tintina Trench, which has seen at least 450 kilometres of lateral movement, and the Denali (or Shakwak) Fault, with 350 kilometres of lateral movement, have dramatically changed the landscape. Other processes have shaped the land, such as the erosive forces of climate and glaciation. The more coastal regions generally have younger rocks and have had more recent tectonic activity, and are therefore more topographically extreme, or rugged. The more interior regions, being composed of older rocks and having been uplifted earlier and to a lesser extent, have gentler topography.

As you travel down Bennett Lake, the rugged Boundary Ranges of the Coast Mountains quickly pass behind you. By Carcross, you have entered what is referred to as the Yukon Plateau, and you will remain in it until Dawson City. Although the word

A study of olivine basalt cliffs of Miles Canyon.

"plateau" conjures up images of flatlands, this very large region is quite mountainous in many places. The Yukon Plateau is divided into several secondary plateaus, as shown on the map below: the Teslin Plateau, which covers the area from Marsh Lake

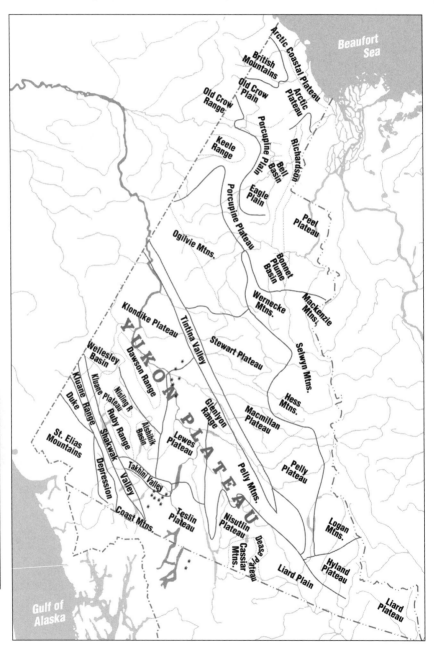

*Physiographic features of the Yukon. The * indicates sites where there has been volcanic activity.*

Whitehorse comglomerate.

to the south end of Lake Laberge; the Lewes Plateau from Lake Laberge to the Minto area; and the Klondike Plateau north to Dawson City.

The Yukon Plateau terrain is typified by high hills and gently sloping mountains, with most of the land above 1,400 metres of elevation. These plateaus are separated by broad valleys at about 600 to 700 metres in elevation. At the time of the last great ice age, the area was situated near the western extent of the Laurentide ice sheet and the eastern extent of the Cordilleran ice sheet. Large glaciers filled the valleys but left the higher elevations bare.

The clay cliffs near Whitehorse were laid down under Glacial Lake Champagne between 12,000 and 8,000 years ago.

■ FURTHER READING

Mammals

Peterson Field Guides — Mammals, by W.H. Burt and R.P. Grossenheider

Peterson Field Guides — Animal Tracks, by O.J. Murie

National Audubon Society Field Guide to North American Mammals,
    by John O. Whitaker, Jr.

Birds

Peterson Field Guides — Western Birds, by Roger Tory Peterson

National Audubon Society Field Guide to North American Birds — Western Region,
    by Miklos D.F. Udvardy

*The Birder's Handbook — A Field Guide to the Natural History of North American
    Birds*, by Paul R. Erhlich, David S. Dobkin and Darryl Wheye

Trees, shrubs and/or wildflowers

Wildflowers of the Yukon, Alaska and Northwestern Canada, by John G. Trelawny

Peterson Field Guides — Pacific States Wildflowers, by Niehous & Ripper

Peterson Field Guides — Rocky Mountain Wildflowers, by Craighead, Craighead
    & Davis

*National Audubon Society Field Guide to North American Wildflowers — Western
    Region*, by Richard Spellenberg

National Audubon Society Field Guide to North American Trees — Western Region,
    by Elbert L. Little

Trees, Shrubs and Flowers to know in British Columbia, by C.P. Lyons

Discovering Wild Plants, Alaska, Western Canada, the Northwest, by Janice J.
    Schofield

Newcomb's Wildflower Guide, by Lawrence Newcomb

Coastal Wildflowers of British Columbia and the Pacific Northwest, by
    Elizabeth H. Horn

Whitehorse & Area Hikes & Bikes, by Yukon Conservation Society

CHAPTER 7...REFERENCES

*T*his chapter contains contacts and details to help you plan your trip. Included are the following:

- gear checklist;
- local services;
  - transportation
  - outfitters
  - government services
  - emergency services
- references;
- glossary of terms; and
- index.

Relaxing at the end of a day of travel.

■ GEAR CHECKLIST

C = Canoeing only   O = Optional   B = Backpacking only

Clothing

___ 1 peaked sun hat
___ 1 brimmed rain hat or hood
___ 1 toque (warm hat)
___ 1 or 2 pair mittens
___ 1 wind shell (O)
___ 1 set rain gear (top and bottom)
___ 1 bug shirt (O)
___ 2 sets poly long underwear
___ 1 or 2 warm wool or poly tops
___ 1 turtleneck
___ 1 light long sleeved top
___ 2 light T-shirts
___ 1 to 2 pair warm pants
___ 1 pair light quick-dry pants
___ 1 pair quick-dry shorts
___ several pairs silk or poly underwear
___ several pairs poly or wool socks
___ 1 belt (O)
___ 1 pair "day" footwear
___ 1 pair "camp" footwear
___ 1 bandana (O)
___ 1 light towel (O)
___ 1 pair river gloves/pogies (C)
___ 1 pillowcase (O)

Camping

___ 3-4 season synthetic sleeping bag
___ sleeping bag liner (O,C)
___ sleeping mattress
___ ground sheet (O)
___ 3-4 season tent (with poles!)
___ repair stuff (duct tape, tools)
___ tarp
___ ropes for tarp and caching
___ camping saw (O,C)
___ full axe (O,C)
___ some form of chair (O,C)
___ clothes pegs (O)
___ leisure items (O)

Kitchen

___ plate, cup and bowl
___ eating and cooking utensils
___ washclothes and dishtowels
___ biodegradable soap
___ food
___ stove and fuel (1 litre/person/week)
___ grill (O,C)
___ nesting, lightweight pot set
___ coffee percolator or cone filter (O,C)
___ matches and/or lighter
___ garbage bags
___ extra plastic bags, elastics and tupperware (O)
___ small cutting board (O,C)

Travelling

___ canoe (don't laugh, even Bill Mason forgot his once!) (C)
___ paddles with spare (C)
___ PFD with knife and whistle (C)
___ painters, bailer and sponge (C)
___ karabiners
___ hiking staff (O,B)
___ water bottles
___ packs — canoe/backpack
___ maps and compass
___ throw bag or rescue rope (O,C)
___ bear spray and holster (O)

Personal

___ bug repellent
___ toilet paper, double waterproofed
___ water filter and spare parts
___ Swiss army knife
___ spade/trowel (C)
___ sunglasses
___ sunscreen for body and lips
___ camera gear with film, batteries (O)
___ binoculars (O)
___ first aid kit
___ flashlight and batteries
___ field guides (O)

■ LOCAL SERVICES

You will likely require the services of local outfitters to complete your trip, whether it is professionally guided or self-guided. There are plenty of service providers in the area, whether you need canoes, float planes, vehicles, gear rentals, bus or shuttle services.

To some extent, local service providers change from time to time. Some outfitters have been around for several decades; others come and go. We therefore recommend that when planning your trip to the Yukon and Alaska, you contact government tourism departments for the most up-to-date list. For air or ferry transportation to and from Whitehorse, your local travel agent is the best contact for current rates and carriers.

Transportation

Air

Air Canada flies scheduled jet service into Whitehorse via Vancouver, British Columbia, usually three times per day in the summer. Charter airlines from Europe and points in southern Canada often provide direct air service to Whitehorse. A travel agent can get you the most current options, schedules and rates.

If you are travelling the entire route from Dyea to Dawson and need to shuttle your ground transportation to Dawson, you may want to fly back to Whitehorse on a regional air carrier, such as Air North. It is unlikely you will need a float plane, unless you are accessing the Yukon River via a remote point, such as on one of the tributaries.

Ferry

• Alaska Marine Highway System
1591 Glacier Avenue, Juneau, Alaska 99801-1427
Phone: 1-800-642-0066, Fax: 907-277-4829
www.dot.state.ak.us/amhshome.html
Ferry service to Skagway, from Prince Rupert, British Columbia or Bellingham, Washington

• B.C. Ferries
1112 Fort Street, Victoria, British Columbia V8V 4V2
Phone: 250-386-3431
Phone: 1-888-223-3779 (within British Columbia), Fax: 250-381-5452
www.bcferries.bc.ca
Ferry service between Port Hardy and Prince Rupert (connects to Alaska Marine Highway)

Rail

(between Skagway and Fraser or Bennett at the end of the Chilkoot Trail)
• White Pass & Yukon Route Railway
P.O. Box 435, Department B, Skagway, Alaska 99840
Phone: 907-983-2217, 1-800-343-7373
Fax: 907-983-2734
info@whitepass.net, www.whitepassrailroad.com
Train from Bennett to Fraser or Skagway for hikers; bus/train between Whitehorse and Skagway. White Pass can also link you with a bus service to Whitehorse; may take canoes to Bennett.

7

REFERENCES

Bus

Bus service is not always the same from year to year. Here is a brief list that was in effect as this book went to press in early 2001. A number of the companies listed below also offer bus service to other locations you may wish to visit in the Yukon or Alaska.

• Between Skagway and Whitehorse
Alaska Direct 1-800-770-6652, 867-668-4833
Alaskon Express (Gray Line), 867-668-3225

• Between Whitehorse and Dawson
Dawson City Courier & Taxi, 867-393-3334

• To Whitehorse from the United States and southern Canada
Greyhound, 867-668-2223, 1-800-661-8747
Your local travel agent, or the CAA or AAA may be able to provide you with current bus schedules and assist with reservations.

Water taxi

Water taxis between Carcross and Bennett may not always be available. The best source for current water taxi services is Parks Canada at the Trail Centre. They can be found under Government services, below.

Trailhead shuttle

Shuttle service between Skagway and the Chilkoot trailhead near Dyea is usually available through private companies in Skagway. Contact the Skagway Convention and Visitors Bureau, found on page 262.

Commercial outfitters and guides

For those with little wilderness canoe trip experience, or those who would rather leave the logistics of trip organization to others, guided canoe, raft and kayak trips down sections of the Yukon River are possible through local outfitters. Available from many of these sources is also rental gear and shuttle services. For a current list, contact Tourism Yukon or the Skagway Convention and Visitors Bureau.

Government services

There are government services available to provide specific information about your trip, including the parks offices, tourism organizations, mapping outlets and international customs offices.

Parks and protection

• U.S. Parks Service — Skagway Unit
Klondike Gold Rush National Historical Park
Box 517, Skagway, Alaska 99840
Phone: 907-983-2921, Fax: 907-983-9249
KLGO_Ranger_Activities@nps.gov, www.nps.gov

Red fox pups.

• Parks Canada — Department of Canadian Heritage, Yukon District
205-300 Main Street, Whitehorse, Yukon Y1A 2B5
Phone: 867-667-3910, 1-800-661-0486

• Parks Canada Trail Centre (summer only)
Broadway & 2nd Avenue, Skagway, Alaska
Phone: 1-800-661-0486, 907-983-3655
Information on permit fees and reservations to hike the Chilkoot Trail.

• Canadian Heritage Rivers System
c/o Parks Canada
Ottawa, Ontario K1A 0M5
Phone: 819-994-2913, Fax: 819-997-0835
donald_gibson@pch.gc.ca, www.chrs.ca

• Yukon board member for Canadian Heritage Rivers System
c/o Parks and Outdoor Recreation Branch
Department of Renewable Resources, Yukon Government
Box 2703, Whitehorse, Yukon Y1A 2C6
Phone: 867-667-5261, Fax: 867-667-393-6223

Tourism information
• Alaska Division of Tourism
Box 110801, Juneau, Alaska 99811-0801
Phone: 907-465-2010, Fax: 907-586-8399
www.travelalaska.com, www.state.ak.us/tourism

7

REFERENCES

- Tourism Yukon, Yukon Government
Box 2703, Whitehorse, Yukon Y1A 2C6
Phone: 867-667-5340, Fax: 867-667-2634
info@touryukon.com, www.touryukon.com

- Skagway Convention and Visitors Bureau
Box 1025, Skagway, Alaska 99840
Phone: 1-888-762-1898, 907-983-2854, Fax: 907-983-3854

- Klondike Visitors Association
Box 389C, Dawson City, Yukon Y0B 1G0
Phone: 867-993-5575, Fax: 867-993-6415
KVA@Dawson.net

Customs

- Canada Customs — Fraser, British Columbia
open 24 hours
Phone: 867-821-4111

- Canada Customs — Whitehorse, Yukon
open Monday to Friday, 8:30 a.m. to 4:30 p.m.
Phone: 867-667-3943, 867-667-3944
www.ccra-adrc.gc.ca

- U.S. Customs – Skagway, Alaska
open daily, 6:00 a.m. to 12:00 midnight
Phone: 907-983-2325
www.customs.ustreas.gov

Maps

- Canada Maps Office
130 Bentley Street, Ottawa, Ontario K1A 0E9
Phone: 613-952-7000, 1-800-465-6277

- Geological Survey of Canada
Suite 101, 605 Robson Street, Vancouver, British Columbia V6B 5J3
Phone: 604-666-0271, Fax: 604-666-1337

- United States Geological Survey, Maps Office, Geophysical Institute
University of Alaska, Fairbanks
903 Koyukuk Drive, P.O. Box 757320, Fairbanks, Alaska 99775
Phone: 907-474-6960

Hunting and fishing information

- Alaska Department of Fish & Game
Box 25526, Juneau, Alaska 99802
Phone: 907-465-4180, Fax: 907-465-2772
www.state.ak.us/local/akpages/FISH.GAME/adfghome.htm
Information about fishing licenses and regulations in Alaska.

- Yukon Government, Department of Renewable Resources
Fish & Wildlife Branch
Box 2703, Whitehorse, Yukon Y1A 2C6
Phone: 867-667-5221, Fax: 867-667-2691
Information about fishing licenses and regulations in the Yukon.

Field Services Branch
Box 2703, Whitehorse, Yukon Y1A 2C6
Phone: 867-667-5221, Fax: 867-667-2691
Information about hunting licenses and regulations for the Yukon.

- Fisheries Management, British Columbia Ministry of Environment Lands and Parks
10470 152 Street, Surrey, BC
Phone: 604-582-5222
Information about fishing in British Columbia.

- Federal Firearms Office, Government of Canada
Phone: 867-667-5969
Canada.justice.gc.ca
Information about Canadian firearm regulations. Any gun must be declared at the Canadian border or any other point of entry.

Emergency services

In case of an emergency, there are several communication repeaters in the Yukon watershed which can be utilized by VHF radio. Coverage is spotty along the river. If you take a VHF radio, you will need to get the "receive" and "transmit" frequencies and channels for repeaters in the area, and have these pre-programmed into the phone. Repeater information can be obtained from the Northwestel operator or through the Yukon Amateur Radio Association, at 867-668-8400.

You should leave a detailed itinerary with a contact. The RCMP used to take itineraries, but now prefer that you leave one with someone you know. Your contact should know at which point to call for help, and should be given the appropriate emergency numbers.

The main medical facilities in the area are located in Skagway, Whitehorse, and Dawson City. Skagway has a medical clinic with a physician's assistant on duty. Whitehorse has a 24-hour general hospital, while Dawson City has a 24-hour clinic with physicians. Carcross and Carmacks have a nurse on call 24 hours a day.

Emergency numbers	RCMP	Medical
Carcross	867-821-5555	867-821-4444
Carmacks	867-863-5555	867-863-4444
Dawson City	867-993-5555	867-993-4444
Skagway	911	911, 907-983-2255
Whitehorse	911	911
Toll free for the Yukon	1-867-667-5555	1-867 667-3333

Reporting forest fires, 1-888-798-3473

7

REFERENCES

■ REFERENCES

Banfield, A.W., *The mammals of Canada;* University of Toronto Press, 1974

Berton, P., *Klondike — The last great gold rush 1896-1899;* Penguin Books, 1972

Burt, W.H. and R.P. Grossenheider, *Peterson field guides — mammals;* Houghton Mifflin Company, 1980

Canadian Recreational Canoe Association, *A canoeist manual for the promotion of environmental and ethical concerns*

Clark, L.J., *Lewis Clark's field guide to wild flowers of the mountains in the Pacific northwest;* Douglas and McIntyre, 1975

Coates, K.S. and W.R. Morrison *Land of the midnight sun — A history of the Yukon;* Hurtig Publishers, 1988

Coutts, R.C., *Yukon: places and names;* Grays Publishing Ltd., 1980

Hacking, N., *Captain William Moore — B.C.'s amazing frontiersman;* Heritage House Publishing Company Ltd., 1993

Herrero, S., *Bear attacks: their causes and avoidance;* Winchester Press, 1985

Kaiper, D. and N. Kaiper, *Tlingit — their art, culture and legends;* Hancock House Publishers, 1978

Karpes, A.C., *The Big Salmon River from Quiet Lake to the Yukon River;* Kugh Enterprises, 1995

Karpes, A.C., *Exploring the upper Yukon River — Part 1 — Whitehorse to Carmacks;* Kugh Enterprises, 1993

Karpes, A.C., *The Teslin River — Johnson's Crossing to Hootalinqua Yukon, Canada;* Kugh Enterprises, 1995

Karpes, A.C., *The Upper Yukon River — Carmacks to Dawson City, Yukon;* Kugh Enterprises, 1994

Krause, A., *The Tlingit Indians — The results of a trip to the northwest coast of America and the Bering Strait;* Douglas and McIntyre, 1956

LeLaguna, Frederica, *Tlingit;* pp. 203-228

Lyons, C.P., *Trees, shrubs and flowers to know in British Columbia;* J.M. Dent and Sons, 1954

Madsen K. and G. Wilson, *Rivers of the Yukon;* Primrose Publishing, 1990

Mason, B., *Path of the paddle;* Key Porter Books, 1980

Mason, B., *Song of the paddle — An illustrated guide to wilderness camping;* Key Porter Books, 1988

Ministry of Forests, *Bear aware student manual;* unpublished manual

Ministry of Forests, *Biogeoclimatic zones of British Columbia, 1992;* unpublished map

Morris Communications, *The milepost — all-the-north travel guide;* Morris Communications, 1999

Murie, O.J., *Peterson field guides — animal tracks;* Houghton Mifflin Company, 1982

Neering, R., *Continental dash — the Russian American telegraph;* Horsdal and Schubart, 1989

Neufeld, D.H. and Norris, F., *Chilkoot Trail — Heritage Route to the Klondike;* Lost Moose, the Yukon Publishers, 1996

Page, L.M. and B.M. Burr, *Peterson field guides — freshwater fishes;* Houghton Mufflin Company, 1991

Peterson, R.T., *Peterson Field Guides — Western Birds;* Houghton Mifflin Company, 1990

Rourke, M., *Pelly River;* Rivers North Publications, 1995

Rourke, M., *Yukon River — Marsh Lake to Dawson City;* Rivers North Publications, 1997

Satterfield, A., *Chilkoot Pass — A hiker's historical guide to the Klondike Gold Rush National Historical Park;* Alaska Northwest Books, 1983

Stedham, G., *Bush basics — a common sense guide to backwoods adventure;* Orca Book Publishers, 1997

Sturtevant, W.C. and J. Helm, *The handbook of North American Indians, volume 6, subarctic;* Smithsonian Institution, Washington, 1990

Sturtevant, W.C. and W. Suttles, *The handbook of North American Indians, volume 7, northwest coast;* Smithsonian Institution, Washington, 1990

Townsend, C., *The backpacker's handbook;* Ragged Mountain Press, Maine, 1997

Trelawny, J.G., *Wildflowers of the Yukon, Alaska and northwestern Canada;* Sono Nis Press, 1993

Twichell, H., *Northwest epic — the building of the Alaska Highway;* St. Martin's Press, 1992

Voss, J.S., *Stikine River — A guide to paddling the great river;* Rocky Mountain Books, 1998

Whitaker, J.O. Jr., *National Audubon Society field guide to North American mammals;* Alfred A. Knopf Inc., 1996

Yardley, J., *Yukon riverboat days;* Hancock House Publishers, 1996

British Columbia coastal mountains.

7

REFERENCES

▊ GLOSSARY OF TERMS

alpine .... an area of mountainous terrain above the timberline, generally with no upright trees, but often abundant plant life low to the ground

arête .... a knife-edged ridge caused by glaciation on both sides

barrel pack .... a container designed primarily for wilderness canoeing, generally with 30 or 60 litres of capacity, in which to carry gear and keep it relatively safe from bears

batholith .... a large pluton, or intrusion of magma, that has hardened

bear bangers .... when a threatening bear is present, a deployed bear banger sends a small projectile towards the bear, making a loud noise designed to scare it away

bear cache .... a place to store food and other items out of reach of bears

bear spray .... a pressurized container filled with a capsicum solution (from cayenne pepper) designed to be sprayed at a bear in the event of an attack

bench .... a raised flat area on top of a river bank

cheechako .... a person new to the north, a greenhorn

cirque .... a bowl- or amphitheatre-shaped depression, with steep sides and a headwall, formed in the side of a mountain at the top of a glacier

class .... the level of difficulty of a rapid, as defined by the International River Classification System

colours .... if prospectors see gold in their pans, it is referred to as "colours"

corduroy bridge .... a rough bridge built of poles

Windswept beach on Tagish Lake.

7

REFERENCES

crust.....................the hard layer of the earth's surface, which is divided into many plates, both oceanic and continental

cutbank................a bank of the river that is cut steeply into sediments due to the action of the river

DEET ....a chemical found in many insect repellents

eddy.....................in a flowing river, a relatively calm area of water behind an obstruction such as a rock

electrolytes...........essential components in the body which are lost through sweating

EPIRB..................Emergency Position Indicating Radio Beacon; a device which, when activated, sends a signal by satellite to alert rescue services and indicate the position of the device

fauna....................animal life of all types, including mammals, birds, invertebrates

ferry ....means of moving across the river, by paddling in an upstream direction and pointing the leading edge of the boat at an angle towards the far shore

flora.....................plant life

geology ....the study of the development of the earth's crust, its rocks and fossils

Giardia ....a cyst sometimes found in surface water which, when ingested, can cause Giardiasis, an uncomfortable intestinal condition, commonly known as "beaver fever"

glacial rebound.....the process by which the land rises or rebounds after the weight of continental ice sheets has disappeared

grade...................the level of difficulty of a river, as defined by the International River Classification System

gradient...............the steepness of a river, usually measured in vertical metres per horizontal kilometre (m/km)

hawser ....a rope or cable by which a ship is anchored or towed

HBC ....the Hudson's Bay Company, the oldest company in Canada, which established trading posts in Canada throughout the 18th and 19th centuries

heath...................open meadows and the plants that grow on them, such as heathers

lichens ....moss-like plants growing on rocks, soil, wood; actually a combination of algae and moss

magma................molten rock

7

REFERENCES

metamorphic........rocks which have changed in structure over time, due to intense pressure and/or heat

metamorphose.....to change in appearance, character or condition, such as a rapid from year to year, or in different flow conditions

microblades..........a type of tool used by ancient people in the Yukon, consisting of small, sharp stone blades placed into bone or antler handles

microclimate........a small area that has environmental characteristics differing from that around it; e.g. many alpine flowers create a "microclimate" within the petals that is warmer than the surrounding air

millennia..............in geological terms, thousands of years

moieties...............in native culture, society was divided into two halves, or moieties, which served to bring order and cooperation to their society; also known as clans

moraine................a mass of soil of mixed grain size (silt, sand, gravel) left behind by retreating glaciers

nunatak................a high rugged peak formed by alpine glaciation

painter..................a rope tied to the end of a canoe to assist in rescues, lining and docking

pepper spray........see bear spray

plate tectonics......the movement of the plates of the earth's crust, the resulting forces and formations

plateau.................an elevated area in which the summits commonly have gentler slopes than those of nearby incised valleys

pluton...................a mass of molten magma (hot, liquid rock) that has melted due to the friction of plates of the earth's crust

poly......................a general term to describe several synthetic materials, such as polypropylene and spun polyester, which wick moisture away from the skin

prevailing winds...due to the movement of the earth, winds most commonly come from the west; along the Alaska coast and inland, these west winds are also often forced somewhat north towards the interior

put-in...................the point at which your canoe journey begins, and the canoe is put in the water

raptors.................birds of prey, such as eagles, hawks, ospreys, falcons, vultures and harriers

riffles....................ripples in a river, caused by obstructions such as rocks and other debris

river left................the left bank or side of a river, when looking downstream

river right.............the right bank or side of a river, when looking downstream

7

KLONDIKE TRAIL: THE COMPLETE HIKING AND PADDLING GUIDE

scurvy .... a condition of weakness brought about by a lack of vitamin C

sedge .... a coarse grasslike plant growing in wet areas

sedimentary .... rocks which have been laid down in layers over the years, often as a result of particles settling out of an ancient water body

shuttle .... the movement of people and gear, usually between the end and the beginning of a route

sourdough .... a person who has experienced a Yukon winter

speeder .... a small, diesel-powered train car, commonly used for track maintenance, but in the case of WP&YR, used as a hiker shuttle between Bennett and Fraser

sweeper .... a tree that has fallen over the river, and is partially in the water, creating a hazard to paddlers

subalpine .... generally a transition zone between alpine and forested areas, with a harsh environment and resulting stunted tree growth

subduction .... the action of two plates of the earth's crust pushing towards each other, when one is pushed underneath the other

take-out .... the point at which your canoe journey ends and you take the canoe out of the water

Taylor & Drury ..... a company established in the Yukon during the Klondike gold rush that ultimately ran a series of trading and supply posts throughout the Yukon

tectonic .... relating to the movement of plates, or sections, of the earth's crust

telegraph line .... a wire that allows communication through the transmission of electrical impulses; the precursor to the modern telephone line

toque .... a warm, winter hat

tram .... a system to transport gear and/or people; along the Klondike trail these consisted of an aerial tramway suspended by overhead cables from Canyon City, Alaska to the Chilkoot summit, and a horse drawn tram on rudimentary rails from Canyon City, Yukon to Whitehorse

tributary .... a river or stream which enters a larger river

watershed .... the area of land which drains into a river

ways .... long wooden skidways placed perpendicular to the shoreline, on which steam boats were hauled out of the water for the winter

WP&YR .... the White Pass & Yukon Route, a railway company established in 1898

wrap .... the result of a boat hitting a rock or obstruction broadside and rolling upstream, where the force of the water on the inside of the boat folds the boat around the obstruction

7

REFERENCES

■ INDEX

Bold indicates map location. *Italic* indicates name of book or report.

A

Ab Mountain **156**
Accreted Terranes 252
Air Canada 259
air horn 32
Air North 259
air travel 7, 15, 16, 17, 19,
259
Aishihik Basin **254**
Alaska Department of Fish
& Game 262
Alaska Direct 260
Alaska Division of Tourism
261
Alaska Highway 7, 9, 10,
15, 16, 18, 84, 89, 90,
91, 98, **99**, 116, **168**,
169, 170, 171, 172,
225-226, 265
Alaska Marine Highway 7,
16, 49, 259
Alaska Railroad and
Transport Company 218
Alaskon Express 260
alder 231
Aleutian Islands 210
All-Canadian Route 116
allergies 30, 42
alpine 46, 69, 230, 230,
235-238, 239, 266, 268,
269
Alsek River **24**, 113, 129
American Automobile
Association (AAA) 21,
260
ammunition 213
amphibian 233, 237, 241,
251
Amtrak 16
Anchor Bar **177**
Anchorage 17
Ancient North America
252
anemone 236
Annie Lake 212
anti-freeze 252
Anvil Range 13
aqua socks 38
archeological sites 36,
208
Arctic Circle **24**
Arctic Coastal Plateau
254
Arctic grayling 26
Arctic Plateau **254**
arête 238, 266
arnica 242
artifacts 10, 36

Ashcroft 116, 217
aspen 231, 239, 246, 248
Athabasca River 217
Athapaskan 208, 210, 212,
214
Atlin 211
Atlin Lake 84
aurora borealis 21, 22, 128
Austins Creek **167, 168**
avalanche 21, 50, 217, 235
Axcell, Claudia 43

B

B.C. Ferries 16, 259
Babbage River **24**
*Backpacker's handbook,
The* 37, 265
bacon 32
Baker Creek **205**
Ballarat Creek 141, **196**,
197
Banfield, A.W. 264
Bare Loon Lake 46, 71,
72, 73, 75, 80, **160, 161**,
162
barrel pack 27, 41, 266
basalt 94, 95, 136, 253
bat 232, 249
batholith 266
Bayer's Woodyard 119,
179
beach **175**, 218, 248, 266
*Bear attacks: their causes
and avoidance* 33, 37,
264
Bear aware student manual
264
bear banger 32, 266
bear pole 57
bear spray 20, 29, 33, 266
bearberries 239
Beardslee, Captain 216
bears 25, 28, 29, 31-34,
37, 54, 57, 127, 139, 211,
224, 232, 240, 245, 249,
264, 266, 268
Beaufort Sea **24, 254**
beaver fever, see giardiasis
beavers 44, 92, 212, 214,
240, 245, 249, 267
Becker's Island 143, **199**,
200
beetles 251
Bell Basin **254**
Bell Creek **205**
Bell River 217
Bellinger's Slough 143,
199

Bellingham 16, 259
Bennett 8, 9, 10, 14, 17,
18, 19, 20, 45, 46, 50,
53, 57, 69, 70, 72, 74, 75,
76-79, **79**, 80, 81, 83,
85, 90, 112, **154, 161**,
162, 163, 212, 217, 219,
221, 226, 259, 269
Bennett Lake 25, 46, 48,
71, 72, 73, 75, 76, 81, 82,
83, 85, **161, 162, 163**,
164, 165, 219, 220, 230,
239, 241, 243, 251, 253
Bennett Range 83, 85,
163, 164
Bennett Station 76
Benson Creek **206**
Bering land bridge 211,
245
Bering Sea 117, 152
Bering Strait 3, 210, 264
Beringia 208, 245, **245**
Bernard, J 49
berries 211, 212, 239, *see
also specific berries*
berry picking 210, 212,
215
Berton, Pierre 26, 264
Best of Robert Service 26
Big Creek 135, **189, 190**
Big Eddy Woodyard
119-120, **180**
Big Fish Hook Rapids 137
Big Horn Crossing **188**
Big Salmon **154**, 180
Big Salmon Lake 121
Big Salmon Range 13
Big Salmon River 3, 8, 9,
12, 13, 23, 24, 48, 112,
116, 120-122, **180**, 216,
264
*Big Salmon River from
Quiet Lake to the Yukon
River, The* 121, 264
Big Salmon village 12, 13,
101, 119, 120-122, **180**
*Biogeoclimatic zones of
British Columbia* 264
birch 235, 248
*Birder's handbook – A field
guide to the natural
history of North American
birds, The* 256
birds 229, 232, 237, 240,
249-250, 256, 265, 267
birth certificates 20
bison 245
Biwell 39

Black Creek **192**
black bears, *see bears*
black flies 34, 251
black-tail deer 211
Blackstone River **24**
blankets 212, 214
blisters 37, 39
Blodgett, Astrid 43
blueberries 239
Bluefish Caves 208
boat wrecks 11, 12, **176**,
177, 183, 187, 206
boats 67, 68, 219-224,
265
boilers 58, 151
Bonanza Creek 2, 120,
146, 148, 150, 151, **206**,
217, 225
Bonnet Plume Basin **254**
Bonnet Plume River **24**
boots 38, 39
borders 14, 17, 19, 20,
158, 159, 164
boreal toad 233, 241, 251
Boronite City 134
Boundary Ranges 234,
238, 243, 253
Bove Island 86, 87, **166**
British Mountains **254**
British Yukon Navigation
Company 117
Brittania **154**, 196
Brittania Creek 127, 141,
195, 196
Brittania Island **196**
brook trout 26
Brute Mountain **164**
Bryant Creek **205, 206**
buffalo berry 239
bug hats 34
bug jackets 34
bugs 21, 22, 34, 139, 232,
233, 237, 242, 246, 249,
251, 252
burbot 108, 251
Burian family 142, 144
burn, *see forest fires*
Burr, B.M. 251, 264
Burt, W.H. 256, 264
bus travel 15, 16, 18, 260
Bush basics 37
*Bush basics — a common
sense guide to
backwoods adventure*
265
butterflies 251

C

cable crossing **172**, **177**
cache 25, 32, 266
California Gulch **206**
camel, Alaskan 245
Campbell, Robert 137, 138, 143, 147, 216
campfires 34, 35
camping 7, 10, 11, 12, 13, 19, 21, 25, 32, 34, 35, 44, 45, 153, **163**, **174**, **175**, 258, 264
Canada Maps Office 15, 262
Canadian Automobile Association (CAA) 21, 260
Canadian Heritage Rivers System 11, 227, 261
Canadian Recreational Canoe Association 35, 264
canoe rentals 7, 18
canoe sailing 8, 10, 81, 82-83
Canoeist manual for the promotion of environmental and ethical concerns, A 35. 264
canoes 8, 10, 17, 18, 19, 29, 40, 41, 42, 43, 44, 45, 47, 48, 81, 82-83, 259, 260, 264, 266, 268
Canyon (Grey) Mountain 92, **171**
Canyon and White Horse Tramway Company 94
Canyon City **154**
Canyon City (Alaska) 46, 53, 56, 57, 58, 69, **157**, 218, 221, 269
Canyon City (Yukon) 10, 90, 92, 93-95, **99**, **171**, 221, 269
Canyon Hotel and Saloon 94
Cape Horn **178**
Captain William Moore — B.C.'s amazing frontiersman 264
Carcross 9, 10, 18, 19, 43, 71, 74, 81, 83, 84, 85, 86, 151, **154**, **165**, 208, 211, 212, 223, **245**, 251, 253, 260, 263
Carcross Desert 85
Carcross/Tagish First Nation 80, 84, 88, 107, 208-**209**, 212-213
caribou 84, 141, 211, 212, 214, 215, 223, 237, 240, 248
Caribou Creek **169**, **205**

Caribou Hotel 84
Caribou Lake **169**
Caribou Mountain 85, **165**
Carlisle Creek **198**
Carmack, George 2, 126, 148, 216, 217
Carmacks 8, 9, 12, 14, 21, 23, **24**, 25, 43, 45, 101, 109, 116, 120, 121, 123, 124, 125-129, **154**, **185**, 208, 214, 223, 224, **245**, 253, 263, 264
Carmacks Visitor Centre 126
Carpenter's Slough **190**
Casca Reef 114, **177**
Cassiar Bar 120, **180**, 216
Cassiar Mountains **254**
cat trail **187**
caterpillars 251
cedar 56, 231
cell phone 36
cemeteries 25, 49, 71, **155**, **156**
Cenozoic era 236
Chadburn Lake **171**
Champagne and Aishihik First Nations **209**
Charlie, Tagish 2, 216
Chechako Hill 150
cheechako 3, 266
chickadees 240
Chilkat River 211
Chilkat Tlingit 211-212, 213, 216
Chilkat Trail 217
Chilkoot Pass 3, 14, 18, 21, 22, 66, 76, 103, **154**, **159**, 210, 217, 221, 235, 238, 265
Chilkoot Pass — A hiker's historical guide to the Klondike Gold Rush National Historical Park 265
Chilkoot Railroad and Transport Company 69, 218
Chilkoot Trail 2, 7, 8, 9, 10, 14, 17, 19, 20, 21, 25, 26, 28, 34, 36, 45, 46, 53-80, **155-162**, 207, 208, 211, 216, 218, 219, 227, 234, 261, 264
Chilkoot Trail National Historic Park 227
Chilkoot Trail National Historic Site 241
Chilkoot Trail — heritage route to the Klondike 26, 264
Chisana Gold Rush 141, 143

chlorine 28
Chris Creek **201**
cinder cones 95, 136
Cinder Cone (Ne Ch'e Ddhawa) **191**
Circle 152
cirque 238, 266
citizenship cards 20
citronella 34
Claim 33 150
Claire Creek **182**
clams 212
Clark, L.J. 264
clay cliffs 92
Clear Creek **206**
climate 21-23, 25, 35, 36, 53, 63, 70, 71, 230, 231, 235, 236, 239, 245, 247, 252, 253
clothing 38, 208, 215, 258
coal 253
Coal River **24**
Coast Mountains 10, 69, 81, 83, 234, 243, 247, 252, 253, 254, 265
Coastal rainforest zone 46, 56, 230-234, 241
Coastal wildflowers of British Columbia and the Pacific northwest 256
Coates, K.S. 264
Coffee Creek 127, 141, **154**, **197**
cold 10, 11, 23, 29, 39, 41, 46
Coltsfoot Creek 70, 71, **159**
Columbia Slough 101, 124, **154**, **184**
Columbia spotted frog 233, 241, 251
communication 36, 37
Compeed 39
Continental dash — the Russian American telegraph 264
Cooke, Diane 43
cooking 25, 32, 34, 35, 42, 43, 44
copper 208, 214
Copper King 102
Cordilleran ice sheet 244, 255
corduroy bridge 266
cotton grass 236
cottonwood 231, 239
Council of Yukon First Nations 114
Coutts, Robert 135, 264
Cowley Creek **171**
coyotes 237, 250
Craighead, Craighead & Davis 256

cranberries 239
Crater Lake 69, 70, **159**
Crawford Island 115, **178**
Crawford, Jack 115
Crawfordsville 115
Cremation of Sam McGee, The 26, 108
Cretaceous period 243
Cripple Creek **194**
Cripple Gulch **206**
crocus 248
crossbills 240
Crossing Creek **187**
Croucher Creek **172**
Crow clan 213, 214
cruise ships 18, 49
currents 10, 11, 21, 23, 47, 220
customs 17, 19, 20, 88, 262
cut-off trail 46, 53, 74, 80, **154**, **161**, **162**
cutthroat 26

D

Dall sheep 145, **201**, 211, 212, 213, 214, 237, 248
Dalton Highway 152
Dalton's Trail 217
Dan Johnson Lake 72, **160**, **161**, **162**
Dan Man Creek **198**
dancing 212, 213
Darling, Linda 43
Davis Point 119, **178**, **179**
Dawson City 2, 3, 4, 8, 9, 12, 13, 14, 15, 17, 18, 19, 21, 22, 23, **24**, 25, 30, 45, 76, 90, 102, 112, 127, 133, 147-149, 150-152, 153, **154**, **206**, 208, 215, 220, 221, 223, 224, 225, 230, 247, 249, 251, 253, 259, 260, 262, 263, 264, 265
Dawson City Courier & Taxi 260
Dawson Creek 15, 16, 226
Dawson Range 12, 128, 139, 141, **195**, **196**, **198**, **199**, 254
Dawson, George 87, 108, 129
Dead Man Island 145, **201**, **202**
Deadwood Creek **206**
Dease Plateau **254**
Deep Creek 11, 109, **174**
Deep Lake 46, 69, 71, 73, **160**, 230, 235, 239
deer flies 251
Deer River 147
DEET 34, 267

7

REFERENCES

Delta Junction 226
Denali Fault 253
Dennis Point **163**
Department of Indian
    Affairs and Northern
    Development 114
Devil's Crossing **190**
devils club 231
Dewey Creek **155**
Dezadeash River 113, 129
Dezadeash Valley 104
Dion Creek **206**
dipper 232
Discovering wild plants,
    Alaska, Western Canada,
    the northwest 256
Discovery claim 151
Dobkin, David S. 256
Dobrowolsky, Helene 26
Dog Island **206**
dogs 32
Dolly Varden 26, 233
Domville Creek 114, **177**
Donahue Creek **199**
Donjek River **24**
dragonflies 251
dredges **181**, **206**, 225,
    227
drought 246
drunken forest 140, 248
dry bags 41
Dry it-you'll like it 43
Dubbin 39
Duchess 84
duct tape 41
Duke Depression **254**
Dundalk Creek **164**
Dundalk Mountain **164**
dunes 75
Dutch Bluff 101, **154**, **181**
Dyea 2, 3, 7, 8, 9, 10, 14,
    17, 18, 19, 21, 30, 45,
    46, 50, **51**, 53, 54, 56,
    57, 153, **154**, **155**, **156**,
    218, 221, 230, 234, 259,
    260
Dyea campground 56
Dyea Point **155**
Dyea Road **155**, **156**
Dyea-Klondike
    Transportation Company
    218

E

Eagle 152
Eagle Plain **254**
Eagle River **24**
Eagle's Nest Bluff 124,
    132, **183**, **184**
eagles 90, 102, 211, 213,
    240, 249, 250, 268
Edmonton 7, 15, 217, 225
Egg Island 103, **173**

Ehlich, Paul R. 256
Elbow Creek **169**
Elbow Lake **169**
Eldorado Creek 2, 146,
    151, 217
Elsa 144
emergencies 27, 28, 29,
    30, 36, 37, 257, 263
Ensley Creek **204**, **205**
environment 230, 231,
    233, 246, 252
EPIRB 36, 267
Erickson's Woodyard 122,
    181
Ete Oho **191**
eulachon 211, 212, 233
Examiner Gulch **206**
Excelsior Creek 127, **154**,
    196, **201**
explorers 3, 210
Exploring the upper Yukon
    River — Part 1 —
    Whitehorse to Carmacks
    264

F

Fairbanks 15, 17, 152, 225,
    245, 262
falcon 237, 249, 268
Falconer Gulch **206**
fall 21, 22, 22, 214, 215
Faro 13, 137, 226
ferns 231
ferries 7, 15, 16, **206**, 259,
    267
Field Services Branch 263
50 Mile, The 90
Finnegan's Point 46, 56,
    157
fir 56, 70, 71, 231, 235,
    239
firearms 20, 213, 263
Fireman Gulch **206**
fireweed 22, 120, 229,
    236, 248
firn 238
first aid 28, 39
First Nation of Nacho Nyak
    Dun **209**
First Nations 2, 4, 11, 12,
    25, 26, 49, 58, 80, 84,
    88, 103, 111, 114, 122,
    125, 126, 138, 139, 141,
    146, 147, 148, 207-208,
    209, 210-216, 221, 265,
    see also specific First
    Nations
Firth River **24**
fish 25-26, 32, 103, 211,
    212, 232, 233, 236, 237,
    241, 249, 251, 262, 263,
    264
fish ladder 97, **99**

fish oils 208, 213
Fisheries Management
    263
fishing 2, 25-26, 42, 108,
    111, 126, 210, 211, 212,
    213, 214, 215, 229, 233,
    241, 251, 262, 263
fishing licenses 25
Five Finger Mountain **186**
Five Finger Rapids 12, 21,
    47, 122, 125, 127, 129,
    130-132, **154**, **186**, 221
Five Fingers Coal
    Company 12, 125, 126,
    129, 129-130, **186**
Flanagan Slough **199**
fleece 40
Fleming, June 43
float planes 10, **99**, 259
flycatchers 249
fog 22, 70
food 27, 32, 42-43, 44, 65,
    85, 125, 142, 149, 211,
    224, 258
footwear 38-39
forest fires 6, 54, 120,
    134, 135, **176**, **177**, **180**,
    183, **199**, 246, 246, 248,
    263
Fort Reliance 145, **154**,
    206
Fort Selkirk 12, 13, 127,
    134, 135, 136, 137, 138,
    154, **191**, 207, 208, 209,
    214, 216, 217, 224, 252
Forty Mile 217
Fossil Point 110, **174**
fossils 87
Fourth Creek **206**
4th of July Bend 122, **181**
fox 261
Fox Lake 111, 246
fox tail 248
Frances River **24**
Frank Creek **178**
Fraser 16, 19, 20, 73, 80,
    259, 262, 269
Frenchman Lake 124
Frisco Creek **199**, **200**
frogs 232, 241, 251
fungi 56, 57, 231, 246
fur seal 211
furs 208, 210, 212, 213
Fyfe Creek **180**

G

Galena Creek 146, **204**
galls 252
Garner Creek **205**
Gatorade 42
gear 7, 17, 18, 27, 28, 29,
    37, 40, 258

Geological Survey of
    Canada 15, 262
geological time scale 236
geology 230, 234, 236,
    238, 243, 244, 245,
    251-255, 267
Geophysical Institute,
    University of Alaska,
    Fairbanks 128
George Black Ferry 147,
    149
giardiasis 28, 267
Glacial Lake Champagne
    92, 244, 255
glaciers and glaciation 23,
    50, 59, 230, 234, 238,
    243, 244, 245, 253, 255,
    266, 267, 268
glass beads 214
Glenlyon Range 137, **254**
Glenora 217
gloves 39, 40
glycerol 252
goats 211, 237, 248
Goddard Point 112, **176**
Goddard, A.J. 112
gold 2, 3, 49, **181**, 216,
    217, 221, 225
gold dredges 12, 102, 122,
    151
gold rush 1, 2, 4, 10, 26,
    49, 50, 148, 150, **150**,
    207, 210, 214, 216-225,
    226, 227, 230, 231, 234,
    245, 264, 265, 269
Gold Rush Cemetery **155**
Golden Horn Mountain 92
Golden Stairs 1, 2, 46, 62,
    63, 64, **158**, **159**, 217,
    219
goldeneye 232
Good food for camp & trail
    – all natural recipes for
    delicious meals outdoors
    43
goose 250
Gore-Tex 38, 39, 40
Gorp, glop and glue stew –
    favourite foods from 165
    outdoor experts 43
goshawk 249
Grady Mountain **182**
Granite Canyon 137
grass of Parnassus 236
grasses 236
gray jay 250
Gray Ridge **165**
grayling 213, 241, 251
Green Creek **199**
Grey Mountain, *see*
    Canyon Mountain
Grey Line 260
Greyhound 260

Greyling Creek **169**
grizzly bears, *see* bears
Grossenheider, R.P. 256, 264
ground sheets 44
grouse 233, 240, 241
Grubstake River 144
Guard Rail Point **163**
Gulf of Alaska 21, **24**, **254**
gyrfalcon 237

H

Hacking, N. 264
Haines 212
Haiyuk Mountains 152
Halfway Creek **197**
Han First Nation 138, 147, 207, 208, 215
Hancock Hills 101, 108, 110, 111, 112, **154**, **175**, **176**
Handbook of North American Indians, volume 7, northwest coast, The 265
Handbook of North American Indians, volume 6, subarctic, The 265
handwear 39-40
Happy Camp 46, 59, 61, 69, 70, 71, **159**, 230, 235
Happy Lapage Woodcamp **186**
Harbour seal 211
harlequin 232, 250
Harper, Arthur 138, 145
harriers 268
Hart River **24**
Harvey, Bruce 71
Hatch's Island 146, **206**
Hatch, George 146
hawks 268
headlights 16
headwater lakes 10, 14, 45, 63, 81-100, 92, **163-171**, 220, 247, 251
heath 267
heaths 236
Hell's Gate 127, 135, 136, **154**, **190**
Helm, J. 265
hemlock 56, 231, 240
Henderson Creek 145, **200**
Henderson Slough **200**
Henderson, Robert 129, 129
Hendrickson Slough **181**
herbs 236
Heritage Branch 94, 139
heron 232
Herrero, Stephen 33, 37, 264

herring 211
Hess Mountains **254**
Hess River **24**
hiking boots 38
Hodgins, Carol 43
Holbrook Creek **193**
Holman's Lake **168**
Homan River **161**, **163**
homesteads **189**, **192**, **193**
Hootalinqua 11, 12, 13, 101, 113, 114, 115, 116, 117, 118, **154**, **178**, 208, 214, 223, 264
Hootalinqua Island, *see* Shipyard Island
Hootchekoo Bluff **188**
Hootchekoo Creek 127, **154**, **188**
Horn, Elizabeth H. 256
horse flies 34, 251
horses 218, 219, 224, 245
Horsfall 141
Horsfall Hills **185**
Horsfall homestead 139
Hosford's Sawmill 54, **156**, **157**
hot springs 15
Hudson's Bay Company 137-139, 144, 216, 267
hummingbirds 57, 233, 241
Hunker Creek Road 151
hunting 2, 25-26, 42, 60, 111, 210, 211, 213, 214, 215, 262, 263
hydraulic mining 151
Hyland Plateau **254**
Hyland River **24**
hypothermia 29

I

ice 21, 22, 23, 76, 91, 107, 108, 117, 133, 140, 144, 146, 208, 220, 223, 224, 234, 238, 243, 244, 245, **245**, 255, 267
ice age 50, 208
immigration 20, 225
Imodium 44
Independence Creek **198**
Indian River 116, 127, 146, **154**, **204**
Ingersoll Islands 136, **190**
Inland Passage 7
Inland Tlingit 211
insects 21, 22, 34, 139, 232, 233, 237, 242, 246, 249, 251, 252
International River Classification System 47, 266, 267
interpretation 59, 71

iodine 28
Irene Glacier 55, 56, **157**, 238
Isaac Creek 127, 141, **154**, **195**
itinerary 29
lyon River 137

J

jackfish 251
Jackfish Bay 109, **174**
Jacob's Landing **189**
Jacobson, Don 43
Jim Boss Cutoff 103, **173**
Jim Creek **204**
Jim, Skookum 2, 216
Joe Creek 111
Joe Mountain 111
Johnson's Crossing 13, 116, 264
Johnston Island **177**
Judas Creek **168**
Judas Mountain **168**
juncos 240
Juneau 7, 17, 259, 261, 262

K

Kaiper, D. 264
Kaiper, N. 264
Kanoe People 97, 102
Karpes, A.C. (Gus) 116, 121, 264
Kaska First Nation 212
Keele Range **254**
Kellyville 130, **186**
Kenny Creek **168**
Keno 225
Keno Bend **179**, **180**
Ketchikan 3
King Solomon's Dome 146
kingfisher 250
Kinmount, Vikki 43
Kirkman **154**, 198
Kirkman Creek 127, 142, **198**
Kirkman Crossing **198**
Klondike 26
Klondike City 147, **206**
Klondike gold rush, *see* gold rush
Klondike Gold Rush National Historic Park 57, 227, 260, 265
Klondike Highway 9, 10, 11, 74, 85, 86, 103, 105, 123, 125, 127, 134, 135, 138, 139, 144, 148, **155**, **162**, **165**, **166**, **171**, **172**, **173**, **174**, **185**, **186**, **187**, **188**, **189**, **206**, 222, 224, 226
Klondike Hills **205**, **206**

Klondike Plateau 12, 104, 128, 254, **254**, 255
Klondike River 24, 145, 147, 148, 151, **206**, 215
Klondike valley 148, 150
Klondike Visitors Association 262
Klondike — The last great gold rush 1896-1899 264
Klondike, Yukon and Copper River Company 115
Kluane First Nation 209
Kluane Plateau **254**
Kluane Range **254**
Klutlan Glacier 106
Knob Creek **164**
Kokrines Hills 152
Koyukuk River 152
Krause, A. 264
Kuskokwim Mountains 152
Kwanlin Dun First Nation 208, **209**, 213, 214

L

Laberge Creek **173**
Labrador tea 236
Ladue, Joseph 145, 148
Lafrance Creek **178**
lagoons **172**
Lake Laberge 8, 9, 11, 21, 25, 46, 90, 91, 101, 102, 103, 105-114, 120, 153, **173**, **174**, **175**, **176**, 213, 214, 220, 224, 246, 251, 255
Lake Lebarge campground 9, 11, 108, 109, **174**
lake trout 26
Lakeview 123-124, **183**
lamp black 192
land claims 210
Land of the midnight sun — A history of the Yukon 264
Laurentide ice sheet 244, 255
Laurier Creek 112, **174**
lava 12
lava cliff **191**
Law of the Yukon 26
legends 212, 264
LeLaguna, Frederica 264
Lepage's woodyard **183**
Lewes Plateau 254, **254**, 255
Lewes River 44, 90, 137, **169**, **170**
Lewes River Bridge 9, 10, 90, 91, **154**, **170**

7

REFERENCES

Lewis Clark's field guide to wild flowers of the mountains in the Pacific northwest 264
Liard First Nation **209**
Liard Plain **254**
Liard Plateau **254**
Liard River **24**, 217
lichen 56, 57, 140, 213, 231, 236, 239, 246, 248, 267
life jackets 29, 29, 46, 132
Lightning Slough **191**
Lime Creek **166**
Lime Mountain 86, 87, 88, **166**
Lime Peak 11, 111
limestone 11
Lindeman 46, 48, 53, 69, 71, 72, **154**, **160**, 219, 221, 227
Lindeman Creek 71, 75, **159**, **160**, **161**, **162**
Lindeman Lake 48, 67, 71, 72, 75, **160**, **161**, **162**, 219, 241, 242, 243
Lindeman Rapids 71
Lindholm, Claudia 43
lions, American 245
litter 35
Little cookbook for the great outdoors, The 43
Little Fish Hook Rapids 137
Little Salmon **154**, 183
Little Salmon Lake 13
Little Salmon River 3, 8, 9, 12, 13, 24, 122-123, 124, **183**
Little Salmon village 9, 12, 13, 101, 109, 122-123, **183**
Little Salmon/Carmacks First Nation 125, 126, 208, **209**, 214
Little Takhini Creek 103, **172**
Little, Elbert L. 256
Livingstone 112
Livingstone Creek 116
Livingstone Trail 13, 112, **174**
locks 92, **170**
loess 245
Log Cabin 8, 9, 10, 19, 20, 57, 70, 74, 80, **154**, **162**, 212, 240
log jams 13, 47
Logan Mountains **254**
London, Jack 145
Long Hill, The 61, 62, **158**, 235

Long Lake 70, 71, **159**, **160**, 219
Long Lake Ridge 70, **160**
loons 125, 240
Los Angeles Creek **198**
Lousetown 147
Lovett Hill **206**
Lower Dewey Lake **155**
Lower Laberge 11, 101, 113, 114, **154**, **176**, 224
Lucky Joe Creek **202**
lumber 226
lupine 236
Lynn Canal 217
lynx 232, 249, 250
Lyons, C.P. 256, 264

M

M'Clintock Bay **169**
M'Clintock River 9, 10, 81, 89, **154**, **169**
Mackenzie Mountains **254**
Mackenzie River **24**, 217
Macmillan Plateau **254**
Macmillan River 13, **24**, 137
Madsen, Ken 144, 264
magpies 240
mail 224
mammals 232, 237, 240, 248-249, 256, 264, 265, 267
Mammals of Canada, The 264
mammoth 245
Mandanna Creek 124, **183**
Mandenhall, Ruth Dyar 43
Maniman, Gen 43
maple 56
maps and mapping **front of book**, 7, 9, 10, 11, 12, 14, 15, **24**, 25, 36, **51**, 44, **60**, **78-79**, **99**, **104**, **106**, **140**, **150**, **152**, 153, **154-206**, **209**, **245**, **254**, 262
marmot 237
marriage 211, 212
Marsh Lake 9, 10, 25, 46, 81, 88-90, 93, 107, **154**, **167**, **168**, **169**, 213, 250, 254-255, 265
Marsh Lake campground 9
Marsh Lake Control Structure 21, 90, 91-92, 224
Marsh Lake Outlet 10
Marsh, O.C. 88
Marshall's Ranch 141
marten 232, 249
Mascot Creek **195**
Mason Creek **179**
Mason's Landing 13, 116

Mason, Bill 37, 264
mastodon 245
Matthew Watson General Store 84
Mauer, Don 43
Maunoir Butte 114, **177**
mayflies 252
Mayo 214, 225
Mayo, Al 145
Mazie Creek 119, **179**
McCabe Creek 134, **188**, **189**
McClellan, Catharine 215
McConnell continental ice sheet 92
McDonald Creek **164**, **165**
McGregor Creek **187**, **188**
McIntyre Creek 102, **172**
McIntyre, Brenda 43
McKay's Roadhouse 133
McClintock, Sir Francis 89
McQuesten River 13, 144
McQuesten, Jack 139, 145
McRae 95, **171**
Mechem Creek **204**
merganser 250
Merrice Creek 134, **187**, **188**
Merrit Island **187**
Mesozoic era 236
Meziadin Junction 16
mice 44, 232, 240
microblade 126, 208, 268
midge 34, 232, 251
Midnight Dome 147, **206**
midnight sun 21
Milepost, The 16, 264
Miles Canyon 10, 47, 90, 93-96, 97, **99**, 112, **171**, 220-221, 252, 253, 259
Miles Canyon Road 97, **99**
Milhaven Bay **164**
military 226
Miller's Ridge **185**
Miller, C.J. 129
Miller, Dorcas S. 43
miners 4, 7, 245
Miners Range 11, 108
mining 4, 12, 84, 86, 88, 120-122, 125, 126, 128, 129-130, 134, 141-142, 143-144, 145, 146-148, 150-151, 210, 216-226
mink 232, 249
Minto 9, 12, 25, 106, 113, 120, 127, 134, 135, **154**, **189**, 208, 224, 249, 250, 255
Minto Hill **189**
Minto Resort 134
missionaries 216
moieties 211, 268

moleskin 39
Monkey Creek **168**, **169**
Montana Creek **205**
Montana Mountain 85, 86, **165**
Moore, William 49, 264
moose 127, 211, 212, 213, 214, 215, 224, 237, 240, 249
Moose Creek 71, 72, 73, **160**
Moose Creek Canyon 71
Mooseshide **206**
Mooseshide Creek **206**
Mooseshide Slide 146, 147, **206**
moraine 238, 268
Morrison, W.R. 264
Morrow Lake **159**
Morton, Keith 37
mosquitoes 34, 242, 251
moss 56, 57, 140, 213, 236, 246, 248, 267
Mount Cleveland **157**, **158**
Mount Clifford **156**
Mount Daoust **184**, **185**
Mount Gray 85, **165**
Mount Harvey 71, **160**, **161**
Mount Hoffman **158**
Mount Laurier 11, 111, 112
Mount Lewes 177
Mount Miller 129, **186**
Mount Milton **186**
Mount Monson 129, **185**
Mount Nansen Road **185**
Mount Yeatman 56, **156**, **157**
mountain avens 236
mountain goats 211, 232
Mountain Lake **160**
Mt. Stewart **199**
mud flats **173**
Mullins Creek **167**, **168**
Murie, O.J. 256, 264
Murray Creek 129, **186**
mushrooms 52, 56, 57, 231, 242, 243
muskeg 248
muskrat 249
Myer's Creek 129
Myer's Roadhouse **186**

N

Na-Chon-De 143
Nahku Bay **155**
Nares Lake 85, **165**
Nares Mountain **165**
Nares River 84, 85, **165**
Narrows **166**

National Audubon Society field guide to North American birds – western region 256
National Audubon Society field guide to North American mammals 265
National Audubon Society field guide to North American trees – western region 256
National Audubon Society field guide to North American wildflowers – western region 256
National Historic Site (Dawson) 148
National Park Service 26, 51, 53, 227, 260
Ne Ch'e Ddhawa 136, **191**
Neering, R. 264
Nelson Creek **155**
Neufeld, Dave 26, 264
Newcomb's wildflower guide 256
Newcomb, Lawrence 256
Niehous & Ripper 256
nighthawks 250
Nine Mile Creek **171, 172**
Nisling River **24, 254**
Nisutlin Plateau **254**
Nisutlin River **24**
No Name Creek **206**
NOLS cookery, The 43
Nordenskiold River **24**, 126, 129, **185**
Norris, Frank 26, 264
North Fork 121
North West Mounted Police 11, 12, 26, 64, 65, 67, 80, 84, 86, 88, 94, 103, 113, 117, 120, 126, 129, 133, 139, 145, 146, **167, 173, 180**, 218, 220
North, Dick 145
Northern boreal forest zone 230, 239, 247-255
Northern Canada Power Commission 92
northern pike 26
Northern Tutchone 117, 126, 133, 134, 138, 139, 141, 145, 146, 207-208, 214
Northwest epic — the building of the Alaska Highway 285
Northwest Staging Route 225
Northwest Territories 17
Northwestel 36, 263
Nourse River **157**
Nunatak 238, 268

O
Ogilvie Creek 113, **176**
Ogilvie Island 115, 145, **202**
Ogilvie Mountains 152, **254**
Ogilvie River **24**
Ogilvie Valley 113, **176**
OK Creek **206**
Old Braeburn Trail **176**
Old Crow 208, 241, **245**, 251
Old Crow Plain **254**
Old Crow Range **254**
Old Crow River **24**
Old Hootalinqua Village **178**
Old Stage Road **185, 186, 187, 191**
100 Mile Crossing 116
One Mile Rapids 48, **161**, 219
One Mile River 79
One pan gourmet cooks lite, a low-fat guide to outdoor cooking, The 43
One pan gourmet – fresh food on the trail, The 43
Orr, Donna 43
osprey 249, 268
otters 232, 249
outfitters 257, 259
owls 249

P
Pacific Ocean 104, 234
packers 211, 218, 219
paddlewheel graveyard 149, **206**
Paddy Pass **163**
Page, L.M. 251, 264
paintbrush 236
Paleozoic era 236
Palm Sunday 50
Parks Canada 15, 19, 20, 26, 54, 67, 71, 75, 151, 227, 261
Part of the land, part of the water 215
passports 20
Path of the Paddle 37, 264
Pavey **163**
Peace River 217
Pearl Harbour 225
Peel Plateau **254**
Peel River **24**, 217
pelican box 41
Pelly Crossing 12, 13, 137, 139, 208, 214
Pelly Farm 9, 12, 13, 139
Pelly Mountains 13, 104, 254, **254**
Pelly Plateau **254**

Pelly River 3, 8, 9, 12, 13, 23, 24, 48, 128, 136, 137, 138, 139, **191**, 208, 216, 217, 244, 251, 265, 265
Pelly, Sir John Henry 137
Pennington 81, 85, **154, 163, 164**
Pennycook Creek **167**
pepper spray 20, 32, 268
peregrine falcon 135, **189**
permafrost 140, **140**, 149, 151, 245, 248
personal locator beacon 36
Perthes Point **166**
Peterson field guide to freshwater fishes 251, 264
Peterson field guides – animal tracks 256, 264
Peterson field guides – Pacific states wildflowers 256
Peterson field guides – Rocky Mountain wildflowers 256
Peterson field guides — mammals 256, 264
Peterson field guides — western birds 256, 265
Peterson's Pass 64, **159**
Peterson, Roger Tory 256, 264
pets 32, 35
photography 31, 229
pika 237
pike 103, 251
pilot 220, 223
Pilot Island 127, 141, **154, 193**
Pilot Mountain 108
pine 71, 74, 239, 248
Planning a wilderness trip in Canada 37
Pleasant Camp 46, 57, 59, **158**
Pleistocene age 104, 244
pogies 39, 40
Policeman's Point (and road) 9, 11, 103, 105, **173**
polypropylene 39, 268
poplar 239, 246
Porcupine Plain **254**
Porcupine Plateau **254**
Porcupine River **24**, 152, 217, 251
porcupines 232, 240
Port Hardy 16, 259
portages 35, 41, 47
powerlines **173**
Prater, Yvonne 43
Precambrian era 236

Prejevalsky Point **164**
Prince George 15, 16
Prince Rupert 16, 259
prospectors 3, 4, 13, 216, 217, 266
ptarmigan 237
Ptarmigan Point 111, **176**
Pullan, Janet 43
pumphouse **171**

Q
Quiet Lake 13, 121, 264

R
Raabe's Hills **185**
Raabe's Slough 125, **185**, 224
Rabbit Creek 150, 216
rabbits 229
radios 36, 263
railways 16, 18, 19, 46, 259, *see also* White Pass & Yukon Route
rain 10, 22, 23, 34, 38, 41, 63, 231, 235, 239
rainbow trout 26
rapids 10, 13, 23, 47-48, 123, 137, 220, 221, 266
raspberries 239
Rat Creek **167, 168**
ravens 211, 240
Ray Mountains 152
Raymond's Island 173
Raymond's Landing 103, **173**
Recipes for roaming – adventure food for the Canadian Rockies 43
red cedar 56
Red Cross 28
redpolls 240
reef booties 39
Reid Creek **155**
Reid Falls **155**
Reid, Frank 49
Reindeer Creek 127, **154, 203**
Renewable Resources 261, 263
Renton Rock **189**
repair kit 41
reptiles 236
rescue 36, 267, 268
residential schools 210
respect 25, 31, 75, 111, 120, 122, 134, 146
Richard, Sukey 43
Richardson **254**
Richthofen Creek **174**
Richthofen Island 10, 109, 110, 112, **154, 174**

7

REFERENCES

Rink Rapids 12, 21, 47, 127, 128, 131, 132-133, **187**
river flows 21-22, 23, 25
river sandals 38, 39
riverboats 4, 94, 102, 105, 107, 113, 114, 117, 122, 125, 130-131, 132, 133, 134, 136, 138, 142, 146, 214, 217, 222, 224, 265
Rivers of the Yukon 264
roadhouses **193**, 224
Roaring Bull Rapids 116
Robert Campbell Bridge 93, 97
Robert Campbell Highway 13, 122, 123, **183, 184**
Robert E. Lowe Bridge **99**
Robert Service Campground 10, 96, 97, **99**
robins 240
rocks 13, 229
Rosebute Creek **202**
Ross River **24**
Ross River Dena Council 209
Rotary Peace Park 97, **99**
Rourke, Mike 137, 265
Royal Canadian Mounted Police 29, 30, 125, 146, 263
Royal Proclamation of 1763 210
rubber boots 38
Ruby Range **254**
Russians 3, 210, 264

S

S.S. Casca 113, 114, 133, **176, 187**, 223
S.S. Columbia 124, 223
S.S. Dawson 133
S.S. Domville 114, **177**, 223
S.S. Evelyn 117, 118
S.S. Excelsior 2, 217
S.S. Keno 147, 223, 224, 227
S.S. Klondike 12, 97, 98, **99**, 101, 119, 133, **171, 179**, 223, 224, 227
S.S. Norcom 117
S.S. Portland 2, 217
S.S. Schwatka 96
S.S. Tanana 223
S.S. Tutshi 84
S.S. Washburn **183**
S.S. Whitehorse 223
safety 27, 28, 29
sagewort 248
Saintly Hill 54, 56, **156**

salmon 26, 56, 129, 147, 211, 213, 214, 233, 251
Salmon Range **181**
salmonberries 231
Sam McGee's ashes 106, 132, 133, **187**
San Francisco 217, 220, 221
sand dunes 46, **164**
sandhill crane 250
Sandy Lake 121
Saskatoon berries 239
satellite telephones 36
Satterfield, A. 265
Saussure Glacier **158**
Sawmill Gulch **206**
Sawmill Island **199**
Scales, The 46, 50, 62, 63, **158**, 230
Schofield, Janice J. 256
Schwatka Lake 9, 10, 92, 96, 97, **99, 171**
Schwatka, Frederick 87, 88, 89
scimitar cats 245
sea otters 211
seatbelts 16
Seattle 17, 117, 216, 217
seaweed 208, 211, 212, 213
Second Skin 39
sedge 236, 248, 269
sedge tussocks 140
Selkirk First Nation 134, 137-139, 208, 209, 214
Selkirk Rock **182**
Selwyn **154**, 194
Selwyn Dome **195**
Selwyn Mountains **254**
Selwyn River 127, 141, **194**
Selwyn Station 141, **194**
Semenof Hills 13, 101, **154, 179, 180**
Service, Robert 26, 108
Seventeen Mile Creek **193**
Seventeen Mile Woodyard 11, 114, 115, **177**
77 Pup **206**
Shakwak Fault 253
Shamrock Creek **200**
Shamrock Dome **200**
sheep 211, 212, 213, 214, 237
Sheep Camp 46, 53, 56, 57, 59, 60, **60**, 61, 62, 69, **154, 158**, 211, 221, 227, 230, 231
shellfish 211
shells 208, 212, 213
Shipyard Island 117, 118, 122, **178**, 223
shipyards 100

Shooting of Dan McGrew, The 26
shuttles 17-19
Side Stream Navigation 117
silver 225, 226
Simple foods for the pack 43
Sister Island **206**
Sitka 3
Six Mile River 88, **167**
Sixty Mile River 115, 127, 145, 148, **154, 202**
Skaguay 49
Skagway 4, 7, 14, 15, 16, 17, 18, 19, 20, 21, 22, **24**, 49, 54, 57, 73, 80, 85, 86, 98, 151, **154, 155**, 218, 221, 227, 232, **245**, 259, 260, 261, 262, 263
Skagway Convention and Visitors Bureau 19, 260, 262
Skagway River **155**
skippers 242
Slaughterhouse Slough **191**
Slide Cemetery 50, **155, 156**
sloth 245
sluice 151
Smith, Soapy 49
Snake River **24**
sneakers 38, 39
Snoseal 39
snow 10, 21, 22, 23, 25, 63, 231, 235, 238, 239, 241, 251, 252
snow bunting 237
snowshoe hare 232, 240, 249, 250
soap 35
socks 39
solstice 21
Song of the paddle — An illustrated guide to wilderness camping 37, 264
South Canol Road 13, 121
South Fork 121
South Macmillan River **24**
South Nahanni River **24**
Southern Tutchone 126, 207, 208, 213-214
sparrow 237, 241, 249
speeder train 17, 269
Spellenburg, Richard 256
Split Rock Creek **178**
Split-up Island 143, 145, **200**
sprains 39
spray covers 41, 47

spring 23, 212, 213, 215, 219
spruce 46, 56, 71, 140, 231, 239, 246, 248
Spruce Island **178**
Squanga Creek 116
squirrels 232, 237, 240, 249
St. Andrews Church 138
St. Andrews Presbyterian Church 75, 76
St. Cyr Range 13
St. Elias Mountains 92, 104, 106, 143, 252, 254
St. John's Ambulance 28
St. Michael 217
stage road 126, 133, 135, 224
stampeders 2, 4, 46, 50, 211, 217-221, 222, 231, 242
Steamboat Island 12
Steamboat Slough 29, 103, 146, 147, **173, 206**, 224
Stedham, Glen 37, 265
Steele, Samuel B. 65, 218
steelhead 26
Stewart Cassiar Highway 16
Stewart Crossing 13
Stewart Island 127, 142, 143, 144, 145, **154, 200**
Stewart Plateau **254**
Stewart River 3, 8, 9, 12, 13, 24, 104, 143, 144, **200**, 208, 214, 215, 216, 217, 251
Stikine River 116, 211, 217, 265
Stikine River — a guide to paddling the great river 265
Stone Crib 69, **159**
stone sheep 15
storytelling 212, 213
strawberries 239
strawberry blight 248
Sturtevant, W.C. 265
sub-boreal 46
Subalpine boreal forest zone 46, 71, 230, 239-246, 269
Sullivan Island 143, **199**
summer 17, 21, 22, 23, 211, 212, 214, 215, 231, 235, 239, 247
summit 46, 57, 62, 63, 64, 66, 67, 69, 70
sunlight 21, 22
Sunnydale 146, **206**
Sunshine Creek **195**
Suttles, W. 265

swallows 133
Swan Haven 89, **169**, 249
swans 89, 228, 250
Swede Creek 127, 146, **154**, **205**
sweepers 13, 47, 269
switchbacks 35
synthetics 38

T

Ta'an Kwach'an First Nation 114, 208, **209**
Tage Cho Hudan Interpretive Centre 126
Tagish 9, 10, 21, 25, 43, 81, 88, **154**, **167**, 212
Tagish First Nation 84, 208, 212-213
Tagish Lake 25, 46, 81, 84, 85-88, **154**, **165**, **166**, **167**, 266
Tagish language 103
Tagish River 88
Tagish Road **165**, **167**
Taiya Inlet **155**
Taiya River 1, 28, 50, 56, 57, 58, 62, 69, **155**, **156**, **157**, **158**, 232, 233, 234, 238
Taiya River Canyon **157**
Taiya valley 232, 238
Takhini Hot Springs Road **173**
Takhini River 9, 10, 11, 24, 92, 93, 101, 102, 103, 104, 113, 129, **154**, **172**, **173**, 208
Takhini valley 92, 104, **254**
Taku Arm 84, 86, 88, **166**
Taku River **24**
Tanana Reef **177**
Tanana River 152
tanning 215
Tantalus 126
Tantalus Butte 125, 126, **185**
Tantalus Coal Mine 125, 126, 129
Tantalus Formation 253
tarps 42, 44
Tatchun Creek 124, 132, **186**
Tatchun Hills 13, **183**, **186**
Tatchun Lake 124
Tatshenshini River **24**
Taylor & Drury 117, 124, 132, 138, 139, 141, 144, 269
Telegraph Creek 116

telegraph line 10, 57, 90, 103, 113, 114, 115, 117, 126, 144, 145, **170**, **178**, 264, 269
Ten Mile **166**
Ten Mile Point 85, **165**
terns 232
Teslin 211
Teslin Lake 115
Teslin Mountain 11, 108, 111
Teslin Plateau 10, 81, 254, **254**
Teslin River 3, 8, 9, 13, 23, 24, 25, 28, 48, 101, 112, 113, 114, 115-116, 117-118, **178**, 217, 251, 264
Teslin River — Johnson's Crossing to Hootalinqua Yukon, Canada, The 264
Teslin Tlingit First Nation 208, **209**, 211
Teslin Trail 90
Thirty Mile, The 11, 25, 101, 114, 115, 116, **154**, **176**, **177**, **178**, 214, 221, 227
Thistle Creek 142, **198**
Thomas Gulch **206**
Thorsen Creek **199**
3M Scotchguard 39
Threeway Channel 127, **154**, **192**, **193**
Thron-diuck 147, 148
till 244
Tintina Trench 250, 251, 252, 253
Tintina valley **254**
Tlingit 264
Tlingit First Nation 3, 49, 58, 107, 138, 207-213, 216, 219, 233, 264
Tlingit Indians — The results of a trip to the northwest coast of America and the Bering Strait, The 264
lingit — their art, culture and legends 264
toads 232, 241, 251
Together today for our children tomorrow 210
ton of goods 65
tools 208
Top of the World Highway **206**, 226
Torpedo Island **191**
totem poles 211
Touleary Creek **197**
tourism 226
Tourism Yukon 7, 21, 260, 262

Townsend, Chris 37, 265
Tr'ondëk Hwëch'in First Nation 148, 208, 209, 215
trading 2, 208-210, 211, 212, 213, 216, 269
Trail Centre 15, 19, 20, 54, 227, 261
trailhead 54, 56, **155**, **156**, 260
tramways 57, 58, 64, 86, 93, 94, 218, 221
trapping 2, 210, 212, 213, 214
Trees, shrubs and flowers to know in British Columbia 256, 264
Trelawny, John G. 256, 265
trout 108, 251
Tuzlak, Suat 43
12 Mile Island **205**
Twichell, H. 265
Twin Creek 101, **154**, **182**
Twin Falls **192**
Tyrell Bend **178**

U

U.S. Bend 114, **177**
U.S. Geological Survey 14, 15
U.S. Navy 216
Udvardy, Miklos D.F. 256
United States Geological Survey 262
Upper Laberge 11, 101, 103, 111, **154**, **173**, **174**
Upper Yukon River — Carmacks to Dawson City, Yukon, The 264

V

V8 juice 42
Vancouver 7, 15, 17, 259, 262
Vanmeter Bend **179**
vegetation 235-236, 239, 246, 248
VHF radio 36, 263
Victoria 259
Victoria Rock 137, 139, **191**, **192**, 207
visas 20
Volcano Mountain 128, 136, 137
volcanos 95, 243, 252, **254**
Von Wilczek Creek **189**
Voss, J.S. 265
voyageurs 3
vultures 268
Vuntut Gwitchin First Nation **209**

W

Walsh Creek **181**
Wanipitei canoe tripper's cookbook: wilderness cooking for fun and nutrition 43
warblers 237, 249
warden's station 61, 67, 71, **159**
wash 159, 160
Washington 234
water levels 7, 85, 92, 108, 125
water pipit 237
water taxi 18, 19, 260
water treatment 28, 44, 103, 146
waterproofing 14, 39, 40-41, 44, 56
Watson **164**
Watson Lake 16
Watson River 85, **165**
waves 10, 11, 29, 46, 47
ways 117, 223-224, 269
weasels 232, 240
weather 7, 21-23, 25, 36, 42, 54, 63, 247
weaving 212
Well-fed backpacker, The 43
Wellesley **254**
Wernecke Mountains **254**
West Arm 85, **164**
West Branch **155**, **156**
West Creek **156**
West Dawson 149, **206**
wet suit booties 38, 39
wharves **155**
Wheaton River 85, **164**
Wheye, Darryl 256
whipsaw 220
Whistle Bend 102, **172**
Whitaker, John O., Jr. 256, 265
White Channel 150
white gas 44
White Mountains 152
White Pass 76, 210, 217, 221
White Pass & Yukon Route 10, 16, 18, 19, 49, 50, 69, 72, 74, 75, 76, 80, 83, 84, 91, 94, 98, **99**, **155**, **161**, **162**, **171**, 218-219, 221, 224, 226, 259, 269
White Pass ore transfer site **200**
White River 12, 23, 24, 28, 106, 127, 128, 143, 144, **154**, **199**, 223, 249, 251
White River Ash 106, **106**, 114, 132, 133, 143, 252

7

REFERENCES

White River First Nation **209**
whitecaps 46
whitefish 251
Whitehorse 3, 4, 7, 8, 9, 10, 11, 14, 15, 16, 17, 18, 19, 20, 21, 22, 23, 25, 26, 28, 36, 43, 45, 73, 76, 90, 93, 94-100, 101-102, 151, **154, 171, 172,** 208, 213, 220, 223, 224, 244, **245,** 253, 255, 259, 260, 261, 262, 263, 264
Whitehorse & Area Hikes & Bikes 98, 256
Whitehorse dam 10, 47, 90, 92, 96, 97, 98, **99, 171, 171**
Whitehorse Rapids 10, 47, 92, 96, 97, 98, 98, **99,** 112, 220
Whitehorse Trough 113
Wickstrom Woodyard 114, **177**
wildflowers 21, 22, 69, 229, 236, 256, 264, 265

Wildflowers of the Yukon, Alaska and Northwestern Canada 256, 265
wildlife 15, 31, 35, 232, *see also names of specific animals*
Williams Creek 134, **188**
willow 235, 246
Wilson, Graham 144, 264
Wind River **24**
winds 9, 10, 11, 22, 29, 34, 42, 46, 63, 70, 75, 81-83, 86, 88, 89, 90, 101, 105, 111, 116, 220, 231, 235, 237, 246, 268
Windy Arm 85, 86, 87, 88, **166**
Winnipeg 220, 221
winter 22, 23, 211, 212, 213, 214, 215, 219, 220, 223, 224, 231, 235, 239, 247, 252
wintergreen 236
Wolf Bar **182**
Wolf clan 213, 214
Wolf Creek 10, **171**

Wolverine Creek **191**
wolverines 240, 250
wolves 127, 224, 227, 240, 245, 249, 250
Wood Cutters Range **187**
wood frogs 233, 241, 251
Woodburn homestead 139
woodcamps **177, 192, 196**
woodlots 12
woodyards **190**
wool 38, 39, 40
World War II 225
Wrangell 211
Wrangell Mountains 143

Y

Yakutania Point **155**
Yardley, J. 265
Yukatat 211
Yukon Amateur Radio Association 36, 263
Yukon Archives 26
Yukon Conservation Society 98, 256

Yukon Crossing 106, 127, 133, **154, 187**
Yukon Energy Corporation 93, 96, **99**
Yukon Field Force 135, 137, 138, 139, **191**
Yukon Plateau 253, 254, **254,** 255
Yukon River 70, 76, 87, 88, 89, 90-93, 96-97, **99,** 100, 101-152, **170-206,** 207, 208, 214, 215, 216, 217, 220, 222, 223, 224, 228, 251, 252
Yukon River flow reversal 103, 104, **104,** 113, 129
Yukon River — Marsh Lake to Dawson City 265
Yukon riverboat days 265
Yukon: places and names 264

Z

zinc 226

ABOUT THE AUTHOR

Although she has always had a love for the outdoors, Jennifer (Jenn) Voss's passion for canoeing began at the age of 13 while attending summer camp in Ontario. The wilderness canoe trips she experienced there left an unshakeable impression on her which continues to this day. Although Jenn took a short break from canoeing to go to university — to take civil engineering with a speciality in hydrology — her love for canoeing has been an underlying current which affects everything she does.

Jenn has been organizing and participating in wilderness canoe trips for more than 20 years, and has become an acknowledged expert by her peers. Jenn has been a certified flatwater canoe instructor in British Columbia. Living in Port Moody, British Columbia, with her husband, Jan, daughters Kelsey and Katrina, and cat, Psycho, Jenn is an avid photographer and artist, hobbies which complement her canoeing well. While not canoeing, she is often sorting through her many photographs and reflecting on past canoeing adventures, or dreaming of future trips.